Treasury of
WORLD LITERATURE

Treasury of
WORLD
LITERATURE

Edited by
DAGOBERT D. RUNES

PHILOSOPHICAL LIBRARY
New York

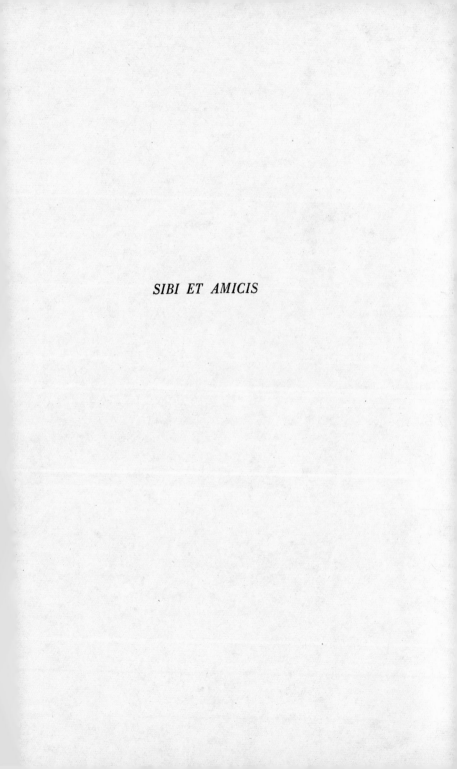

SIBI ET AMICIS

FOREWORD

A TREASURY of literature is a personal matter. It represents one man's choice of creative writing taken from the vast reservoir at his disposal. Thus, what is inspiring to one may seem dull to another, and quite frequently shallow waters appear to have profound depths to one who is distant.

Our libraries abound with anthologies and symposia, housing in their various abodes segments of one or another literary activity. Their scope differs as widely as their taste. It is not my place to sit in judgment upon their failings or their merits. In the last analysis there are no absolutely valid criteria by which we may adjudicate with finality a piece of writing as being creative. Those who have wandered through the ways and bypaths of the world of books know only too well that the same piece which is placed upon a pedestal by some as being the ultimate in beauty and conception, is thrown away by others as just so much trash.

I say in sincere humility that my judgment is biased—as it must be by my background and my experience—and that in all likelihood I have as far as this volume is concerned muted the voices of many who are truly outstanding, and perhaps made some speak who had better remained silent. As I have worked in three continents, my selections must necessarily reflect them all. I should like to remark at this point that in my opinion the Western world, in its books, has not given Asia an appropriate place on the dais.

It may be that some readers will think I have given in this anthology more space to the Asians than they deserve. It is my own opinion that I have given them not enough. But some of our Eastern friends write with a decidedly Oriental mannerism, so that in spite of its enchantment I was afraid I would not help their cause by presenting the available.

The literature before us is of the written word. The literature of the spoken word, which undoubtedly lived for many thousands of years before that, reverberates in some of the early writings. Some of the renowned fabulists of India and China, for instance, wove their stories from legends and tales that had lived with their people for millennia. In later years, the Greeks and the Romans, and in our era the French and the Germans, varied these fables to suit the taste and the milieu of their people. We shall never know some of the great men or women who originated these charming tales that have ever since bewitched young and old.

For the poetry of old in its purest form, we must turn to Israel, where three thousand and more years ago we find such gems as the Psalter brightening the life of a desert people. Whether all or only some of this was written by the Shepherd King, or by his scholarly son Solomon, is not important, but in their gracefulness and the ardor of their appeal to yearning mankind, nothing else of that era can compare to the songs ringing from King David's harp.

China, India, Persia and Japan spread open a glittering wealth of poetry at the beginning of our medieval era, when the Western world had little literature to give its people aside from some imitations of the Hellenic and Roman epochs long gone by. The riches of Asia's literary treasures are still to be explored.

In the choice of my selections I took pains to omit the products of the professional court writers and palace versifiers whether they were stationed in Bagdad, Rome or the Kremlin. Eulogies to Nero are as painful to listen to as those fabricated for the Queen of England or comrade Stalin.

I have given comparatively little space to the novel, for this literary form is a rather recent one, sometimes compounded of little more than journalistic plots and intricate sex situations. Occasionally these novels, though they frantically hoist the flag of some social cause, do little more than wallow in the sordid mudbanks of cruelty, perversion, criminality, and all types of social abuse. The diaries of a slum dweller or the memoirs of a bus driver do not necessarily make literature.

Wherever possible I have used existing translations with only minor adjustments. It is, of course, frequently difficult to translate works of creative literature, especially when cast in the form of poetry.

I should like to thank Mrs. Rose Morse and Mr. Richard Passmore for their assistance in preparing the manuscript.

D. D. R.

NOTE: Western translators have rendered the names of Oriental authors in a bewildering variety of spellings and styles—family name first, family name last, and so on. In this book such names are given in the form which seems to be most frequently encountered and which therefore will be most easily recognized by English-speaking readers.

Treasury of
WORLD LITERATURE

CONTENTS

Aeschylus   1
Aesop   6
Ryunosuke Akutagawa   10
Sholem Aleikhem   15
Vittorio Alfieri   20
Hans Christian Andersen   28
Leonid Nicolayevic Andreyev   31
Guillaume Apollinaire   42
Ludovico Ariosto   45
Aristophanes   53
Sholem Asch   55
Attar   61
Sri Aurobindo   63
Mary Austin   66

Isaak Emmanuilovich Babel   69
Honoré de Balzac   77
James Matthew Barrie   87
Basho   94
Charles Baudelaire   96
Stephen Vincent Benét   97
Pierre Jean de Béranger   110
Bhartrihari   115
Bhasa   118
Bhavabhuti   120
Hayyim Nahman Bialik   125
Bilhana   127
Björnstjerne Björnson   129
Giovanni Boccaccio   133

Charlotte Brontë 140
Elizabeth Barrett Browning 144
Robert Browning 151
Karl Georg Büchner 154
Ivan Bunin 162
John Bunyan 169
Robert Burns 174
George Gordon Byron 180

Pedro Calderón de la Barca 188
Karel Capek 200
Giosue Carducci 207
Miguel de Cervantes y Saavedra 209
Adalbert Von Chamisso 215
François-René de Chateaubriand 224
Bankim Chandra Chatterjee 230
Geoffrey Chaucer 232
Anton Chekhov 236
Chikamatsu Monzaemon 239
Ch'u Yuan 244
Confucius 249
Joseph Conrad 252
James Fenimore Cooper 265
Stephen Crane 271

Dandin 282
Gabriele D'Annunzio 283
Dante Alighieri 285
Alphonse Daudet 289
David 291
Daniel Defoe 293
Richard Dehmel 304
Grazia Deledda 309
Charles Dickens 316
Emily Dickinson 321
John Donne 325
Feodor Mikhaylovich Dostoyevsky 329

John Dryden   335
Alexandre Dumas   342

Joseph Von Eichendorff   351
George Eliot   354
Mihail Eminescu   363
Euripides   365
Abraham Ibn Ezra   370

William Faulkner   376
Firdausi   385
Gustave Flaubert   388
Friedrich De La Motte-Fouque   396
Anatole France   404
Ferdinand Freiligrath   407
Robert Frost   410
Fuzuli   412

Solomon Ibn Gabirol   415
John Galsworthy   418
Vsevolod Garshin   424
Théophile Gautier   433
Khalil Gibran   444
André Gide   446
Jean Giraudoux   449
Johann Wolfgang Von Goethe   456
Nikolai Gogol   467
Carlo Goldoni   480
Oliver Goldsmith   485
Ivan Alexandrovich Goncharov   490
Maxim Gorky   498
Thomas Gray   506
Franz Grillparzer   510

Hafiz   516
Judah Halevi   518
Knut Hamsun   520

Thomas Hardy	524
Bret Harte	533
Gerhart Hauptmann	542
Nathaniel Hawthorne	549
Johann Peter Hebel	557
Heinrich Heine	559
Ernest Hemingway	570
O. Henry	575
Johann Gottfried Von Herder	581
Hermann Hesse	583
Hitomaro Kakinomoto	585
Friedrich Hölderlin	589
Homer	590
Horace	594
Ricarda Huch	599
Victor Hugo	600
Henrik Ibsen	609
Muhammad Iqbal	612
Washington Irving	614
Jens Peter Jacobsen	623
Henry James	629
Jami	638
The Jataka	641
Jayadeva	645
Juan Ramón Jiménez	646
Maurus Jokai	650
Ben Jonson	659
James Joyce	663
Franz Kafka	669
Nagai Kafu	674
Kagawa Kageki	684
Kalidasa	685
John Keats	687
Gottfried Keller	692

Omar Khayyam 696
Kan Kikuchi 700
Rudyard Kipling 706
Joseph Kiss 713
Heinrich Von Kleist 723
Friedrich Gottlieb Klopstock 725
Vladimir Korolenko 731
Zygmunt Krasinski 735

Selma Lagerlöf 745
Lao Shê 749
Lao-Tzu 757
David Herbert Lawrence 760
Lee Hou-Chu 762
Nikolaus Lenau 763
Giacomo Leopardi 768
Mikhail Yuryevich Lermontov 772
Gotthold Ephraim Lessing 775
Sinclair Lewis 782
Lin Ho-Ching 795
Li Po 796
Liu Chi 800
Li Shang-yiu 802
Jack London 803
Henry Wadsworth Longfellow 818
Federico Garcia Lorca 825
Lusin 828

Antonio Machado 837
Maurice Maeterlinck 842
Stéphane Mallarmé 845
Thomas Mann 848
Alessandro Manzoni 855
Christopher Marlowe 858
John Masefield 859
William Somerset Maugham 863
Guy de Maupassant 868

François Mauriac	877
Herman Melville	879
Mêng Hao-Jan	885
George Meredith	887
Adam Mickiewicz	892
Edna St. Vincent Millay	896
John Milton	898
Molière	902
Thomas Moore	904
Mori Ogai	910
Eduard Mörike	915
Multatuli	922
Lady Murasaki	934
Saneatsu Mushakoji	938
Mu'tamid	946
Sarojini Naidu	949
Natsume Soseki	950
Nizami	953
Novalis	955
Eugene O'Neill	959
Jiro Osaragi	963
Ovid	968
Yitskhok Leybush Peretz	971
Benito Pérez Galdós	974
Saint-John Perse	977
Alexander Petöfi	978
Francesco Petrarca	980
Pilpay	982
Pindar	985
David Pinski	990
Luigi Pirandello	994
Po Chü-i	1000
Edgar Allan Poe	1002
Alexander Pope	1007

Marcel Proust	1009
Alexander Sergeyevich Pushkin	1015
François Rabelais	1021
Jean Baptiste Racine	1025
Jean Paul Richter	1029
Rainer Maria Rilke	1031
Jean Arthur Rimbaud	1037
Edwin Arlington Robinson	1041
Romain Rolland	1042
Pierre de Ronsard	1046
Edmond Rostand	1048
Jalal Ud-din Rumi	1050
Sa'di	1054
Priest Saigyo	1057
George Sand	1058
Carl Sandburg	1061
George Santayana	1063
Sappho	1066
Jean-Paul Sartre	1069
Friedrich Von Schiller	1080
Arthur Schnitzler	1083
Sir Walter Scott	1090
Se'ami	1096
Sei Shonagon	1104
Mendele Mocher Sforim	1109
William Shakespeare	1113
George Bernard Shaw	1128
Percy Bysshe Shelley	1148
Shen Ts'ung-wên	1154
Shih Nai-an	1162
Henryk Sienkiewicz	1165
Solomon	1178
Somadeva	1180
Sophocles	1186
Carl Spitteler	1197

Ssü-kung T'u	1201
John Ernst Steinbeck	1203
Stendhal	1211
Wallace Stevens	1221
Robert Louis Stevenson	1224
Theodor Storm	1233
Harriet Beecher Stowe	1245
August Strindberg	1250
Sudraka	1256
Sun Hsi-chen	1263
Su Tung-p'o	1272
Jonathan Swift	1274
Algernon Charles Swinburne	1278
Rabindranath Tagore	1285
Junichiro Tanizaki	1288
T'ao Ch'ien	1291
Torquato Tasso	1293
Alfred Lord Tennyson	1295
William Makepeace Thackeray	1299
Johann Ludwig Tieck	1303
Leo Tolstoy	1313
Anthony Trollope	1325
Tu Fu	1328
Ivan Sergeyevich Turgenev	1330
Mark Twain	1338
Miguel de Unamuno	1344
Paul Valéry	1349
Valmiki	1352
Giovanni Verga	1362
Emile Verhaeren	1368
Paul Verlaine	1370
Jules Verne	1375
François Villon	1378
Virgil	1381
Walther von der Vogelweide	1383

Wang Wei   1387
Jakob Wassermann   1389
Franz Werfel   1392
Walt Whitman   1395
John Greenleaf Whittier   1401
Christoph Martin Wieland   1405
Oscar Wilde   1411
William Wordsworth   1415

Yamanoe No Okura   1422
William Butler Yeats   1426

Emile Zola   1429
Arnold Zweig   1433

A

AESCHYLUS

AESCHYLUS (Greek, 525-456 B.C.). One of the most prolific and original of the ancient dramatists. Believed to have written some 90 plays, of which only 7 remain—including *Prometheus Bound,* the *Oresteia* trilogy, and *Seven Against Thebes.* Using Greek myths to convey philosophic ideas, his tragedies have a moral grandeur unsurpassed to this day.

THE COMPLAINT OF PROMETHEUS

PROMETHEUS (alone)

O Holy Æther, and swift-winged Winds,
    And River-wells, and laughter innumerous
    Of yon Sea-waves! Earth, mother of us all,
And all-viewing cyclic Sun, I cry on you,—
Behold me a god, what I endure from gods!
    Behold, with throe on throe,
    How, wasted by this woe,
I wrestle down the myriad years of Time!
    Behold, how fast around me
The new King of the happy ones sublime
Has flung the chain he forged, has shamed and bound me!
Woe, woe! to-day's woe and coming morrow's
    I cover with one groan. And where is found me
    A limit to these sorrows?
And yet what word do I say? I have foreknown
Clearly all things that should be; nothing done
Comes sudden to my soul—and I must bear
What is ordained with patience, being aware
Necessity doth front the universe
With an invincible gesture. Yet this curse

1

Which strikes me now, I find it hard to brave
  In silence or in speech. Because I gave
  Honor to mortals, I have yoked my soul
  To this compelling fate. Because I stole
The secret fount of fire, whose bubbles went
Over the ferrule's brim, and manward sent
Art's mighty means and perfect rudiment,
  That sin I expiate in this agony,
  Hung here in fetters, 'neath the blanching sky.
    Ah, ah me! what a sound,
What a fragrance sweeps up from a pinion unseen
Of a god, or a mortal, or nature between,
Sweeping up to this rock where the earth has her bound,
To have sight of my pangs, or some guerdon obtain—
Lo, a god in the anguish, a god in the chain!
    The god Zeus hateth sore,
    And his gods hate again,
As many as tread on his glorified floor,
Because I loved mortals too much evermore.
Alas me! what a murmur and motion I hear,
    As of birds flying near!
    And the air undersings
    The light stroke of their wings—
And all life that approaches I wait for in fear.

A PRAYER TO ARTEMIS

Strophe IV

  Though Zeus plan all things right,
Yet is his heart's desire full hard to trace;
    Nathless in every place
  Brightly it gleameth, e'en in darkest night,
Fraught with black fate to man's speech-gifted race.

Antistrophe IV

  Steadfast, ne'er thrown in fight,
The deed in brow of Zeus to ripeness brought;
    For wrapt in shadowy night,
  Tangled, unscanned by mortal sight,
Extend the pathways of his secret thought.

2

Strophe V

From towering hopes mortals he hurleth prone
  To utter doom: but for their fall
  No force arrayeth he; for all
That gods devise is without effort wrought.
A mindful Spirit aloft on holy throne
  By inborn energy achieves his thought.

Antistrophe V

But let him mortal insolence behold:—
  How with proud contumacy rife,
  Wantons the stem in lusty life
My marriage craving;—frenzy over-bold,
Spur ever-pricking, goads them on to fate,
By ruin taught their folly all too late.

Strophe VI

Thus I complain, in piteous strain,
  Grief-laden, tear-evoking, shrill;
    Ah woe is me! woe! woe!
  Dirge-like it sounds; mine own death-trill
I pour, yet breathing vital air.
Hear, hill-crowned Apia, hear my prayer!
    Full well, O land,
My voice barbaric thou canst understand;
  While oft with rendings I assail
My byssine vesture and Sidonian veil.

Antistrophe VI

My nuptial right in Heaven's pure sight
  Pollution were, death-laden, rude;
    Ah woe is me! woe! woe!
Alas for sorrow's murky brood!
Where will this billow hurl me? Where?
Hear, hill-crowned Apia, hear my prayer?
    Full well, O land,
My voice barbaric thou canst understand;
  While oft with rendings I assail
My byssine vesture and Sidonian veil.

3

The oar indeed and home with sails
Flax-tissued, swelled with favoring gales,
Stanch to the wave, from spear-storm free,
Have to this shore escorted me,
Not so far blame I destiny.
But may the all-seeing Father send
In fitting time propitious end;
So our dread Mother's mighty brood
The lordly couch may 'scape, ah me.
      Unwedded, unsubdued!

Antistrophe VII

Meeting my will with will divine,
Daughter of Zeus, who here dost hold
      Steadfast thy sacred shrine—
Me, Artemis unstained, behold.
Do thou, who sovereign might dost wield,
Virgin thyself, a virgin shield;
So our dread Mother's mighty brood
The lordly couch may 'scape, ah me,
      Unwedded, unsubdued!

THE VISION OF CASSANDRA

Cassandra

Phœbus Apollo!

Chorus

Hark!
The lips at last unlocking.

Cassandra

Phœbus! Phœbus!

Chorus

Well, what of Phœbus, maiden? though a name
'Tis but disparagement to call upon
In misery

Cassandra

   Apollo! Apollo! Again!
Oh, the burning arrow through the brain!
   Phœbus Apollo! Apollo!

4

Chorus

Seemingly
Possessed indeed—whether by—

Cassandra

Phœbus! Phœbus!
Through trampled ashes, blood, and fiery rain,
Over water seething, and behind the breathing
War-horse in the darkness—till you rose again,
Took the helm—took the rein—

Chorus

As one that half asleep at dawn recalls
A night of Horror!

Cassandra

Hither, whither, Phœbus? And with whom,
Leading me, lighting me—

Chorus

I can answer that—

Cassandra

Down to what slaughter-house!
Foh! the smell of carnage through the door
Scares me from it—drags me toward it—
   Phœbus Apollo! Apollo!

Chorus

One of the dismal prophet-pack, it seems,
That hunt the trail of blood. But here at fault—
This is no den of slaughter, but the house
Of Agamemnon.

Cassandra

Down upon the towers,
Phantoms of two mangled children hover—and a famished man,
At an empty table glaring, seizes and devours!

Chorus

Thyestes and his children! Strange enough
For any maiden from abroad to know,
Or, knowing—

Cassandra

And look! in the chamber below
The terrible Woman, listening, watching,
Under a mask, preparing the blow
In the fold of her robe—

5

Chorus

Nay, but again at fault:
For in the tragic story of this House—
Unless, indeed the fatal Helen—
No woman—

Cassandra

No Woman—Tisiphone! Daughter
Of Tartarus—love-grinning Woman above,
Dragon-tailed under—honey-tongued, Harpy-clawed,
Into the glittering meshes of slaughter
She wheedles, entices him into the poisonous
Fold of the serpent—

Chorus

Peace, mad woman, peace!
Whose stony lips once open vomit out
Such uncouth horrors.

Cassandra

I tell you the lioness
Slaughters the Lion asleep; and lifting
Her blood-dripping fangs buried deep in his mane,
Glaring about her insatiable, bellowing,
Bounds hither—Phœbus Apollo, Apollo, Apollo!
Whither have you led me, under night alive with fire,
Through the trampled ashes of the city of my sire,
From my slaughtered kinsmen, fallen throne, insulted shrine,
Slave-like to be butchered, the daughter of a royal line!

AESOP

AESOP (Greek, 6th Century B.C.). According to tradition, a foreign slave having great familiarity with the fables of India. Creator of the Animal Fable, a brief tale told to point a simple moral. Believed to have been put to death at Delphi. Later mentioned by Aristophanes and Socrates. Many later collections, in Greek and Latin, freely attributed to him.

THE DOG AND THE SHADOW

A DOG, with a piece of stolen meat between his teeth, was one day crossing a river by means of a plank, when he caught sight of another dog in the water carrying a far larger piece of meat. He opened his jaws to snap at the greater morsel, when the meat dropped in the stream and was lost even in the reflection.

THE DYING LION

A LION, brought to the extremity of weakness by old age and disease, lay dying in the sunlight. Those whom he had oppressed in his strength now came round about him to revenge themselves for past injuries. The Boar ripped the flank of the King of Beasts with his tusks. The Bull came and gored the Lion's sides with his horns. Finally, the Ass drew near, and after carefully seeing that there was no danger, let fly with his heels in the Lion's face. Then, with a dying groan, the mighty creature exclaimed: "How much worse it is than a thousand deaths to be spurned by so base a creature!"

THE MOUNTAIN IN LABOUR

A MOUNTAIN was heard to produce dreadful sounds, as though it were labouring to bring forth something enormous. The people came and stood about waiting to see what wonderful thing would be produced from this labour. After they had waited till they were tired, out crept a Mouse.

HERCULES AND THE WAGGONER

A WAGGONER was driving his team through a muddy lane when the wheels stuck fast in the clay, and the Horses could get no farther. The Man immediately dropped on his knees, and, crying bitterly, besought Hercules to come and help him. "Get up and stir thyself, thou lazy fellow!" replied Hercules. "Whip thy Horses, and put thy shoulder to the wheel. If thou art in need of my help, when thou thyself hast laboured, then shalt thou have it."

THE FROGS THAT ASKED FOR A KING

THE FROGS, who lived an easy, happy life in the ponds, once prayed to Jupiter that he should give them a King. Jupiter was amused by this prayer, and cast a log into the water saying: "There, then, is a King for you." The Frogs, frightened by the great splash, regarded their King with alarm, until at last, seeing that he did not stir, some of them jumped upon his back and began to be merry there, amused

7

ideas for very long, and so once again they petitioned Jupiter to send them a King, a real King who would rule over them, and not lie helpless in the water. Then Jupiter sent the Frogs a Stork, who caught them by their legs, tossed them in the air, and gobbled them up whenever he was hungry. All in a hurry the Frogs besought Jupiter to take away King Stork and restore them to their former happy condition. "No, no," answered Jupiter; "a King that did you no hurt did not please you; make the best of him you now have, lest a worse come in his place!"

THE GNAT AND THE LION

A LIVELY and insolent Gnat was bold enough to attack a Lion, which he so maddened by stinging the most sensitive parts of his nose, eyes and ears that the beast roared with anguish and tore himself with his claws. In vain were the Lion's efforts to rid himself at such a foolish King. However, King Log did not satisfy their of his insignificant tormentor; again and again the insect returned and stung the furious King of Beasts till at last the Lion fell exhausted on the ground. The triumphant Gnat, sounding his tiny trumpet, hovered over the spot exulting in his victory. But it happened that in his circling flight he got himself caught in the web of a Spider, which, fine and delicate as it was, yet had power enough to hold the tiny insect a prisoner. All the Gnat's efforts to escape only held him the more tightly and firmly a prisoner, and he who had conquered the Lion became in his turn the prey of the Spider.

THE WOLF AND THE STORK

A WOLF ate his food so greedily that a bone stuck in his throat. This caused him such great pain that he ran hither and thither, promising to reward handsomely anyone who would remove the cause of his torture. A Stork, moved with pity by the Wolf's cry of pain, and tempted also by the reward, undertook the dangerous operation. When he had removed the bone, the Wolf moved away, but the Stork called out and reminded him of the promised reward. "Reward!" exclaimed the Wolf. "Pray, you greedy fellow, what reward can you expect? You dared to put your head in my mouth, and instead of biting it off, I let you take it out again unharmed. Get away with you! And do not again place yourself in my power."

8

THE FROG WHO WANTED TO BE AS BIG AS AN OX

A VAIN Frog, surrounded by her children, looked up and saw an Ox grazing near by. "I can be as big as the Ox," she said, and began to blow herself out. "Am I as big now?" she inquired. "Oh, no; not nearly so big!" said the little frogs. "Now?" she asked, blowing herself out still more. "No, not nearly so big!" answered her children. "But now?" she inquired eagerly, and blew herself out still more. "No, not even now," they said; "and if you try till you burst yourself you will never be so big." But the Frog would not listen, and attempting to make herself bigger still, burst her skin and died.

THE DOG IN THE MANGER

A DOG lay in a manger which was full of hay. An Ox, being hungry, came near, and was about to eat when the Dog started up, and, with angry snarls, would not let the Ox approach. "Surely, brute," said the Ox; "you cannot eat the hay yourself, and you will let no one else have any."

THE BUNDLE OF FAGGOTS

AN HONEST Man had the unhappiness to have a quarrelsome family of children. One day he called them before him, and bade them try and break a bundle of faggots. All tried, and all failed. "Now," said he, "unbind the bundle and take every stick by itself, and see if you cannot break them." They did his bidding, and snapped all the sticks one by one with the greatest possible ease. "This, my children," said the Father at last, "is a true emblem of your condition. Keep together and you are safe, divide and you are undone."

THE FOX WITHOUT A TAIL

A FOX was once caught in a trap by his tail, and in order to get free was obliged to leave it behind. He knew that his fellows would make fun of his tailless condition, so he made up his mind to induce them all to part with their tails. At the next assemblage of Foxes he made a speech on the uselessness of tails in general, and the inconvenience of a Fox's tail in particular, declaring that never in his whole life had he felt so comfortable as now in his tailless freedom. When he sat down, a sly old Fox rose, and, waving his brush, said, with a sneer, that if he had lost his tail, he would be convinced by the last speaker's arguments, but until such an accident occurred he fully intended to vote in favour of tails.

9

THE BLIND MAN AND THE PARALYTIC

A BLIND Man finding himself stopped in a rough and difficult road, met with a paralytic and begged his assistance. "How can I help you," replied the paralytic, "when I can scarcely move myself along?" But, regarding the blind man, he added: "However, you appear to have good legs and a broad back, and, if you will lift me and carry me, I will guide you safely through this difficulty, which is more than each one can surmount for himself. You shall walk for me, and I will see you you." "With all my heart," rejoined the blind man; and, taking the paralytic on his shoulders, the two went cheerfully forward in a wise partnership which triumphed over all difficulties.

RYUNOSUKE AKUTAGAWA

RYUNOSUKE AKUTAGAWA (Japanese, 1892-1927). Sophisticated story-teller, essayist and poet. A follower of the novelist, Natsume Soseki. Wrote more than 100 stories, highly imaginative, with fantastic, symbolic plots. Best-known works: *Rashomon, Hana, Jigokuhen*. Was teacher and newspaper-man before committing suicide at 35.

RASHOMON

IT WAS a chilly evening. A servant of a samurai stood under the Rashomon, waiting for a break in the rain.

No one else was under the wide gate. On the thick column, its crimson lacquer rubbed off here and there, perched a cricket. Since the Rashomon stands on Sujaku Avenue, a few other people at least, in sedge hat or nobleman's headgear, might have been expected to be waiting there for a break in the rain storm. But no one was near except this man.

For the past few years the city of Kyoto had been visited by a series of calamities, earthquakes, whirlwinds, and fires, and Kyoto had been greatly devastated. Old chronicles say that broken pieces of Buddhist images and other Buddhist objects, with their lacquer, gold, or silver leaf worn off, were heaped up on roadsides to be sold as firewood. Such being the state of affairs in Kyoto, the repair of the Rashomon was out of the question. Taking advantage of the devastation, foxes and other wild animals made their dens in the

10

ruins of the gate, and thieves and robbers found a home there too. Eventually it became customary to bring unclaimed corpses to this gate and abandon them. After dark it was so ghostly that no one dared approach.

Flocks of crows flew in from somewhere. During the daytime these cawing birds circled round the ridgepole of the gate. When the sky overhead turned red in the afterlight of the departed sun, they looked like so many grains of sesame flung across the gate. But on that day not a crow was to be seen, perhaps because of the lateness of the hour. Here and there the stone steps, beginning to crumble, and with rank grass growing in their crevices, were dotted with the white droppings of crows. The servant, in a worn blue kimono, sat on the seventh and highest step, vacantly watching the rain. His attention was drawn to a large pimple irritating his right cheek.

As has been said, the servant was waiting for a break in the rain. But he had no particular idea of what to do after the rain stopped. Ordinarily, of course, he would have returned to his master's house, but he had been discharged just before. The prosperity of the city of Kyoto had been rapidly declining, and he had been dismissed by his master, whom he had served many years, because of the effects of this decline. Thus, confined by the rain, he was at a loss to know where to go. And the weather had not a little to do with his depressed mood. The rain seemed unlikely to stop. He was lost in thoughts of how to make his living tomorrow, helpless incoherent thoughts protesting an inexorable fate. Aimlessly he had been listening to the pattering of the rain on the Sujaku Avenue.

The rain, enveloping the Rashomon, gathered strength and came down with a pelting sound that could be heard far away. Looking up, he saw a fat black cloud impale itself on the tips of the tiles jutting out from the roof of the gate.

He had little choice of means, whether fair or foul, because of his helpless circumstances. If he chose honest means, he would undoubtedly starve to death beside the wall or in the Sujaku gutter. He would be brought to this gate and thrown away like a stray dog. If he decided to steal . . . His mind, after making the same detour time and again, came finally to the conclusion that he would be a thief.

But doubts returned many times. Though determined that he had no choice, he was still unable to muster enough courage to justify the conclusion that he must become a thief.

11

After a loud fit of sneezing he got up slowly. The evening chill of Kyoto made him long for the warmth of a brazier. The wind in the evening dusk howled through the columns of the gate. The cricket which had been perched on the crimson-lacquered column was already gone.

Ducking his neck, he looked around the gate, and drew up the shoulders of the blue kimono which he wore over his thin underwear. He decided to spend the night there, if he could find a secluded corner sheltered from wind and rain. He found a broad lacquered stairway leading to the tower over the gate. No one would be there, except the dead, if there were any. So, taking care that the sword at his side did not slip out of the scabbard, he set foot on the lowest step of the stairs.

A few seconds later, halfway up the stairs, he saw a movement above. Holding his breath and huddling cat-like in the middle of the broad stairs leading to the tower, he watched and waited. A light coming from the upper part of the tower shone faintly upon his right cheek. It was the cheek with the red, festering pimple visible under his stubby whiskers. He had expected only dead people inside the tower, but he had only gone up a few steps before he noticed a fire above, about which someone was moving. He saw a dull, yellow, flickering light which made the cobwebs hanging from the ceiling glow in a ghostly way. What sort of person would be making a light in the Rashomon . . . and in a storm? The unknown, the evil terrified him.

As quickly as a lizard, the servant crept up to the top of the steep stairs. Crouching on all fours, and stretching his neck as far as possible, he timidly peeped into the tower.

As rumor had said, he found several corpses strewn carelessly about the floor. Since the glow of the light was feeble, he could not count the number. He could only see that some were naked and others clothed. Some of them were women, and all were lolling on the floor with their mouths open or their arms outstretched showing no more signs of life than so many clay dolls. One would doubt that they had ever been alive, so eternally silent they were. Their shoulders, breasts, and torsos stood out in the dim light; other parts vanished in shadow. The offensive smell of these decomposed corpses brought his hand to his nose.

The next moment his hand dropped and he stared. He caught sight of a ghoulish form bent over a corpse. It seemed to be an old

12

woman, gaunt, gray-haired, and nunnish in appearance. With a pine torch in her right hand, she was peeping into the face of a corpse which had long black hair.

Seized more with horror than curiosity, he even forgot to breathe for a time. He felt the hair of his head and body stand on end. As he watched, terrified, she wedged the torch between two floor boards and, laying hands on the head of the corpse, began to pull out the long hairs one by one, as a monkey kills the lice of her young. The hair came out smoothly with the movement of her hands.

As the hair came out, fear faded from his heart, and his hatred toward the old woman mounted. It grew beyond hatred, becoming a consuming antipathy against all evil. At this instant if anyone had brought up the question of whether he would starve to death or become a thief—the question which had occurred to him a little while ago—he would not have hesitated to choose death. His hatred toward evil flared up like the piece of pine wood which the old woman had stuck in the floor.

He did not know why she pulled out the hair of the dead. Accordingly, he did not know whether her case was to be put down as good or bad. But in his eyes, pulling out the hair of the dead in the Rashomon on this stormy night was an unpardonable crime. Of course it never entered his mind that a little while ago he had thought of becoming a thief.

Then, summoning strength into his legs, he rose from the stairs and strode, hand on sword, right in front of the old creature. The hag turned, terror in her eyes, and sprang up from the floor, trembling. For a small moment she paused, poised there, then lunged for the stairs with a shriek.

"Wretch! Where are you going?" he shouted, barring the way of the trembling hag who tried to scurry past him. Still she attempted to claw her way by. He pushed her back to prevent her . . . they struggled, fell among the corpses, and grappled there. The issue was never in doubt. In a moment he had her by the arm, twisted it, and forced her down to the floor. Her arms were all skin and bones, and there was no more flesh on them than on the shanks of a chicken. No sooner was she on the floor than he drew his sword and thrust the silver-white blade before her very nose. She was silent. She trembled as if in a fit, and her eyes were open so wide that they were almost out of their sockets, and her breath came in hoarse gasps. The life of this wretch was his now. This

13

thought cooled his boiling anger and brought a calm pride and satisfaction. He looked down at her, and said in a somewhat calmer voice:

"Look here, I'm not an officer of the High Police Commissioner. I'm a stranger who happened to pass by this gate. I won't bind you or do anything against you, but you must tell me what you're doing up here."

Then the old woman opened her eyes still wider, and gazed at his face intently with the sharp red eyes of a bird of prey. She moved her lips, which were wrinkled into her nose, as though she were chewing something. Her pointed Adam's apple moved in her thin throat. Then a panting sound like the cawing of a crow came from her throat:

"I pull the hair . . . I pull out the hair . . . to make a wig."

Her answer banished all unknown from their encounter and brought disappointment. Suddenly she was only a trembling old woman there at his feet. A ghoul no longer: only a hag who makes wigs from the hair of the dead—to sell, for scraps of food. A cold contempt seized him. Fear left his heart, and his former hatred entered. These feelings must have been sensed by the other. The old creature, still clutching the hair she had pulled off the corpse, mumbled out these words in her harsh broken voice:

"Indeed, making wigs out of the hair of the dead may seem a great evil to you, but these that are here deserve no better. This woman, whose beautiful black hair I was pulling, used to sell cut and dried snake flesh at the guard barracks, saying that it was dried fish. If she hadn't died of the plague, she'd be selling it now. The guards liked to buy from her, and used to say her fish was tasty. What she did couldn't be wrong, because if she hadn't, she would have starved to death. There was no other choice. If she knew I had to do this in order to live, she probably wouldn't care."

He sheathed his sword, and, with his left hand on its hilt, he listened to her meditatively. His right hand touched the big pimple on his cheek. As he listened, a certain courage was born in his heart—the courage which he had not had when he sat under the gate a little while ago. A strange power was driving him in the opposite direction of the courage which he had had when he seized the old woman. No longer did he wonder whether he should starve to death or become a thief. Starvation was so far from his mind that it was the last thing that would have entered it.

"Are you sure?" he asked in a mocking tone, when she finished

14

talking. He took his right hand from his pimple, and, bending forward, seized her by the neck and said sharply:

"Then it's right if I rob you. I'd starve if I didn't."

He tore her clothes from her body and kicked her roughly down on the corpses as she struggled and tried to clutch his leg. Five steps, and he was at the top of the stairs. The yellow clothes he had wrested off were under his arm, and in a twinkling he had rushed down the steep stairs into the abyss of night. The thunder of his descending steps pounded in the hollow tower, and then it was quiet.

Shortly after that the hag raised up her body from the corpses. Grumbling and groaning, she crawled to the top stair by the still flickering torchlight, and through the grey hair which hung over her face, she peered down to the last stair in the torch light.

Beyond this was only darkness . . . unknowing and unknown.

SHOLEM ALEIKHEM

SHOLEM ALEIKHEM (Sholem Rabinovitch, Yiddish, 1859-1916). The tragi-comedian of Jewish literature. Folk-lore style, mingling pathos and humor. Born in Russia, left for Switzerland in 1904, came to America in 1914. Most famous works: *Menakhem Mendel, Tevye der Milkhiker, Motel dem Khazans, Funem Yarid*. Many tales dramatized for stage and films.

THE PASSOVER GUEST

"I HAVE a Passover guest for you, Reb Yoneh, such a guest as you never had since you became a householder."

"What sort is he?"

"A real Oriental citron!"

"What does that mean?"

"It means a 'silken Jew,' a personage of distinction. The only thing against him is—he doesn't speak our language."

"What does he speak, then?"

"Hebrew."

"Is he from Jerusalem?"

"I don't know where he comes from, but his words are full of a's."

Such was the conversation that took place between my father and the beadle, a day before Passover, and I was wild with curiosity to

15

see the "guest" who didn't understand Yiddish, and who talked with a's. I had already noticed, in synagogue, a strange-looking individual, in a fur cap, and a Turkish robe striped blue, red, and yellow. We boys crowded round him on all sides, and stared, and then caught it hot from the beadle, who said children had no business "to creep into a stranger's face" like that. Prayers over, every one greeted the stranger, and wished him a happy Passover, and he, with a sweet smile on his red cheeks set in a round gray beard, replied to each one, "Shalom! Shalom!" instead of our Sholom. This "Shalom! Shalom!" of his sent us boys into fits of laughter. The beadle grew very angry, and pursued us with slaps. We eluded him, and stole deviously back to the stranger, listened to his "Shalom! Shalom!" exploded with laughter, and escaped anew from the hands of the beadle.

I am puffed up with pride as I follow my father and his guest to our house, and feel how all my comrades envy me. They stand looking after us, and every now and then I turn my head, and put out my tongue at them. The walk home is silent. When we arrive, my father greets my mother with "a happy Passover!" and the guest nods his head so that his fur cap shakes. "Shalom! Shalom!" he says. I think of my comrades, and hide my head under the table, not to burst out laughing. But I shoot continual glances at the guest, and his appearance pleases me; I like his Turkish robe, striped yellow, red, and blue, his fresh red cheeks set in a curly gray beard, his beautiful black eyes that look out so pleasantly from beneath his bushy eyebrows. And I see that my father is pleased with him, too, that he is delighted with him. My mother looks at him as though he were something more than a man, and no one speaks to him but my father, who offers him the cushioned reclining-seat at table.

Mother is taken up with the preparations for the Passover meal, and Rikel the maid is helping her. It is only when the time comes for saying Kiddush that my father and the guest hold a Hebrew conversation. I am proud to find that I understand nearly every word of it. Here it is in full.

My father: "Nu?" (That means, "Won't you please say Kiddush?")

The guest: "Nu-nu!" (meaning, "Say it rather yourself!")

My father: "Nu-O?" ("Why not you?")

The guest: "O-nu?" ("Why should I?")

My father: "I-O!" ("You first!")

The guest: "O-ai!" ("*You* first!")

My father: "È-o-i!" ("I beg of you to say it!")

The guest: "Ai-o-ê!" (I beg of you!")

My father: "Ai-e-o-nu?" ("Why should you refuse?")

The guest: "Oi-o-e-nu-nu!" ("If you insist, then I must.")

And the guest took the cup of wine from my father's hand, and recited a Kiddush. But what a Kiddush! A Kiddush such as we had never heard before, and shall never hear again. First, the Hebrew—all a's. Secondly, the voice, which seemed to come, not out of his beard, but out of the striped Turkish robe. I thought of my comrades, how they would have laughed, what slaps would have rained down, had they been present at that Kiddush.

Being alone, I was able to contain myself. I asked my father the Four Questions, and we all recited the Haggadah together. And I was elated to think that such a guest was ours, and no one else's.

Our sage who wrote that one should not talk at meals (may he forgive me for saying so!) did not know Jewish life. When shall a Jew find time to talk, if not during a meal? Especially at Passover, when there is so much to say before the meal and after it. Rikel the maid handed the water, we washed our hands, repeated the Benediction, mother helped us to fish, and my father turned up his sleeves, and started a long Hebrew talk with the guest. He began with the first question one Jew asks another:

"What is your name?"

To which the guest replied all in a's and all in one breath:

"Ayak Bakar Gashal Damas Hanoch Vassam Za'an Chafaf Tatzatz."

My father remained with his fork in the air, staring in amazement at the possessor of so long a name. I coughed and looked under the table, and my mother said, "Favele, you should be careful eating fish, or you might be choked with a bone," while she gazed at our guest with awe. She appeared overcome by his name, although unable to understand it. My father, who understood, thought it necessary to explain it to her.

"You see, Ayak Bakar, that is our Alef-Bes inverted. It is apparently their custom to name people after the alphabet."

"Alef-Bes! Alef-Bes!" repeated the guest with the sweet smile on his red cheeks, and his beautiful black eyes rested on us all, including Rikel the maid, in the most friendly fashion.

Having learned his name, my father was anxious to know whence, from what land, he came. I understand this from the names of countries and towns which I caught, and from what my father translated for my mother, giving her a Yiddish version of nearly every phrase. And my mother was quite overcome by every single thing she heard, and Rikel the maid was overcome likewise. And no wonder! It is not every day that a person comes from perhaps two thousand miles away, from a land only to be reached across seven seas and a desert, the desert journey alone requiring forty days and nights. And when you get near to the land, you have to climb a mountain of which the top reaches into the clouds, and this is covered with ice, and dreadful winds blow there, so that there is peril of death! But once the mountain is safely climbed, and the land is reached, one beholds a terrestrial Eden. Spices, cloves, herbs, and every kind of fruit—apples, pears, and oranges, grapes, dates, and olives, nuts and quantities of figs. And the houses there are all built of deal, and roofed with silver, the furniture is gold (here the guest cast a look at our silver cups, spoons, forks, and knives), and brilliants, pearls, and diamonds bestrew the roads, and no one cares to take the trouble of picking them up, they are of no value there. (He was looking at my mother's diamond earrings, and at the pearls round her white neck.)

"You hear that?" my father asked her, with a happy face.

"I hear," she answered, and added: "Why don't they bring some over here? They could make money by it. Ask him that, Yoneh!"

My father did so, and translated the answer for my mother's benefit:

"You see, when you arrive there, you may take what you like, but when you leave the country, you must leave everything in it behind, too, and if they shake out of you no matter what, you are done for."

"What do you mean?" questioned my mother, terrified.

"I mean, they either hang you on a tree, or they stone you with stones."

The more tales our guest told us, the more thrilling they became, and just as we were finishing the dumplings and taking another sip or two of wine, my father inquired to whom the country belonged. Was there a king there? And he was soon translating, with great delight, the following reply:

"The country belongs to the Jews who live there, and who are called Sefardîm. And they have a king, also a Jew, and a very pious one, who wears a fur cap, and who is called Joseph ben Joseph. He is the high priest of the Sefardîm, and drives out in a gilded carriage, drawn by six fiery horses. And when he enters the synagogue, the Levites meet him with songs."

"There are Levites who sing in your synagogue?" asked my father, wondering, and the answer caused his face to shine with joy.

"What do you think?" he said to my mother. "Our guest tells me that in his country there is a temple, with priests and Levites and an organ."

"Well, and an altar?" questioned my mother, and my father told her:

"He says they have an altar, and sacrifices, he says, and golden vessels—everything just as we used to have it in Jerusalem."

And with these words my father sighs deeply, and my mother, as she looks at him, sighs also, and I cannot understand the reason. Surely we should be proud and glad to think we have such a land, ruled over by a Jewish king and high priest, a land with Levites and an organ, with an altar and sacrifices—and bright, sweet thoughts enfold me, and carry me away as on wings to that happy Jewish land where the houses are of pine-wood and roofed with silver, where the furniture is gold, and diamonds and pearls lie scattered in the street. And I feel sure, were I really there, I should know what to do—I should know how to hide things—they would shake nothing out of *me*. I should certainly bring home a lovely present for my mother, diamond ear-rings and several pearl necklaces. I look at the one mother is wearing, at her ear-rings, and I feel a great desire to be in that country. And it occurs to me, that after Passover I will travel there with our guest, open my heart to him, tell him the whole truth, and beg him to take me there, if only for a little while. He will certainly do so, he is a very kind and approachable person, he looks at every one, even at Rikel the maid, in such a friendly, such a very friendly way!

So I think, and it seems to me, as I watch our guest, that he has read my thoughts, and that his beautiful black eyes say to me:

"Keep it dark, little friend, wait till after Passover, then we shall manage it!"

I dreamt all night long. I dreamt of a desert, a temple, a high priest, and a tall mountain. I climb the mountain. Diamonds and pearls grow on the trees, and my comrades sit on the boughs, and shake the jewels down onto the ground, whole showers of them, and I stand and gather them, and stuff them into my pockets, and, strange to say, however many I stuff in, there is still room! I stuff and stuff, and still there is room! I put my hand into my pocket, and draw out—not pearls and brilliants, but fruits of all kinds—apples, pears, oranges, olives, dates, nuts, and figs. This makes me very unhappy, and I toss from side to side. Then I dream of the temple, I hear the priests chant, and the Levites sing, and the organ play. I want to go inside and I cannot—Rikel the maid has hold of me, and will not let me go. I beg of her and scream and cry, and again I am very unhappy, and toss from side to side. I wake —and see my father and mother standing there, half dressed, both pale, my father hanging his head, and my mother wringing her hands, and with her soft eyes full of tears. I feel at once that something has gone very wrong, very wrong indeed, but my childish head is incapable of imagining the greatness of the disaster.

The fact is this: our guest from beyond the desert and the seven seas has disappeared, and a lot of things have disappeared with him: all the silver wine-cups, all the silver spoons, knives, and forks; all my mother's ornaments, all the money that happened to be in the house, and also Rikel the maid!

A pang goes through my heart. Not on account of the silver cups, the silver spoons, knives, and forks that have vanished; not on account of mother's ornaments or of the money, still less on account of Rikel the maid, a good riddance! But because of the happy, happy land whose roads were strewn with brilliants, pearls, and diamonds; because of the temple with the priests, the Levites, and the organ; because of the altar and the sacrifices; because of all the other beautiful things that have been taken from me, taken, taken, taken!

I turn my face to the wall, and cry quietly to myself.

VITTORIO ALFIERI

VITTORIO ALFIERI (Italian, 1749-1803). The greatest tragedian of the Italian drama. Of noble birth, began writing at 25, and was an instant success. Plays notable for their intense patriotism and attacks on tyrants and tyranny. Among his 19 tragedies, best are: *Saul, Filippo, Virginia, Mirra*. Wrote in classical style. Called the Shakespeare of Italy.

DAVID SOOTHES SAUL'S MADNESS

Jonathan. Ah come, beloved father; to thy thoughts
Allow a little respite: the pure air

Will bring thee some refreshment; come and sit
A little while among thy children now.
    Saul. What are those words I hear?
    Michal. Beloved father!
    Saul. Who, who are ye? Who speaks of pure air here?
This? 'tis a thick impenetrable gloom;
A land of darkness and the shades of death—
O see! Come nearer me; dost thou observe it?
A fatal wreath of blood surrounds the sun.
Heardst thou the singing of ill-omen'd birds?
The vocal air resounds with loud laments
That smite my ears, compelling me to weep.—
But what? Ye, ye weep also.
    Jon. Mighty God
Of Israel, dost Thou thus Thy face avert
From Saul the king? Is he, Thy servant once,
Abandoned to the adversary thus?
    Michal. Father, thy much-loved daughter is beside thee:
If thou art cheerful, she is also cheerful;
She, if thou weepest, weeps. But, wherefore now
Should we shed tears? For joy hath reappeared.
    Saul. David thou meanest. Ah! Why doth not David
Also embrace me with my other children?
    David. O father! I have been restrained by fear
Of importuning thee. Ah! why canst thou
Not read my heart? I evermore am thine.
    Saul. Thou lovest then—the house of Saul?
    David. I love it?
O Heavens! Dear as the apple of mine eye
To me is Jonathan; I neither know
Nor heed a peril in the world for thee;
Let my wife, if she can, say with what love,
And how much love, I love her.
    Saul. Yet thyself
Thou mightily dost prize.
    David. I prize myself?
No despicable soldier in the camp,
In court thy son-in-law, I deem myself;
And nothing, nothing in the sight of God.
    Saul. Incessantly to me of God thou speakest;
Yet thou well knowest that the crafty rage,

Cruel, tremendous, of perfidious priests,
Has for a long time severed me from God.
Dost thou thus name Him to insult me?

   David. I
Name Him, to give Him glory. Why dost thou
Believe that He no longer is with thee?
He doth not dwell with him who loves Him not:
But doth He ever fail to succor him
Who doth invoke Him, and who hath reposed
In Him implicit trust? He to the throne
Appointed thee; and on that throne He keeps thee:
And if in Him, in Him exclusively
Thou dost confide, He's thine, and thou art His.

   Saul. Who speaks of Heaven? Is he in snowy vest
Enrobed who thus his sacred lip unseals?
Let's see him—No: thou art a warrior: thou
Graspest the sword: approach; and let me see,
If David thus or Samuel doth accost me.—
What sword is this? 'Tis not the same, methinks,
Which I, with my own hands, on thee bestow'd.

   David. This is the sword that my poor sling acquired.
The sword that over me in Elah hung
Threatening my life; in fierce Goliath's hands
I saw it flash a horrid glare of death
Before my eyes: he grasped it: but it bears
Not mine, but his coagulated blood.

   Saul. Was not that sword, a consecrated thing,
In Nob, within the tabernacle hung?
Was it not wrapped within the mystic ephod,
And thus from all unhallowed eyes concealed?
Devoted to the Lord of hosts forever?

   David. 'Tis true; but—

   Saul. Whence didst thou obtain it then?
Who dared to give it? who?

   David. I will explain.
Powerless and fugitive to Nob I came:
Wherefore I fled, thou knowest. Every path
Was crowded with unhappy wretches; I,
Defenceless, found myself at every step
Within the jaws of death. With humble brow
I kneel'd within the tabernacle, where

22

God's Spirit doth descend: and there, these arms
(Which if a living man might to his side
Refit them, David surely was that man)
Myself demanded of the priest.

  Saul. And he?

  David. Gave them to me.

  Saul. He was?

  David. Ahimelech.

  Saul. Perfidious traitor! Vile!—Where is the altar?
O rage! Ah, all are miscreants! traitors all!
The foes of God; are ye his ministers?
Black souls in vestments white—Where is the axe?
Where is the altar? let him be destroyed.
Where is the victim? I will slay him.

  Michal. Father!

  Jon. O Heav'ns! What mean these words? Where dost thou fly?
Be pacified, I pray thee: there are not
Or altars here, or victims: in the priests
Respect that God who hears thee evermore.

  Saul. Who thus restrains me? Who resists me thus?
Who forces me to sit?

  Jon. My father—

  David. Thou,
Great God of Israel, do Thou succor him!
Thy servant kneels to Thee, and this implores.

  Saul. I am bereft of peace; the sun, my kingdom,
My children, and my power of thought, all, all
Are taken from me! Ah, unhappy Saul!
Who doth console thee? who is now the guide,
The prop of thy bewildered feebleness?
Thy children all are mute, are harsh and cruel.
And of the doting and infirm old man
They only wish the death: and nought attracts
My children, but the fatal diadem,
Which now is twined around thy hoary head.
Wrest it at once: and at the same time sever
From this now tremulous decaying form
Your father's palsied head.—Ah, wretched state!
Better were death. I wish for death.

  Michal. O father!
We all desire thy life: we each of us

23

Would die ourselves, to rescue thee from death.

Jon. Now, since in tears his fury is dissolved,
Brother, do thou, to recompose his soul,
Exert thy voice. So many times already
Hast thou enthralled him with celestial songs
To calm oblivion.

Michal. Yes; thou seest now,
The breathing in his panting breast subsides;
His looks, just now so savage, swim in tears:
Now is the time to lend him thy assistance.

David. May God in mercy speak to him through me.—

Omnipotent, eternal, infinite,
　　Thou, who dost govern each created thing;
Thou, who from nothing mad'st me by Thy might,
　　Blest with a soul that dares to Thee take wing;
Thou, who canst pierce the abyss of endless night,
　　And all its mysteries into daylight bring;
The universe doth tremble at Thy nod,
And sinners prostrate own the outstretched arm of God.

Oft on the gorgeous blazing wings ere now
　　Of thousand cherubim wert Thou revealed;
Oft did Thy pure divinity endow
　　Thy people's shepherd in the martial field:
To him a stream of eloquence wert Thou;
　　Thou wert his sword, his wisdom and his shield:
From Thy bright throne, O God, bestow one ray
To cleave the gathering clouds that intercept the day.

In tears of darkness we——

Saul. Hear I the voice
Of David? From a mortal lethargy
It seems to wake me, and displays to me
The cheering radiance of my early years.
David. Who comes, who comes, unseen, yet heard?
A sable cloud of dust appeared,
　　Chased by the eastern blast.—
But it has burst; and from its womb
A thousand brandished swords illume
　　The track through which it passed.

24

Saul, as a tower, his forehead rears,
His head a flaming circlet wears.
　　The earth beneath his feet
Echoes with tramp of horse and men:
The sea, the sky, the hills, the plain,
　　The warlike sounds repeat.

In awful majesty doth Saul appear;
　　Horsemen and chariots from before him fly:
Chilled by his presence is each heart with fear;
　　And god-like terrors lighten in his eye.

Ye sons of Ammon, late so proud,
Where now the scorn, the insults loud,
　　Ye raised against our host?
Your corpses more than fill the plain;
The ample harvest of your slain
　　Invalidates your boast.
See what it is thus to depend
On gods unable to defend.—
　　But wherefore from afar
Hear I another trumpet sound?
'Tis Saul's:—he levels with the ground
　　All Edom's sons of war.

Thus Moab, Zobah, by his arms laid low,
　　With impious Amalek, united fall:
Saul, like a stream fed by dissolving snow,
　　Defeats, disperses, overwhelms them all.

　　Saul. This is the voice of my departed years,
That from the tomb to glory now recalls me.
I live again in my victorious youth,
When I hear this—What do I say? Alas!
Should cries of war be now addressed to me?
Oblivion, indolence, and peace, invite
The old man to themselves.
　　David. Let peace be sung.—

Weary and thirsty, see he lies
　　Beside his native stream;
God's champion, whose past victories
　　Wake many a glorious dream.

25

The sighed-for laurel's evergreen
  Doth screen his head from heat;
His children, all around him seen,
  His sighs and smiles repeat.

They weep and smile, then smile and weep,
  With sympathy endued;
And still a strict accordance keep
  To every varying mood.

One daughter's gentle hand unfits
  His crested helm and sword;
His consort fond beside him sits,
  Embracing her loved lord.

The other doth clear water bring
  From the pure ambient flood,
To cleanse his stately brows, where cling
  Commingled dust and blood.

A cloud of odorous flowers she spreads,
  Which breathe their perfumes near;
And on his honor'd hand she sheds
  The duteous filial tear.

But why sits one apart reclined,
  In pensive mood alone?
Alas, she mourns that others find
  A task, while she has none.

But diff'rent thoughts, with eager haste,
  Attract the band of boys;
Till his turn comes to be embraced,
  One son himself employs

To make the blood-encrusted blade
  From spot and blemish clear:
With envy fired, another said:
  "When shall I poise that spear?

"That pond'rous lance when shall I wield,
  That now defies my strength?"
Another grasps the blazoned shield,
  And stalks behind its length.

26

Then tears of sweet surprise,
From forth the swimming eyes
  Of Saul are seen to roll:
For of his blooming race,
So full of royal grace,
  He knows that he's the soul.

The pleasure how entire,
How happy is the sire,
Whose waking thoughts inspire
  Affections so sincere!
But now the day is o'er;
The zephyrs breathe no more;
And sleep's soft powers restore
  The monarch we revere.

  Saul. Happy the father of a race like this!
O peace of mind, how precious are thy gifts!
Through all my veins balsamic sweetness flows.

THE DEATH OF SAUL

  Abner. O hapless king! Now whither dost thou fly?
This is a dreadful night.
  Saul. But, why this battle?
  Abner. The foe assailed us unawares: we
Wholly discomfited.
  Saul. Discomfited?
And liv'st thou, traitor!
  Abner. I? I live to save thee.
Hither perchance Philistia's hordes are streaming:
We are compelled to shun the first attack:
Meanwhile the day will dawn. Thee will I lead,
With my few followers, to yonder slopes.
  Saul. Shall I then live, while all my people fall?
  Abner. Ah, come! Alas! the tumult grows: approaches.
  Saul. My children—Jonathan—do they too fly?
Do they abandon me?
  Abner. O Heavens! Thy children,—
No, no; they fled not—ill-starred progeny!
  Saul. I understand thee: they are all destroyed.
  Michal. Alas! My brothers!

27

Abner. Thou no more hast sons.

Saul. What now remains for me?—Thou, thou alone,
But not for me, remainest.—In my heart
Have I been long time finally resolved:
And now the hour is come. This, Abner, is
The last of my commands. My daughter now
Guide to some place of safety.

Michal. Father, no;
Around thee will I twine myself: the foe
Will never aim a sword against a woman.

Saul. O daughter! say no more: compel me not
To weep. A conquered king should never weep.
Save her, O Abner, go: but, if she fall
Within the foeman's hands, say not, O no,
That she's the child of Saul; but rather tell them
That she is David's wife; they will respect her.
Go; fly.

Abner. She shall, I swear to thee, be safe,
If I can aught avail; but thou meantime.

Michal. My father—ah!—I will not, will not leave thee.

Saul. I will it: and I yet am king. But see,
The armed bands approach. Fly, Abner, fly:
Drag her by force with thee, if it be needful.

Michal. O father!—and forever?

Saul (alone). O my children!
I was a father. See thyself alone,
O king; of thy so many friends and servants,
Not one remains. Inexorable God,
Is Thy retributory wrath appeased?—
But, thou remain'st to me, O sword: now come,
My faithful servant in extremity.—
Hark, hark! the howlings of the haughty victors:
The flashing of their burning torches glare
Before my eyes already, and I see
Their swords by thousands.—O thou vile Philistia,
Me thou shalt find, but like a king, here—dead!

HANS CHRISTIAN ANDERSEN

HANS CHRISTIAN ANDERSEN (Danish, 1805-1875). One of the truly great modern storytellers. Childhood and youth of grinding poverty. After failing to achieve theatrical career, finally found success as a writer. Experimented in every field of literature, but universal fame rests on 168 fairy tales and stories, such as "The Ugly Duckling," "The Red Shoes," and "The Emperor's New Clothes."

THE LOVERS

A whip Top and a little Ball were together in a drawer among some other toys; and the Top said to the Ball, "Shall we not be bridegroom and bride, as we live together in the same box?"

But the Ball, which had a coat of morocco leather, and was just as conceited as any fine lady, would make no answer to such a proposal.

Next day the little boy came to whom the toys belonged; he painted the Top red and yellow, and hammered a brass nail into it; and it looked splendid when the Top turned round!

"Look at me!" he cried to the Ball. "What do you say now? Shall we not be engaged to each other? We suit one another so well! You jump and I dance! No one could be happier than we two should be."

"Indeed! Do you think so?" replied the little Ball. "Perhaps you do not know my papa and mamma were morocco slippers, and that I have a Spanish cork inside me?"

"Yes, but I am made of mahogany," said the Top; "and the mayor himself turned me. He has a turning lathe of his own and it amuses him greatly."

"Can I depend upon that?" asked the little Ball.

"May I never be whipped again if it is not true!" replied the Top.

"You can speak well for yourself," observed the Ball, "but I cannot grant your request. I am as good as engaged to a swallow; every time I leap up into the air she puts her head out of her nest and says, 'Will you?' And now I have silently said 'Yes,' and that is as good as half engaged; but I promise I will never forget you."

"Yes, that will be much good!" said the Top.

And they spoke no more to each other.

The next day the Ball was taken out by the boy. The Top saw how high it flew into the air, like a bird; at last one could no longer see it. Each time it came back again, but gave a high leap when it touched the earth, and that was done either from its longing to mount up again, or because it had a Spanish cork in its body. But the ninth time the little Ball remained absent, and did not come back again; and the boy sought and sought, but it was gone.

29

"I know very well where it is!" sighed the Top. "It is in the swallow's nest, and has married the swallow."

The more the Top thought of this, the more it longed for the Ball. Just because it could not get the Ball, its love increased; and the fact that the Ball had chosen another formed a peculiar feature in the case. So the Top danced round and hummed, but always thought of the little Ball, which became more and more beautiful in his fancy. Thus several years went by, and now it was an old love.

And the Top was no longer young! But one day he was gilt all over; never had he looked so handsome; he was now a golden Top, and sprang till he hummed again. Yes, that was something worth seeing! But all at once he sprang up too high, and—he was gone.

They looked and looked, even in the cellar, but he was not to be found. Where could he be?

He had jumped into the dust box, where all kinds of things were lying: cabbage stalks, sweepings, and dust that had fallen down from the roof.

"Here's a nice place to lie in! The gilding will soon leave me here. Among what a rabble have I alighted."

And then he looked sideways at a long, leafless cabbage stump, and at a curious round thing that looked like an old apple; but it was not an apple—it was an old Ball, which had lain for years in the gutter on the roof, and was quite saturated with water.

"Thank goodness, here comes one of us, with whom one can talk!" said the little Ball, and looked at the gilt Top. "I am really morocco, worked by maiden's hands, and have a Spanish cork within me; but no one would think it, to look at me. I was very nearly marrying a swallow, but I fell into the gutter on the roof, and have lain there full five years, and become quite wet through. You may believe me; that's a long time for a young girl."

But the Top said nothing. He thought of his old love; and the more he heard, the clearer it became to him that this was she.

Then came the servant girl, and wanted to turn out the dust box.

"Aha! there's a gilt Top!" she cried.

And so the Top was brought again to notice and honor, but nothing was heard of the little Ball. And the Top spoke no more of his old love; for that dies away when the beloved object has lain for five years in a gutter and got wet through; yes, one does not know her again when he meets her in the dust box.

LEONID NICOLAYEVIC ANDREYEV

LEONID NIKOLAYEVIC ANDREYEV (Russian, 1871-1919). Dramatist and
novelist of Russian realistic school, following Chekhov. Later developed his
own pessimistic philosophy of nihilism. Bitterly opposed Bolshevik regime,
and died in exile. Best-known works: *He Who Gets Slapped, The Black
Maskers, The Seven Who Were Hanged.* His writing sometimes journalistic,
but always worth while.

VALIA

VALIA was reading a huge, very huge book, almost half as large as
himself, with very black letters and pictures occupying the entire
page. To see the top line Valia had to stretch out his neck, lean far
over the table, kneeling in his chair, and putting his short chubby
finger on the letters for fear they would be lost among the other
ones like it, in which case it was a difficult task to find them again.
Owing to these circumstances, unforeseen by the publishers, the
reading advanced very slowly, notwithstanding the breath-catching
interest of the book.

It was a story about a very strong boy whose name was Prince
Bova, and who could, by merely grasping the legs or arms of
other boys, wrench them away from the body.

But Valia was suddenly interrupted in his reading; his mother
entered with some other woman.

"Here he is," said his mother, her eyes red with weeping. The
tears had evidently been shed very recently as she was still crushing
a white lace handkerchief in her hand.

"Valichka, darling!" exclaimed the other woman, and putting
her arms about his head, she began to kiss his face and eyes,
pressing her thin, hard lips to them. She did not fondle him as did
his mother, whose kisses were soft and melting; this one seemed
loath to let go of him. Valia accepted her pricking caresses with a
frown and silence; he was very much displeased at being interrupted, and he did not at all like this strange woman, tall, with
bony, long fingers upon which there was not even one ring. And
she smelled so bad: a damp, moldly smell, while his mother always
exhaled a fresh, exquisite perfume.

At last the woman left him in peace, and while he was wiping
his lips she looked him over with that quick sort of glance which
seemed to photograph one. His short nose with its indication of a

31

future little hump, his thick, unchildish brows over dark eyes, and the general appearance of stern seriousness, recalled some one to her, and she began to cry. Even her weeping was unlike mama's: the face remained immovable while the tears quickly rolled down one after the other—before one had time to fall another was already chasing after it. Her tears ceased as suddenly as they had commenced, and she asked: "Valichka, do you know me?"—"No."

"I called to see you. Twice I called to see you."

Perhaps she had called upon him, perhaps she had called twice, but how should Valia know of it? With her questions she only hindered him from reading.

"I am your mama, Valia!" said the woman.

Valia looked around in astonishment to find his mama, but she was no longer in the room.

"Why, can there be two mamas?" he asked. "What nonsense you are telling me."

The woman laughed, but this laugh did not please Valia; it was evident that the woman did not wish to laugh at all, and did it purposely to fool him. For some moments they were both silent.

"And what book is it you are reading?"

"About Prince Bova," Valia informed her with serious self-esteem and an evident respect for the big book.

"Ach, it must be very interesting! Tell me, please!" the woman asked with an ingratiating smile.

And once more something unnatural and false sounded in this voice, which tried to be soft and round like the voice of his mother, but remained sharp and prickly. The same insincerity appeared also in all the movements of the woman; she turned on her chair and even stretched out her neck with a manner as if preparing for a long and attentive listening; and when Valia reluctantly began the story, she immediately retired within herself, like a dark-lantern on which the cover is suddenly thrown. Valia felt the offense toward himself and Prince Bova, but, wishing to be polite, he quickly finished the story and added: "That is all."

"Well, good-by, my dear, my dove!" said the strange woman, and once more pressed her lips to Valia's face. "I shall soon call again. Will you be glad?"

"Yes, come please," politely replied Valia, and to get rid of her more quickly he added: "I will be very glad."

The visitor left him, but hardly had Valia found in the book again the word at which he had been interrupted, when mama entered, looked at him, and she also began to weep. He could easily understand why the other woman should have wept; she must have been sorry that she was so unpleasant and tiresome—but why should his mama weep?

"Listen, mama," he said musingly, "how that woman bored me! She says that she is my mama. Why, could there be two mamas to one boy?"

"No, baby, there could not; but she speaks the truth; she is your mother."

"And what are you, then?"

"I am your auntie."

This was a very unexpected discovery, but Valia received it with unshakable indifference; auntie, well, let it be auntie—was it not just the same? A word did not, as yet, have the same meaning for him as it would for a grown person. But his former mother did not understand it, and began to explain why it had so happened that she had been a mother and had become an aunt. Once, long ago, when Valia was very little—

"How little? So?" Valia raised his hand about a quarter of a yard from the table. "Like Kiska?" Valia exclaimed, joyfully surprised, with mouth opened and brow lifted. He spoke of his kitten that had been presented to him.

"Yes."

Valia broke into a happy laugh, but immediately resumed his usual earnestness, and with the condescension of a grown person recalling the mistakes of his youth, he remarked: "How funny I must have been!"

When he was so very little and funny, like Kiska, he had been brought by that woman and given away forever, also like Kiska. And now, when he had become so big and clever, the woman wanted him.

"Do you wish to go to her?" asked his former mother and reddened with joy when Valia resolutely and sternly said: "No, she does not please me!" and once more took up his book.

Valia considered the affair closed, but he was mistaken. This strange woman, with a face as devoid of life as if all the blood had been drained out of it, who had appeared from no one knew where, and vanished without leaving a trace, seemed to have set the whole house in turmoil and filled it with a dull alarm. Mama-auntie often cried and repeatedly asked Valia if he wished to leave her; uncle-papa grumbled, patted his bald pate so that the sparse, gray hair on it stood up, and when auntie-mama was absent from the room he also asked Valia if he would like to go to that woman. Once, in the evening, when Valia was already in his little bed but was not yet sleeping, he heard his uncle and auntie speaking of him and the woman. The uncle spoke in an angry basso at which the crystal pendants of the chandelier gently trembled and sparkled with bluish and reddish lights.

"You speak nonsense, Nastasia Philippovna. We have no right to give the child away."

"She loves him, Grisha."

"And we! Do we not love him? You are arguing very strangely, Nastasia Philippovna. It seems as if you would be glad to get rid of the child—"

"Are you not ashamed of yourself?"

"Well, well, how quick you are to take offense. Just consider this matter cold-bloodedly and reasonably. Some frivolous thing or other gives birth to children, light-heartedly disposes of them by placing them on your threshold, and afterward says: 'Kindly give me my child, because, on account of my lover having abandoned me, I feel lonesome. For theatres and concerts I have no money, so give me the child to serve as a toy to play with.' No, madam, be easy, we shall see who wins in this case!"

"You are unjust to her, Grisha. You know well how ill and lonely she is—"

"You, Nastasia Philippovna, can make even a saint lose patience, by God! And the child you seem to have forgotten? For you is it wholly immaterial whether he is brought up an honest man or a scoundrel? And I could bet my head that he would be brought up by her a scoundrel, rascal, and—scoundrel."

"Grisha!"

"I ask you, for God's sake, not to irritate me! And where did you get this devilish habit of contradicting? 'She is so lonely.' And are *we* not lonely? The heartless woman that you are, Nastasia Philippovna! And why did I marry you!"

The heartless woman broke into tears, and her husband immediately begged her pardon, declaring that only a born fool could pay any attention to the words of such an old ass as he was. Gradually she became calmer and asked: "What does Talonsky say?"

"And what makes you think that he is such a clever fellow?" Gregory Aristarchovich again flew into a passion. "He says that everything depends on how the court will look at it. . . Something new, is it not, as if we did not know without his telling that everything depends on how the court will look at it! Of course it matters little to him—what does he care?—he will have his bark and then safely go his way. If I had *my* way, it would go ill with all these empty talkers—"

But here Nastasia Philippovna shut the dining-room door and Valia did not hear the end of the conversation. But he lay for a long time with open eyes, trying to understand what sort of woman it was who wished to take him away from his home and ruin him.

On the next day he waited from early morning expecting his auntie to ask him if he wished to go to his mother; but auntie did not ask. Neither did his uncle. Instead of this, they both gazed at Valia as if he were dangerously ill and would soon die; they caressed him and brought him large books with colored pictures. The woman did not call any more, but it seemed to Valia that she must be lurking outside the door watching for him, and that as soon as he would pass the threshold she would seize him and carry him out into a black and dismal distance where cruel monsters were wriggling and breathing fire.

In the evenings while his uncle Gregory Aristarchovich was occupied in his study and Nastasia Philippovna was knitting something, or playing a game of solitaire, Valia read his books, in which the lines would grow gradually thicker and the letters smaller. Everything in the room was quiet, so quiet that the only thing to be heard was the rustling of the pages he turned, and occasionally the uncle's loud cough from the study, or the striking of the abacus counters. The lamp, with its blue shade, threw a bright light on the blue plush table-cover, but the corners of the room were full of a quiet, mysterious gloom. There stood large plants with curious leaves and roots crawling out upon the surface and looking very much like fighting serpents, and it seemed as if something large and dark was moving amidst them. Valia read, and before his wide-open eyes passed terrible, beautiful and sad images which awakened in him pity and love, but more often fear. Valia was sorry for the poor water-nymph who so dearly loved the handsome prince that for him she had given up her sisters and the deep, peaceful ocean; and the prince knew nothing of this love, because the poor water-nymph was dumb, and so he married a gay princess; and while great festivities in honor of the wedding were in full swing on board the ship, and music was playing and all were enjoying themselves, the poor water-nymph threw herself into the dark waves to die. Poor,

35

sweet little water-nymph, so quiet and sad, and modest! But often terrible, cruel, human monsters appeared before Valia. In the dark nights they flew somewhere on their prickly wings, and the air whistled over their heads, and their eyes burned like red-hot coals. And afterward, they were surrounded by other monsters like themselves while a mysterious and terrible something was happening there. Laughter as sharp as a knife, long and pitiful wailing; strange weird dances in the purplish light of torches, their slanty, fiery tongues wrapped in the red clouds of smoke; and dead men with long, black beards— All this was the manifestation of a single enigmatic and cruel power, wishing to destroy man. Angry and mysterious spectres filled the air, hid among the plants, whispered something, and pointed their bony fingers at Valia; they gazed at him from behind the door of the adjoining unlit room, giggled and waited till he would go to bed, when they would silently dart around over his head; they peeped at him from out of the garden through the large, dark windows, and wailed sorrowfully with the wind.

In and out among all this vicious and terrible throng appeared the image of that woman who had come for Valia. Many people came and went in the house of Gregory Aristarchovich, and Valia did not remember their faces, but this face lived in his memory. It was such an elongated, thin, yellow face, and smiled with a sly, dissembling smile, from which two deep lines appeared at the two corners of the mouth. If this woman took Valia he would die.

"Listen," Valia once said to his aunt, tearing himself away from his book for a moment. "Listen," he repeated with his usual earnestness, and with a glance that gazed straight into the eyes of the person with whom he spoke: "I shall call you mama, not auntie. You talk nonsense when you say that the woman—is mama. You are mama, not she."

"Why?" asked Nastasia Philippovna, blushing like a young girl who had just received a compliment. But along with her joy there could also be heard in her voice the sound of fear for Valia. He had become so strange of late, and timid; feared to sleep alone, as he used to do, raved in his sleep and cried.

"But, Valichka, it is true, she is your mother."

"I really wonder where you get this habit of contradicting!" Valia said after some musing, imitating the tone of Gregory Aristarchovich.

Nastasia Philippovna laughed, but while preparing for bed that night she spoke for a considerable time with her husband, who

36

boomed like a Turkish drum, abused the empty talkers, and frivolous, hare-brained women, and afterward went with his wife to see
Valia.

They gazed long and silently into the face of the sleeping child.
The flame of the candle swayed in the trembling hand of Gregory
Aristarchovich and lent a fantastic, death-like coloring to the face
of the boy, which was as white as the pillows on which it rested.
It seemed as if a pair of stern, black eyes looked at them from the
dark hollows, demanding a reply and threatening them with misfortune and unknown sorrow, and the lips twitched into a strange,
ironic smile as if upon his helpless child-head lay a vague reflection
of those cruel and mysterious spectre monsters that silently hovered
over it.

"Valia!" whispered the frightened Nastasia. The boy sighed deeply
but did not move, as if enchained in the sleep of death.

"Valia! Valia!" the deep, trembling voice of her husband was
added to that of Nastasia Philippovna.

Valia opened his eyes, shaded by thick eyelashes; the light of
the candle made him wink, and he sprang to his knees, pale and
frightened. His uncovered, thin little arms, like a pearl necklace
encircled his auntie's full, rosy neck, and hiding his little head
upon her breast and screwing up his eyes tight as if fearing that
they would open of themselves, he whispered: "I am afraid, mama,
I am afraid! Do not go!"

That was a bad night for the whole household; when Valia at
last fell asleep, Gregory Aristarchovich got an attack of asthma. He
choked, and his full, white breast rose and fell spasmodically under
the ice compresses. Toward morning he grew more tranquil, and
the worn Nastasia fell asleep with the thought that her husband
would not survive the loss of the child.

After a family council at which it was decided that Valia ought
to read less and to see more of children of his own age, little girls
and boys were brought to the house to play with him. But Valia
from the first conceived a dislike for these foolish children who, in
his eyes, were too noisy, loud and indecorous. They pulled flowers,
tore books, jumped over chairs, and fought like little monkeys; and
he, serious and thoughtful, looked on at their pranks with amazement and displeasure, and, going up to Nastasia Philippovna, said:
"They tire me! I would rather sit by you." And in the evenings he
once more took up his book, and when Gregory Aristarchovich,
grumbling at all the deviltry the child read about, and by which he

was losing his senses, gently tried to take the book from Valia's hands, the child silently and irresolutely pressed it to himself. And the improvised pedagogue beat a confused retreat and angrily scolded his wife:

"Is this what you call bringing up! No, Nastasia Philippovna, I see you are more fit to take care of kittens than to bring up children. The boy is so spoiled that one can not even take a book away from him."

One morning while Valia was sitting at breakfast with Nastasia Philippovna, Gregory Aristarchovich suddenly came rushing into the dining-room. His hat was tilted on the back of his head, his face was covered with perspiration; while still at the other side of the door he shouted joyfully into the room:

"Refused! The court has refused!"

The diamond earrings in Nastasia Philippovna's ears began to sparkle, and the little knife she held in her hand dropped to the plate.

"Is it true?" she asked, breathlessly.

Gregory Aristarchovich made a serious face, just to show that he had spoken the truth, but immediately forgetting his intention, his face became covered with a whole network of merry wrinkles. Then once more remembering that he lacked that earnestness of demeanor with which important news is usually imparted, he frowned, pushed a chair up to the table, placed his hat upon it, forgot that it was his hat, and thinking the chair to be already occupied by some one, threw a stern look at Nastasia Philippovna, then on Valia, winked his eye at Valia; and only after all these solemn preliminaries did he declare:

"I always said that Talonsky was a devilish clever fellow; can't fool him easily, Nastasia Philippovna."

"So it is true?"

"You are always ready with your eternal doubts. I said the case of Mme. Akimova is dismissed. Clever, is it not, little brother?" he turned to Valia and added in a stern, official tone: "And that said Akimova is to pay the costs."

"That woman will not take me, then?"

"I guess she won't, brother mine! Ach, I have entirely forgotten, I brought you some books!"

Gregory Aristarchovich rushed into the corridor, but halted on hearing Nastasia Philippovna's scream. Valia had fallen back on his chair in a faint.

A happy time began for the family. It was as if some one who had lain dangerously ill in the house had suddenly recovered and all began to breathe more easily and freely. Valia lost his fear of the terrible monsters and no longer suffered from nightmares. When the little monkeys, as he called the children, came to see him again, he was the most inventive of the lot. But even into the most fantastic plays he introduced his habitual earnestness and staidness, and when they played Indians. he found it indispensable to divest himself of almost all his clothing and cover his body with red paint.

In view of the businesslike manner in which these games were conducted, Gregory Aristarchovich now found it possible to participate in them, as far as his abilities allowed. In the rôle of a bear he did not appear to great advantage, but he had a great and well deserved success in his rôle of elephant. And when Valia, silent and earnest as a true son of the Goddess Kali, sat upon his father's shoulders and gently tapped upon his rosy bald pate with a tiny toy hammer, he really reminded one of a little Eastern prince who despotically reigns over people and animals.

The lawyer Talonsky tried to convey a hint to Gregory Aristarchovich that all was not safe yet, but the former could not comprehend how three judges could reverse the decision of three other judges, when the laws are the same here and everywhere. And when the lawyer insisted, Gregory Aristarchovich grew angry, and to prove that there was nothing to be feared from the higher court, he brought forward that same Talonsky on whom he now implicitly relied:

"Why, are you not going to be present when the case is brought before the court? Well, then what is there to be talked about. I wish you, Nastasia Philippovna, would make him ashamed of himself."

Talonsky smiled, and Nastasia Philippovna gently chided him for his purposeless doubts. They also spoke of the woman who had caused all the trouble, but now that she could menace them no more, and the court had decided that she must bear all the costs of the trial, they often dubbed her "poor woman."

Since the day Valia had heard that the woman had no longer any power to take him, she had lost in his eyes the halo of mysterious fear, which enveloped her like a mist and distorted the features of her thin face, and Valia began to think of her as he did of all other people. He now repeatedly heard that she was unhappy and could not understand why; but this pale bloodless face grew more simple, natural and near to him, the "poor woman," as they called her, began to interest him, and recalling other poor women of whom he had read, he felt a growing pity and a timid tenderness for her.

He imagined that she must sit alone in some dark room, fearing something and weeping, always weeping, as she had wept then when she had come to see him. And he felt sorry that he had not told her the story of Prince Bova better than he had at the time.

.   .   .   .

It appeared that three judges could, after all, disagree with the decision of three other judges. The higher court had reversed the decision of the district court, the child was adjudged to his real mother. And the appeal was not considered by the senate.

When the woman came to take Valia away with her, Gregory Aristarchovich was not at home, he was at Talonsky's house and was lying in Talonsky's bedroom, and only the bald, rosy pate was visible above the snow-white pillows.

Nastasia Philippovna did not leave her room, and the maid led Valia forth from it already dressed for the road. He wore a fur coat and tall overshoes in which he moved his feet with difficulty. From under his fur cap looked out a pale little face with a frank and serious expression in the dark eyes. Under his arm Valia carried a book in which was the story of a poor water-nymph.

The tall, gaunt woman pressed the boy to her shabby coat and sobbed out: "How you have grown, Valichka! You are unrecognizable," she said, trying to joke, but Valia adjusted his cap and, contrary to habit, did not look into the eyes of the one who from this day on was to be his mother, but into her mouth. It was large, but with beautiful, small teeth; the two wrinkles on the corners of the mouth were still on the same place where Valia had seen them first, only now they were deeper.

"You are not angry with me?" asked mama; but Valia, not replying to her question, said: "Let us be gone."

"Valichka!" came a pitiful scream from Nastasia Philippovna's room, and she appeared on the threshold with eyes swollen from weeping, and clasping her hands she rushed toward the child, sank on her knees, and put her head on his shoulder. She did not utter a sound, only the diamonds in her ears trembled.

"Come, Valia," sternly said the tall woman, taking his hand. "We must not remain any longer among people who have subjected your mother to such torture—such torture!"

Her dry voice was full of hatred and she longed to strike the kneeling woman with her foot.

"Ugh! heartless wretches! You would be glad to take even my only child from me!" she wrathfully whispered, and pulled Valia away by his hand. "Come! Don't be like your father, who abandoned me."

"Ta-ke ca-re of him," Nastasia called after them.

The hired sleigh which stood waiting for them flew softly and lightly over the snow and noiselessly carried Valia away from the quiet house with its wonderful plants and flowers, its mysterious fairy-tale world, immeasurable and deep as the sea, with its windows gently screened by the boughs of the tall trees of the garden. Soon the house was lost in the mass of other houses, as similar to each other as the letters in Valia's book, and vanished forever from Valia.

It seemed to him as if they were swimming in a river, the banks of which were constituted of rows of lanterns as close to each other as beads on a string, but when they approached nearer, the beads were scattered, forming large, dark spaces and merging behind into just such a line of light. And then Valia thought that they were standing motionless on the very same spot; and everything began to be like a fairy tale—he himself and the tall woman who was pressing him to her, and everything around him.

The hand in which he carried his book was getting stiff with cold, but he would not ask his mother to take the book from him.

The small room into which Valia's mother had taken him was untidy and hot; in a corner near the large bed stood a little curtained bed such as Valia had not slept in for a long, long time.

"You are frozen! Well, wait, we shall soon have some tea! Well, now you are with your mama. Are you glad?" his mother asked with the hard, unpleasant look of one who has been forced to smile beneath blows all her life long.

"No," Valia replied shyly, frightened at his own frankness.

"No? And I had bought some toys for you. Just look, there they are on the window.

Valia approached the window and examined the toys. They were wretched paper horses with straight, thick legs, Punch with a red cap on, with an idiotically grinning face and a large nose, and little tin soldiers with one foot raised in the air.

Valia had long ago given up playing with toys and did not like them, but from politeness he did not show it to his mother. "Yes, they are nice toys," he said.

She noticed the glance he threw at the window, and said with that unpleasant, ingratiating smile:

"I did not know what you liked, darling, and I bought them for you a long time ago."

Valia was silent, not knowing what to reply.

"You must know that I am all alone, Valia, all alone in the wide world; I have no one whose advice I could ask; I thought they would please you." Valia was silent.

Suddenly the muscles of the woman's face relaxed and the tears began to drop from her eyes, quickly, quickly, one after the other, and she threw herself on the bed which gave a pitiful squeak under the weight of her body, and with one hand pressed to her breast, the other to her temples, she looked vacantly through the wall with her pale, faded eyes, and whispered:

"He was not pleased! Not pleased!—"

Valia promptly approached the bed, put his little hand, still red with the cold, on the head of his mother, and spoke with the same serious staidness which distinguished this boy's speech:

"Do not cry, mama. I will love you very much. I do not care to play with toys, but I will love you ever so much. If you wish, I will read to you the story of the poor water-nymph."

GUILLAUME APOLLINAIRE

GUILLAUME APOLLINAIRE (French, 1880-1918). The ancestor of poetic surrealism. Born in Italy, became French citizen in 1914. Died of wounds received in World War I. Fought for new movements in painting and literature: impressionism, cubism, surrealism. Chief works: *Alcools, Calligrammes, Les Mamelles de Tirésias*. The leader of his generation, influenced modern poetry.

FAREWELL

I have culled this twig of heather
Remember the autumn now too late
We shall meet no more in any weather
Odor of the season twig of heather
And remember that I wait.

HUNTING HORNS

Our story is noble and tragic
As a tyrant's mask;
No dangerous drama or magic;
No detail unpoetic
Makes our love-dream pathetic.

And Thomas De Quincey drinking
His opiate hippocras
Of his poor Ann wandered thinking
Let us pass, since all things pass
I shall return at my ease.

Memories are hunting horns
Whose sound dies on the breeze.

SALOME

So that John the Baptist might once more seem glad
Sire I'd dance to the Seraphim's pride
Mother tell me why it is you are so sad
In your robe of a countess at the Dauphin's side

My heart beat beat more loudly at his word
While I danced in the fennel hearkening
And I broidered lilies for a pennon-bird
At the end of his lance for to swing

Now for whom do you want me to broider this thing
His lance buds again on the Jordan banks
And the lilies by your soldiers O Herod king
When they bore him away drooped dead in their ranks

Come all of you with me below the quincunce
Weep not pretty royal jester steady
Take this head dance with it for your motley dunce
Don't touch his brow mother dear is cold already

Sire march before your troops will follow arter
We'll dig a ditch and lay him underground
We'll plant some flowers and we'll dance a round
Till I have lost my garter
The king his sneeze-starter
The child his prayer-charter
The priest his soul-barter

MEADOW-SAFFRON

The meadow is pretty but poisonous in the fall.
The cows at pasture there
Slowly absorb the venom;
The meadow-saffron, lilac, ringed,
Flourishes there your eyes are like that flower
Violet as its dark ring and as the fall
And from your eyes my days seep in slow poison.

With a clamor the children pour out of school
With their jackets on, playing harmonicas.
They gather the meadow-saffrons, which are like mothers there
Daughters of their daughters and color of your eyelids

Waving as flowers wave in the wild wind

The shepherd of the flock sings sweetly
While slowly lowing the cows leave once for all
This great field ill-flowered by the fall.

THE LORELEI

At Bacharach was a sorceress with flaxen locks
For love of whom the men around died in flocks

She was called to the tribunal at the bishop's manse
But because of her beauty he absolved her in advance

O beauteous Lorelei with eyes of jeweled smiles
From what magician have you learned your wiles

I am tired of living and mine eyes are accurst
Those who have beheld them, bishop, died of lusting thirst

Mine eyes are flames they are not sparkling jewels
Throw throw to the flames these devil's fuels

I flare in the flames O beauteous Lorelei
Let another condemn you you have bewitched me I

Bishop you jest pray I find the Virgin's breast
Send me to die with the Lord may you rest

My love has gone to a far-off coast
Send me to die for my love is lost

My heart is sore stricken indeed I must die
If I could behold myself it would glaze my eye

44

My heart is sore stricken since he went away
My heart is sore stricken from his parting day

The bishop summoned three lance-tall cavaliers
Take her to the convent with her insane tears

Go crazy Lora go Lora with trembling sight
You will be a sister robed in black and white

Then off they started all four on the way
The Lorelei besought them and her eyes were like the day

Cavaliers let me mount that distant height
Once more to glimpse my castle ere it pass fore'er from sight

Once more to behold myself mirrored in the flood
Then to the convent of maid- and widowhood

There her loosened locks in the wind waved high
And the cavaliers shouted Lorelei Lorelei

Below on the Rhine a slow skiff crawls
And my lover guides it he has seen me and he calls

My heart becomes calm again 'tis my lover mine
Then she leaned over and she fell into the Rhine

For seeing in the water the beauteous Lorelei
With hair of the sunlight and with eyes of the sky.

LUDOVICO ARIOSTO

LUDOVICO ARIOSTO (Italian, 1474-1533). The outstanding poet of the
Cinquecento. Held political posts at the court of Ferrara, and was governor
of Garfagnana. Wrote first in Latin, later in Italian. His masterpiece is the
epic poem, *Orlando Furioso*, though he wrote numerous comedies and satires.
He added romantic imagination and humor to the traditional Latin epic.

ALCINA THE ENCHANTRESS

Not so much does the palace, fair to see,
   In riches other princely domes excel,
   As that the gentlest, fairest company
   Which the whole world contains, within it dwell:
   Of either sex, with small variety
   Between, in youth and beauty matched as well:
   The fay alone exceeds the rest as far
   As the bright sun outshines each lesser star.

Her shape is of such perfect symmetry,
  As best to feign the industrious painter knows,
  With long and knotted tresses; to the eye
  Not yellow gold with brighter luster glows.
  Upon her tender cheek the mingled dye
  Is scattered, of the lily and the rose.
  Like ivory smooth, the forehead gay and round
  Fills up the space, and forms a fitting bound.

Two black and slender arches rise above
  Two clear black eyes, say suns of radiant light;
  Which ever softly beam and slowly move;
  Round these appears to sport in frolic flight,
  Hence scattering all his shafts, the little Love,
  And seems to plunder hearts in open sight.
  Thence, through mid visage, does the nose descend,
  Where Envy finds not blemish to amend.

As if between two vales, which softly curl,
  The mouth with vermeil tint is seen to glow:
  Within are strung two rows of orient pearl,
  Which her delicious lips shut up or show.
  Of force to melt the heart of any churl,
  However rude, hence courteous accents flow;
  And here that gentle smile receives its birth,
  Which opes at will a paradise on earth.

Like milk the bosom, and the neck of snow;
  Round is the neck, and full and large the breast;
  Where, fresh and firm, two ivory apples grow,
  Which rise and fall, as, to the margin pressed
  By pleasant breeze, the billows come and go.
  Not prying Argus could discern the rest.
  Yet might the observing eye of things concealed
  Conjecture safely, from the charms revealed.

To all her arms a just proportion bear,
  And a white hand is oftentimes descried,
  Which narrow is, and somedeal long; and where
  No knot appears, nor vein is signified.

For finish of that stately shape and rare,
A foot, neat, short, and round, beneath is spied.
Angelic visions, creatures of the sky,
Concealed beneath no covering veil can lie.

A springe is planted in Rogero's way,
On all sides did she speak, smile, sing, or move;
No wonder then the stripling was her prey,
Who in the fairy saw such show of love,
With him the guilt and falsehood little weigh,
Of which the offended myrtle told above.
Nor will he think that perfidy and guile
Can be united with so sweet a smile.

No! he could now believe, by magic art,
Astolpho well transformed upon the plain,
For punishment of foul ungrateful heart,
And haply meriting severer pain.
And, as for all he heard him late impart,
'Twas prompted by revenge, 'twas false and vain.
By hate and malice was the sufferer stung,
To blame and wound the fay with slanderous tongue.

The beauteous lady whom he loved so well
Is newly banished from his altered breast;
For (such the magic of Alcina's spell)
She every ancient passion dispossessed:
And in his bosom, there alone to dwell,
The image of her love and self impressed.
So witched, Rogero sure some grace deserves,
If from his faith his frail affection swerves.

At board lyre, lute, and harp of tuneful string,
And other sounds, in mixed diversity,
Made, round about, the joyous palace ring,
With glorious concert and sweet harmony.
Nor lacked there well-accorded voice to sing
Of love, its passion and its ecstasy;
Nor who, with rare inventions, choicely versed,
Delightful fiction to the guests rehearsed.

47

What table, spread by whatsoever heir
　　Of Ninus, though triumphant were the board,
　　Or what more famous and more costly, where
　　Cleopatra feasted with the Latian lord,
　　Could with this banquet's matchless joys compare,
　　By the fond fairy for Rogero stored?
　　I think not such a feast is spread above,
　　Where Ganymede presents the cup to Jove.

They form a ring, the board and festive cheer
　　Removed, and sitting, play a merry game:
　　Each asks, still whispering in a neighbor's ear,
　　What secret pleases best; to knight and dame
　　A fair occasion, without let or fear,
　　Their love, unheard of any, to proclaim.
　　And in conclusion the two lovers plight
　　Their word, to meet together on that night.

Soon, and much sooner than their wont, was ended
　　The game at which the palace inmates play:
　　When pages on the troop with torches tended,
　　And with their radiance chased the night away.
　　To seek his bed the paladin ascended,
　　Girt with that goodly squadron, in a gay
　　And airy bower, appointed for his rest,
　　'Mid all the others chosen as the best.

And when of comfits and of cordial wine
　　A fitting proffer has been made anew,
　　The guests their bodies reverently incline,
　　And to their bowers depart the courtly crew.
　　He upon perfumed sheets, whose texture fine
　　Seemed of Arachne's loom, his body threw:
　　Hearkening the while with still attentive ears,
　　If he the coming of the lady hears.

At every movement heard on distant floor,
　　Hoping 'twas she, Rogero raised his head:
　　He thinks he hears; but it is heard no more,
　　Then sighs at his mistake: ofttimes from bed

He issued, and undid his chamber door,
  And peeped abroad, but still no better sped:
  And cursed a thousand times the hour that she
  So long retarded his felicity.

"Yes, now she comes," the stripling often said,
  And reckoned up the paces, as he lay,
  Which from her bower were haply to be made
  To that where he was waiting for the fay.
  These thoughts, and other thoughts as vain, he weighed
  Before she came, and, restless at her stay,
  Often believed some hindrance, yet unscanned,
  Might interpose between the fruit and hand.

At length, when dropping sweets the costly fay
  Had put some end to her perfumery,
  The time now come she need no more delay,
  Since all was hushed within the palace, she
  Stole from her bower alone, through secret way,
  And passed towards the chamber silently,
  Where on his couch the youthful cavalier
  Lay, with a heart long torn by Hope and Fear.

When the successor of Astolpho spies
  Those smiling stars above him, at the sight
  A flame, like that of kindled sulphur, flies
  Through his full veins, as ravished by delight
  Out of himself; and now up to the eyes
  Plunged in a sea of bliss, he swims outright.
  He leaps from bed and folds her to his breast,
  Nor waits until the lady be undressed;

Though but in a light sendal clad, that she
  Wore in the place of farthingale or gown;
  Which o'er a shift of finest quality,
  And white, about her limbs the fay had thrown:
  The mantle yielded at his touch, as he
  Embraced her, and that veil remained alone,
  Which upon every side the damsel shows,
  More than clear glass the lily or the rose.

The plant no closer does the ivy clip,
    With whose green boughs its stem is interlaced,
    Than those fond lovers, each from either's lip
    The balmy breath collecting, lie embraced:
    Rich perfume this, whose like no seed or slip
    Bears in sweet Indian or Sabæan waste;
    While so to speak their joys is either fixed,
    That oftentimes those meeting lips are mixed.

These things were carried closely by the dame
    And youth, or if surmised, were never bruited;
    For silence seldom was a cause for blame,
    But oftener as a virtue well reputed.
    By those shrewd courtiers, conscious of his claim,
    Rogero is with proffers fair saluted:
    Worshiped of all those inmates, who fulfill
    In this the enamored fay, Alcina's will.

No pleasure is omitted there; since they
    Alike are prisoners in Love's magic hall.
    They change their raiment twice or thrice a day,
    Now for this use, and now at other call.
    'Tis wrestling, tourney, pageant, bath, and ball;
    Now underneath a hill by fountain cast,
    They read the amorous lays of ages past;

Now by glad hill, or through the shady dale,
    They hunt the fearful hare, and now they flush
    With busy dog, sagacious of the trail,
    Wild pheasant from the stubble field or bush.
    Now where green junipers perfume the gale,
    Suspend the snare, or lime the fluttering thrush;
    And casting now for fish, with net or hook,
    Disturb their secret haunts in pleasant brook.

Rogero revels there, in like delight,
    While Charles and Agramant are troubled sore.
    But not for him their story will I slight,
    Nor Bradamant forget; who evermore,
    'Mid toilsome pain and care, her cherished knight,
    Ravished from her, did many a day deplore;

Whom by unwonted ways, transported through
Mid air, the damsel saw, nor whither knew.

Of her I speak before the royal pair,
  Who many days pursued her search in vain;
By shadowy wood, or over champaign bare,
  By farm and city, and by hill and plain;
But seeks her cherished friend with fruitless care,
  Divided by such space of land and main:
Often she goes among the Paynim spears,
Yet never aught of her Rogero hears.

Of hundreds questioned, upon every side,
  Each day, no answer ever gives content.
She roams from post to post, and far and wide
  Searches pavilion, lodging, booth, or tent,
And this, 'mid foot or horseman, unespied,
  May safely do, without impediment,
Thanks to the ring, whose more than mortal aid,
When in her mouth, conceals the vanished maid.

She cannot, will not, think that he is dead;
  Because the wreck of such a noble knight
Would from Hydaspes' distant waves have spread,
  To where the sun descends with westering light.
She knows not what to think, nor whither sped,
  He roams in earth or air; yet, hapless wight,
Him ever seeks, and for attendant train
Has sobs and sighs, and every bitter pain.

At length to find the wondrous cave she thought,
  Where the prophetic bones of Merlin lie,
And there lament herself until she wrought
  Upon the pitying marble to reply;
For thence, if yet he lived, would she be taught,
  Or this glad life to hard necessity
Had yielded up; and, when she was possessed
Of the seer's counsels, would pursue the best.

With this intention, Bradamant her way
  Directed thither, where in Poictier's wood

51

The vocal tomb, containing Merlin's clay,
Concealed in Alpine place and savage, stood.
But that enchantress sage, who night and day
Thought of the damsel, watchful for her good,
She, I repeat, who taught her what should be
In that fair grotto her posterity;

She who preserved her with protecting care,
That same enchantress, still benign and wise,
Who, knowing she a matchless race should bear
Of men, or rather semi-deities,
Spies daily what her thoughts and actions are,
And lots for her each day, divining, tries;—
She all Rogero's fortune knew, how freed;
Then borne to India by the griffin steed:

Him on that courser plainly she had eyed,
Who would not the controlling rein obey;
When, severed by such interval, he hied,
Borne through the perilous, unwonted way,
And knew that he sport, dance, and banquet plied,
And lapt in idleness and pleasure lay;
Nor memory of his lord nor of the dame,
Once loved so well, preserved, nor of his fame.

And thus such gentle knight ingloriously
Would have consumed his fairest years and best
In long inaction, afterwards to be,
Body and soul, destroyed; and *that*, possessed
Alone by us in perpetuity,
That flower, whose sweets outlive the fragile rest
Which quickens man when he in earth is laid,
Would have been plucked or severed in the blade,

But that enchantress kind, who with more care
Than for himself he watched, still kept the knight,
Designed to drag him, by rough road and bare,
Towards true virtue, in his own despite;
As often cunning leech will burn and pare
The flesh, and poisonous drug employ aright:
Who, though at first his cruel art offend,
Is thanked, since he preserves us, in the end.

She, not like old Atlantes, rendered blind
　　By the great love she to the stripling bore,
　　Set not on gifting him with life her mind,
　　As was the scope of that enchanter hoar;
　　Who, reckless all of fame and praise declined,
　　Wished length of days to his Rogero more
　　Than that, to win a world's applause, the peer
　　Should of his joyous life forego one year.

By him he to Alcina's isle had been
　　Dispatched, that in her palace he might dwell,
　　Forgetting arms; and, as enchanter seen
　　In magic and the use of every spell,
　　The heart had fastened of that fairy queen,
　　Enamored of the gentle youth, so well,
　　That she the knot would never disengage,
　　Though he should live to more than Nestor's age.

ARISTOPHANES

ARISTOPHANES (Greek, *ca.* 450-385 B.C.). The great satirical dramatist of
his time. Used comedy as vehicle for political, literary, and social criticism.
Of possibly 44 plays, 11 survive complete. Best-known: *The Birds, The Frogs,
The Clouds, Lysistrata.* Humor is often Rabelaisian, but is motivated by
serious moral purpose. His plays are good theater rather than great drama.

GRAND CHORUS OF BIRDS

Come on then, ye dwellers by nature in darkness, and like to the
　　leaves' generations,
That are little of might, that are molded of mire, unenduring and
　　shadowlike nations,
Poor plumeless ephemerals, comfortless mortals, as visions of
　　shadows fast fleeing,
Lift up your mind unto us that are deathless, and dateless the
　　date of our being;
Us, children of heaven, us, angels of aye, us, all of whose thoughts
　　are eternal:
That ye may from henceforth, having heard of us all things aright
　　as to matters supernal,

Of the being of birds, and beginning of gods, and of streams, and
the dark beyond reaching,
Trustfully knowing aright, in my name bid Prodicus pack with
his preaching!
It was Chaos and Night at the first, and the blackness of darkness,
and Hell's broad border,
Earth was not, nor air, neither heaven: when in depths of the womb
of the dark without order
First thing, first-born of the black-plumed Night, was a wind-egg
hatched in her bosom,
Gold wings glittering forth of his back, like whirlwinds gustily
turning.
He, after his wedlock with Chaos, whose wings are of darkness,
in Hell broad-burning,
For his nestlings begat him the race of us first, and upraised us
to light new-lighted.
And before this was not the race of the gods, until all things by
Love were united:
And of kind united in kind with communion of nature the sky
and the sea are
Brought forth, and the earth, and the race of the gods everlasting
and blest. So that we are
Far away the most ancient of all things blest. And that we are
of Love's generation
There are manifest manifold signs. We have wings, and with us
have the Love's habitation;
And manifold fair young folk that forswore love once, ere the
bloom of them ended,
Have the men that pursued and desired them subdued by the help
of us only befriended,
With such baits as a quail, a flamingo, a goose, or a cock's comb
staring and splendid.
All best good things that befall men come from us birds, as is
plain to all reason:
For first we proclaim and make known to them spring, and the
winter and autumn in season;
Bid sow, when the crane starts clanging for Afric in shrill-voiced
emigrant number,
And calls to the pilot to hang up his rudder again for the season
and slumber;

54

And then weave a cloak for Orestes the thief, lest he strip men of
theirs if it freezes.
And again thereafter the kite reappearing announces a change in
the breezes,
And that here is the season for shearing your sheep of their spring
wool. Then does the swallow
Give you notice to sell your great-coat, and provide something
light for the heat that's to follow.
Thus are we as Ammon or Delphi unto you, Dodona, nay, Phœbus
Apollo.
For, as first ye come all to get auguries of birds, even such is in
all things your carriage,
Be the matter a matter of trade, or of earning your bread, or of
any one's marriage.
And all things ye lay to the charge of a bird that belong to dis-
cerning prediction:
Winged fame is a bird, as you reckon; you sneeze, and the sign's
as a bird for conviction;
All tokens are "birds" with you—sounds, too, and lackeys and
donkeys. Then must it not follow
That we are to you all as the manifest godhead that speaks in
prophetic Apollo?

SHOLEM ASCH

SHOLEM ASCH (Yiddish, 1880-). Versatile novelist and playwright. Foremost exponent of Yiddish literature in contemporary world. Born in Poland,
settled in America in 1910. Early plays produced by Max Reinhardt, and
throughout Europe and America. Later novels conceived on epic scale, idealistic
in concept, realistic in treatment. Major works: *Three Cities, Moses, The
Nazarene, The Apostle.*

A JEWISH CHILD

THE mother came out of the bride's chamber, and cast a piercing
look at her husband, who was sitting beside a finished meal, and
was making pellets of bread crumbs previous to saying grace.

"You go and talk to her! I haven't a bit of strength left!"

"So, Rochel-Leon has brought up children, has she, and can't manage them! Why! People will be pointing at you and laughing —a ruin to your years!"

"To my years! A ruin to *yours! My* children, are they? Are they not yours, too? Couldn't you stay at home sometimes to care for them and help me to bring them up, instead of trapesing round —the black year knows where and with whom?"

"Rochel, Rochel, what has possessed you to start a quarrel with me now? The bridegroom's family will be arriving directly."

"And what do you expect me to do, Moishehle, eh?! For God's sake! Go in to her, we shall be made a laughing-stock."

The man rose from the table, and went into the next room to his daughter. The mother followed.

On the little sofa that stood by the window sat a girl about eighteen, her face hidden in her hands, her arms covered by her loose, thick, black hair. She was evidently crying, for her bosom rose and fell like a stormy sea. On the bed opposite lay the white silk wedding-dress, the Chuppeh-Kleid, with the black, silk Shool-Kleid, and the black stuff morning-dress, which the tailor who had undertaken the outfit had brought not long ago. By the door stood a woman with a black scarf round her head and holding boxes with wigs.

"Channehle! You are never going to do me this dishonour? to make me the talk of the town?" exclaimed the father. The bride was silent.

"Look at me, daughter of Moisheh Groiss! It's all very well for Genendel Freindel's daughter to wear a wig, but not the daughter of Moisheh Groiss? Is that it?"

"And yet Genendel Freindel might very well think more of herself than you: she is more educated than you are, and has a larger dowry," put in the mother.

The bride made no reply.

"Daughter, think how much blood and treasure it has cost to help us to a bit of pleasure, and now you want to spoil it for us? Remember, for God's sake, what you are doing with yourself! We shall be excommunicated, the young man will run away home on foot!"

"Don't be foolish," said the mother who took a wig out of a box from the woman by the door, and approached her daughter.

"Let us try on the wig, the hair is just the colour of yours," and she laid the strange hair on the girl's head.

The girl felt the weight, put up her fingers to her head, met among her own soft, cool, living locks, the strange, dead hair of the wig, stiff and cold, and it flashed through her, Who knows where the head to which this hair belonged is now? A shuddering enveloped her, and as though she had come in contact with something unclean, she snatched off the wig, threw it onto the floor and hastily left the room.

Father and mother stood and looked at each other in dismay.

The day after the marriage ceremony, the bridegroom's mother rose early, and, bearing large scissors, and the wig and a hood which she had brought from her home as a present for the bride, she went to dress the latter for the "breakfast."

But the groom's mother remained outside the room, because the bride had locked herself in, and would open her door to no one.

The groom's mother ran calling aloud for help to her husband, who, together with a dozen uncles and brothers-in-law, was still sleeping soundly after the evening's festivity. She then sought out the bridegroom, an eighteen-year-old boy with his mother's milk still on his lips, who, in a silk caftan and a fur cap, was moving about the room in bewildered fashion, his eyes on the ground, ashamed to look anyone in the face. In the end she fell back on the mother of the bride, and these two went in to her together, having forced open the door between them.

"Why did you lock yourself in, dear daughter. There is no need to be ashamed."

"Marriage is a Jewish institution!" said the groom's mother, and kissed her future daughter-in-law on both cheeks.

The girl made no reply.

"Your mother-in-law has brought you a wig and a hood for the procession to the Shool," said her own mother.

The band had already struck up the "Good Morning" in the next room.

"Come now, Kallehshi, Kalleh-leben, the guests are beginning to assemble."

The groom's mother took hold of the plaits in order to loosen them.

The bride bent her head away from her, and fell on her own mother's neck.

57

"I can't, Mame-leben! My heart won't let me, Mame-krön!"

She held her hair with both hands, to protect it from the other's scissors.

"For God's sake, my daughter, my life," begged the mother.

"In the other world you will be plunged for this into rivers of fire. The apostate who wears her own hair after marriage will have her locks torn out with red hot pincers," said the other with the scissors.

A cold shiver went through the girl at these words.

"Mother-life, mother-crown!" she pleaded.

Her hands sought her hair, and the black silky tresses fell through them in waves. Her hair, the hair which had grown with her growth, and lived with her life, was to be cut off, and she was never, never to have it again—she was to wear strange hair, hair that had grown on another person's head, and no one knows whether that other person was alive or lying in the earth this long time, and whether she might not come any night to one's bedside, and whine in a dead voice:

"Give me back my hair, give me back my hair!"

A frost seized the girl to the marrow, she shivered and shook.

Then she heard the squeak of scissors over her head, tore herself out of her mother's arms, made one snatch at the scissors, flung them across the room, and said in a scarcely human voice:

"My own hair! May God Himself punish me!"

That day the bridegroom's mother took herself off home again, together with the sweet-cakes and the geese which she had brought for the wedding breakfast for her own guests. She wanted to take the bridegroom as well, but the bride's mother said: "I will not give him back to you! He belongs to me already!"

The following Sabbath they led the bride in procession to the Shool wearing her own hair in the face of all the town, covered only by a large hood.

But may all the names she was called by the way find their only echo in some uninhabited wilderness.

A summer evening, a few weeks after the wedding: The young man had just returned from the Stübel, and went to his room. The wife was already asleep, and the soft light of the lamp fell on her pale face, showing here and there among the wealth of silky-black hair that bathed it. Her slender arms were flung round her head, as though she feared that someone might come by night to shear them off while she slept. He had come home excited and irritable: this was the fourth week of his married life, and they had not yet called him up to the Reading of the Law, the Chassidim pursued him, and to-day Chayyim Moisheh had blamed him in the presence of the whole congregation, and had shamed him, because *she*, his wife, went about in her own hair. "You're no better than a clay image," Reb Chayyim Moisheh had told him. "What do you mean by a woman's saying she won't. It is written: 'And he shall rule over thee.'"

And he had come home intending to go to her and say: "Woman, it is a precept in the Torah! If you persist in wearing your own hair, I may divorce you without returning the dowry," after which he would pack up his things and go home. But when he saw his little wife asleep in bed, and her pale face peeping out of the glory of her hair, he felt a great pity for her. He went up to the bed, and stood a long while looking at her, after which he called softly:

"Channehle . . . Channehle . . . Channehle. . . ."

She opened her eyes with a frightened start, and looked round in sleepy wonder:

"Nosson, did you call? What do you want?"

"Nothing, your cap has slipped off," he said, lifting up the white nightcap, which had fallen from her head.

She flung it on again, and wanted to turn towards the wall.

"Channehle, Channehle, I want to talk to you."

The words went to her heart. The whole time since their marriage he had, so to say, not spoken to her. During the day she saw nothing of him, for he spent it in the house-of-study or in the Stübel. When he came home to dinner, he sat down to the table in silence. When he wanted anything, he asked for it speaking into the air, and when really obliged to exchange a word with her, he did so with his eyes fixed on the ground, too shy to look her in the face. And now he said he wanted to talk to her, and in such a gentle voice, and they two alone together in their room!

"What do you want to say to me?" she asked softly.

"Channehle," he began, "please don't make a fool of me, and don't make a fool of yourself in people's eyes. Has not God decreed that we should belong together? You are my wife and I am your husband, and is it proper, and what does it look like, a married woman wearing her own hair?"

Sleep still half dimmed her eyes, and had altogether clouded her thought and will. She felt helpless, and her head fell lighty towards his breast.

"Child," he went on still more gently, "I know you are not so depraved as they say. I know you are a pious Jewish daughter, and His Blessed Name will help us, and we shall have pious Jewish children. Put away this nonsense! Why should the whole world be talking about you? Are we not man and wife? Is not your shame mine?"

It seemed to her as though *someone*, at once far away and very near, had come and was talking to her. Nobody had ever yet spoken to her so gently and confidingly. And he was her husband, with whom she would live so long, so long, and there would be children, and she would look after the house!

She leant her head lightly against him.

"I know you are very sorry to lose your hair, the ornament of your girlhood. I saw you with it when I was a guest in your home. I knew that God gave you grace and loveliness, I know. It cuts me to the heart that your hair must be shorn off, but what is to be done? It is a rule, a law of our religion, and after all we are Jews. We might even, God forbid, have a child conceived to us in sin, may Heaven watch over and defend us."

She said nothing, but remained resting lightly in his arm, and his face lay in the stream of her silky-black hair with its cool odour. In that hair dwelt a soul, and he was conscious of it. He looked at her long and earnestly, and in his look was a prayer, a pleading with her for her own happiness, for her happiness and his.

"Shall I?" . . . he asked, more with his eyes than with his lips.

She said nothing, she only bent her head over his lap

He went quickly to the drawer, and took out a pair of scissors.

She laid her head in his lap, and gave her hair as a ransom for their happiness, still half-asleep and dreaming. The scissors squeaked over her head, shearing off one lock after the other, and Channehle lay and dreamt through the night.

On waking next morning, she threw a look into the glass which hung opposite the bed. A shock went through her, she thought she had gone mad, and was in the asylum! On the table beside her lay her shorn hair, dead!

She hid her face in her hands, and the little room was filled with the sound of weeping!

ATTAR

ATTAR (Farid ud-Din, Persian, 1119-1230). One of the three main Persian mystic poets (with Sanai and Rumi). A physician who traveled widely in the East. Said to have been killed during Mongol invasion. His copious works, devoted to teachings of the Sufis, generally written in couplets, include: Pand-Namah, Mantiq ut-Tayr, Elahi-Namah.

THE BIRD PARLIAMENT

Once on a time from all the Circles seven
Between the steadfast Earth and rolling Heaven,
The Birds, of all Note, Plumage, and Degree,
That float in Air, and roost upon the Tree;
And they that from the Waters snatch their Meat,
And they that scour the Desert with long Feet:
Birds of all Natures, known or not to Man,
Flock'd from all Quarters into full Divan,
On no less solemn business than to find
Or choose, a Sultan Khalif of their kind,
For whom, if never theirs, or lost, they pin'd.
The Snake had his, 'twas said; and so the Beast
His Lion-lord: and Man had his, at least:
And that the Birds, who nearest were the Skies,
And went apparel'd in its Angel Dyes,
Should be without—under no better Law
Than that which lost all others in the Maw—
Disperst without a Bond of Union—nay,
Or meeting to make each the other's Prey—
This was the Grievance—this the solemn Thing
On which the scatter'd Commonwealth of Wing,
From all the four Winds, flying like to Cloud
That met and blacken'd Heav'n, and Thunder-loud
With sound of whirring Wings and Beaks that clash'd
Down like a Torrent on the Desert dash'd:
Till by Degrees, the Hubbub and Pellmell
Into some Order and Precedence fell,
And, Proclamation made of Silence, each
In special Accent, but in general Speech
That all should understand, as seem'd him best,
The Congregation of all Wings Addrest.

61

And first, with Heart so full as from his Eyes
Ran Weeping, up rose Tajidar the Wise;
The mystic Mark upon whose Bosom show'd
That He alone of all the Birds THE ROAD
Had travel'd: and the Crown upon his head
Had reach'd the Goal; and He stood forth and said:—
"Oh Birds, by what Authority divine
I speak, you know, by His authentic Sign,
And Name, emblazon'd on my Breast and Bill:
Whose Counsel I assist at, and fulfill:
At his Behest I measured as he plann'd
The Spaces of the Air and Sea and Land;
I gaug'd the secret sources of the Springs
From Cloud to Fish: the Shadow of my wings
Dream'd over sleeping Deluge: piloted
The Blast that bore Sulayman's Throne: and led
The Cloud of Birds that canopied his Head;
Whose Word I brought to Balkis: and I shar'd
The Counsel that with Ásaf he prepar'd.
And now You want a Khalif: and I know
Him, and his whereabout, and How to go:
And go alone I could, and plead your cause
Alone for all: but, by the eternal laws,
Yourselves by Toil and Travel of your own
Must for your old Delinquency atone.
Were you indeed not blinded by the Curse
Of Self-exile, that still grows worse and worse,
Yourselves would know that, though *you* see him not,
He is with you this Moment, on this Spot,
Your Lord through all Forgetfulness and Crime,
Here, There, and Everywhere, and through all Time.
But as a Father, whom some wayward Child
By sinful Self-will has unreconcil'd,
Waits till the sullen Reprobate at cost
Of long Repentance should regain the Lost;
Therefore, yourselves to see as you are seen,
Yourselves must bridge the Gulf you made between
By such a Search and Travel to be gone
Up to the mighty mountain Káf, whereon
Hinges the World, and round about whose Knees
Into one Ocean mingle the Sev'n Seas;

In whose impenetrable Forest-folds
Of Light and Dark 'Symurgh' his presence holds;
Not to be reach'd, if to be reach'd at all
But by a Road the stoutest might appall;
Of Travel not of Days or Months, but Years—
Lifelong perhaps: of Dangers, Doubts, and Fears
As yet unheard of: Sweet of Blood and Brain
Interminable—often all in vain—
And, if successful, no Return again:
A Road whose very Preparation scar'd
The Traveler who yet must be prepar'd.
Who then this Travel to Result would bring
Needs both a lion's Heart beneath the Wing,
And even more, a Spirit purified
Of Worldly Passion, Malice, Lust, and Pride:
Yea, ev'n of *Worldly* Wisdom, which grows dim
And dark, the nearer it approaches *Him,*
Who to the Spirit's Eye alone reveal'd;
By sacrifice of Wisdom's self unseal'd;
Without which none who reach the Place could bear
To look upon the Glory dwelling there."

SRI AUROBINDO

SRI AUROBINDO (Sri Aurobindo Ghose, Indian, 1872-1950). Philosopher-
poet of modern India. Son of Bengalese physician, educated in England.
Anticipatated Gandhi in organizing passive resistance as a political weapon
in Bengal. After imprisonment by British, went to live in French Pondicherry.
Author of 3 volumes of poetry and 2 major philosophic works: *The Life
Divine* and *The Synthesis of Yoga.*

MUSA SPIRITUS

O word concealed in the upper fire,
    Thou who has lingered through centuries,
Descend from thy rapt white desire,
    Plunging through gold eternities.

Into the gulfs of our nature leap,
    Voice of the spaces, call of the Light!

Break the seals of Matter's sleep,
  Break the trance of the unseen height.

In the uncertain glow of human mind,
  Its waste of unharmonied thronging thoughts,
Carve thy epic mountain-lined
  Crowded with deep prophetic grots.

Let thy hue-winged lyrics hover like birds
  Over the swirl of the heart's sea.
Touch into sight with thy fire-words
  The blind indwelling deity.

O Muse of the Silence, the wideness make
  In the unplumbed stillness that hears thy voice,
In the vast mute heavens of the spirit awake
  Where thy eagles of Power flame and rejoice.

Out, out with the mind and its candle flares,
  Light, light the suns that never die.
For my ear the cry of the seraph stars
  And the forms of the Gods for my naked eye!

Let the little troubled life-god within
  Cast his veils from the still soul,
His tiger-stripes of virtue and sin,
  His clamour and glamour and thole and dole;

All make tranquil, all make free.
  Let my heart-beats measure the footsteps of God
As He comes from His timeless infinity
  To build in their rapture His burning abode.

Weave from my life His poem of days,
  His calm pure dawns and His noons of force.
My acts for the grooves of His chariot-race,
  My thoughts for the tramp of His great steeds' course!

BRIDE OF THE FIRE

Bride of the Fire, clasp me now close,—
  Bride of the Fire!
I have shed the bloom of the earthly rose,
  I have slain desire.

Beauty of the Light, surround my life,—
  Beauty of the Light!
I have sacrificed longing and parted from grief,
  I can bear thy delight.

Image of ecstasy, thrill and enlace,—
  Image of bliss!
I would see only thy marvellous face,
  Feel only thy kiss.

Voice of Infinity, sound in my heart,—
  Call of the One!
Stamp there thy radiance, never to part,
  O living Sun.

THE BLUE BIRD

I am the bird of God in His blue;
  Divinely high and clear
I sing the notes of the sweet and the true
  For the god's and the seraph's ear.

I rise like a fire from the mortal's earth
  Into a griefless sky
And drop in the suffering soil of his birth
  Fire-seeds of ecstasy.

My pinions soar beyond Time and Space
  Into unfading Light;
I bring the bliss of the Eternal's face
  And the boon of the Spirit's sight.

I measure the worlds with my ruby eyes;
  I have perched on Wisdom's tree
Thronged with the blossoms of Paradise
  By the streams of Eternity.

Nothing is hid from my burning heart;
  My mind is shoreless and still;
My song is rapture's mystic art,
  My flight immortal will.

65

MARY AUSTIN

MARY AUSTIN (American, 1868-1934). A spirited student of anthropological and social problems. Investigated American Indian and early Spanish cultures in the Southwest. Her novels and plays also dealt with social injustices and problems of machine age. Important works: *The Land of Little Rain, A Woman of Genius, No. 26 Jayne Street.*

PAPAGO WEDDING

THERE was a Papago woman out of Panták who had a marriage paper from a white man after she had borne him five children, and the man himself was in love with another woman. This Shuler was the first to raise cotton for selling in the Gila Valley—but the Pimas and Papagoes had raised it long before that—and the girl went with him willingly. As to the writing of marriage, it was not then understood that the white man is not master of his heart, but is mastered by it, so that if it is not fixed in writing it becomes unstable like water and is puddled in the lowest place. The Sisters at San Xavier del Bac had taught her to clean and cook. Shuler called her Susie, which was nearest to her Papago name, and was fond of the children. He sent them to school as they came along, and had carpets in the house.

In all things Susie was a good wife to him, though she had no writing of marriage and she never wore a hat. This was a mistake which she learned from the sisters. They, being holy women, had no notion of the *brujeria* which is worked in the heart of the white man by a hat. Into the presence of their God also, without that which passes for a hat, they do not go. Even after her children were old enough to notice, Susie went about the country with a handkerchief tied over her hair, which was long and smooth on either side of her face, like the shut wings of a raven.

By the time Susie's children were as tall as their mother, there were many white ranchers in the Gila country, with their white wives, who are like Papago women in this, that if they see a man upstanding and prosperous, they think only that he might make some woman happy, and if they have a cousin or a friend, that she should be the woman. Also the white ones think it so shameful for a man to take a woman to his house without a writing that they have no scruple to take him away from her. At Rinconada there was a woman with large breasts, surpassing well looking, and with many

66

hats. She had no husband and was new to the country, and when Shuler drove her about to look at it, she wore each time a different hat.

This the Papagoes observed, and, not having visited Susie when she was happy with her man, they went now in numbers, and by this Susie understood that it was in their hearts that she might have need of them. For it was well known that the white woman had told Shuler that it was a shame for him to have his children going about with a Papago woman who had only a handkerchief to cover her head. She said it was keeping Shuler back from being the principal man among the cotton growers of Gila Valley, to have in his house a woman who would come there without a writing. And when the other white women heard that she had said that, they said the same thing. Shuler said, "My God, this is the truth, I know it," and the woman said that she would go to Susie and tell her that she ought to go back to her own people and not be a shame to her children and Shuler. There was a man from Panták on the road, who saw them go, and turned in his tracks and went back, in case Susie should need him, for the Papagoes, when it is their kin against whom there is *brujeria* made, have inknowing hearts. Susie sat in the best room with the woman and was polite. "If you want Shuler," she said, "you can have him, but I stay with my children." The white woman grew red in the face and went out to Shuler in the field where he was pretending to look after something, and they went away together.

After that Shuler would not go to the ranch except of necessity. He went around talking to his white friends. "My God," he kept saying, "what can I do, with my children in the hands of that Papago?" Then he sent a lawyer to Susie to say that if she would go away and not shame his children with a mother who had no marriage writing and no hat, he would give her money, so much every month. But the children all came in the room and stood by her, and Susie said, "What I want with money when I got my children and this good ranch?" Then Shuler said "My God!" again, and "What can I do?"

The lawyer said he could tell the Judge that Susie was not a proper person to have care of his children, and the Judge would take them away from Susie and give them to Shuler. But when the day came for Susie to come into court, it was seen that though she had a handkerchief on her hair, her dress was good, and the fringe of her shawl was long and fine. All the five children came also, with new clothes, well looking. "My God!" said Shuler, "I must get those kids away from that Papago and into the hands of a white woman." But the white people who had come to see the children taken away saw that although the five looked like Shuler, they had their mouths shut like Papagoes; so they waited to see how things turned out.

Shuler's lawyer makes a long speech about how Shuler loves his children, and how sorry he is in his heart to see them growing up like Papagoes, and water is coming out of Shuler's eyes. Then the Judge asks Susie if she has anything to say why her children shall not be taken away.

"You want to take these children away and giff them to Shuler?" Susie asks him. "What for you giff them to Shuler?" says Susie, and the white people are listening. She says, "Shuler's not the father of them. Thees children all got different fathers," says Susie. "Shuler——"

Then she makes a sign with her hand. I tell you if a woman makes that sign to a Papago he could laugh himself dead but he would not laugh off that. Some of the white people who have been in the country a long time know that sign and they begin to laugh.

Shuler's lawyer jumps up. . . . "Your Honour, I object——"

The Judge waves his hand. "I warn you the Court cannot go behind the testimony of the mother in such a case. . . ."

By this time everybody is laughing, so that they do not hear what the lawyer says. Shuler is trying to get out of the side door, and the Judge is shaking hands with Susie.

"You tell Shuler," she says, "if he wants people to think hees the father of thees children he better giff me a writing. Then maybe I think so myself."

"I *will*," said the Judge, and maybe two, three days after that he takes Shuler out to the ranch and makes the marriage writing. Then all the children come around Susie and say, "Now, Mother, you will have to wear a hat." Susie, she says, "Go, children, and ask your father." But it is not known to the Papagoes what happened after that.

B

ISAAK EMMANUILOVICH BABEL

ISAAK EMMANUILOVICH BABEL (Russian, 1894-193?). Classical story writer of Communist era. *Konarmiya*, his masterpiece, a collection of powerful tales based on experiences in Red Army. *Benia Creak*, a novel about a famous Jewish bandit. Disappeared around 1935; is presumed, like many of his race, to have died in Soviet concentration camp.

THE BIRTH OF A KING

I WAS the one to begin.

"Reb Arie-Leib," I said to the old man, "let us talk about Benia Creak. Let us talk about his lightning beginnings and his terrible end. Three black shadows stand in the way of my imagination. The first is the one-eyed Froim Grach. The rusted steel of his exploits —can it stand comparison with the new power of the King? The second is Kolka Paskovsky. The simple-minded audacity of that man should have been sufficient for successful domination. And as for Haim Drong—couldn't he recognize the brilliance of the new star? Why then was Benia Creak the only one to climb to the top of the rope ladder, while all the others were left hanging below on its wobbly rungs?"

Reb Arie-Leib remained silent, perched on the wall of the cemetery. Before us spread the green quietude of the graves. A man who thirsts for knowldge must learn to be patient. Gravity befits the man who possesses knowledge. That is why Arie-Leib remained silent as he sat on the cemetery wall. At last he spoke:

"Why he? Why not they, you want to know? Now listen—forget for a moment that you have spectacles on your nose and autumn in your heart. Stop making rows at your writing-table and stammering when you have to face an audience. Imagine for a moment that you are making rows in public squares and stammer only on paper. You're a tiger, a lion, a tom-cat. You can spend the night with a Russian woman, and the Russian woman will be satisfied with you. You are twenty-five. If the sky and the earth had a couple of rings attached to them, you would seize these rings and draw the sky and the earth together. And you have for a father a carter, Mendel Creak. What does such a father think of? He thinks of having a good drink of vodka, he thinks of swiping some one across the face, he thinks of his horses—that's all. You want to live, and he makes you die twenty times a day. What would you have done if you were Benia Creak? You would have done nothing. But he did. That's why he's King, and you haven't got a brass farthing in your pocket.

"He, little Benia, went to see Froim Grach, who then was already looking at the world with one eye only, and was what he is now. He said to Froim:

'Take me, Froim. I want to be washed up on your shore. The shore on which I'm washed up will gain by it.'

"Grach asked him:

'Who are you, where do you come from, and what do you live by?'

'Try me, Froim,' said Benia, 'and let us stop smearing the clean table with porridge.'

'All right, let us stop smearing porridge about,' said Grach. 'I will try you.'

"Then the gangsters called a meeting to think over Benia Creak. I was not present at that meeting. But I was told that they held a council. The late Levka Byk was then the elder.

'What's happening under his hat—the hat of this little Benia?' asked the late Byk.

"The one-eyed Grach then gave his opinion:

'Benia talks little but his talk is full of meat. He says little, but you wish he would say more.'

'If that is so,' cried the late Levka, 'then let us try him on Tartakovsky,' decided the council, and all in whom a little conscience was still alive, blushed when they heard this decision. Why did they blush? You'll know why if you follow me where I shall lead you.

"Tartakovsky was nicknamed in Odessa 'Jew-and-a-half' or 'Nine Raids.' He was nicknamed 'Jew-and-a-half' because no one Jew could contain in himself so much insolence and money as possessed Tartakovsky. In height he was taller than the tallest policeman in Odessa, and in weight—heavier than the fattest Jewess. As for

'Nine Raids', he was so-called because the gang of Levka Byk and Co. made neither eight nor ten raids on his office, but exactly nine. It was Benia's lot—and he wasn't yet King then—to make the tenth raid on the 'Jew-and-a-half.' When Froim passed this on to him, Benia said: 'Yes,' and walked out, slamming the door. Why did he slam the door? You will find out if you follow me where I shall lead you.

"Tartakovsky has the soul of a murderer, but he belongs to us. He came from our midst. He's our flesh, as if one mother had born us. Half Odessa works in his shops. And he has suffered through his own people of Moldavanka. Twice they kidnapped him in order to get a ransom, and once during a pogrom they staged his funeral with a choir. It was when the hooligans from Sloboda were beating up the Jews. Tartakovsky escaped them, and met a funeral procession with a choir in the Sophia Square.

'Who's being buried with a choir?' he asked.

"Passers-by told him it was Tartakovsky. The procession got as far as the cemetery in Sloboda. Then our people, who had staged the procession, took a machine-gun out of the coffin and opened fire on the hooligans of Sloboda. But the 'Jew-and-a-half' had not foreseen that. He was scared to death. And what fellow would not have been scared in his position?

"A tenth raid on a man who had already been buried once—you must agree, it was downright rudeness. Benia, who was not yet King then, understood that better than any other. But he had said 'yes' to Grach, and on the same day he wrote Tartakovsky a letter, resembling all the letters of that sort:

'HIGHLY-RESPECTED ROOVIM OSIPOVICH,

'Be so kind as to put under the tank of rain-water by next Saturday' . . . and so on. 'In case of refusal, as you have presumed to do on the last few occasions, a very serious disappointment in your family life will await you.

'I sign respectfully, as some one well known to you,

BENCION CREAK'

"Tartakovsky was not a lazy man and answered this letter without delay.

'Benia! If you were an idiot, I would have written to you as to an idiot. But I don't know you as such, and the Lord forbid that I should ever know you as such. You must be pretending that you're a baby. Don't you know that there has been a bumper crop of wheat in Argentina this year, and that we cannot even begin selling ours? And I will tell you, with my hand on my heart, that I'm tired of eating such a bitter crust of bread in my old age and to experience all these upsets, after I've been working like a cart-horse all my life. And what have I got after all these years of hard forced labour? Ulcers, sores, worries, and sleeplessness. Drop this nonsense, Benia. Your friend, much more so than you think,

ROOVIM TARTAKOVSKY'

"The 'Jew-and-a-half' did his part. He wrote the letter. But the post-office failed to deliver it. Having received no answer, Benia got angry. On the following day he arrived with three friends at Tartakovsky's office. Four young men, wearing masks and armed with revolvers, burst into the room.

'Hands up!' they shouted, and began to brandish their revolvers in the air.

'Work more calmly, Solomon,' Benia told the one who was shouting louder than the others, 'don't get into such nervous habits when you work.' And turning to the assistant, who was as white as death and as yellow as parchment, he asked:

'Is the "Jew-and-a-half" at the works?'

'He's not at the works,' answered the assistant, whose surname was Mughinstein, and who was called Joseph. He was an unmarried son of Aunt Pessia, a woman who sold chickens in Seredinsky Square.

'But who's in charge here?' they questioned the unfortunate Mughinstein.

'I'm in charge here," answered the assistant, as green as green grass.

'Then open the cash-box with God's help," Benia ordered him.

"And in this way an opera in three acts began.

"The highly strung Solomon was packing bank-notes, papers, watches, and monograms into a suit-case, while the late Joseph stood in front of him with his hands raised, and Benia was telling stories from the past of the Hebrew people.

'If he likes to believe he's a Rothschild,' Benia was saying of Tartakovsky, 'then let him burn like a bonfire. Explain it to me, Mughinstein, like a friend: he got a business letter from me, didn't he? Why didn't he get on a tram for five copecks, and drive up to my flat, and have a glass of vodka with my family and a bite of

72

something, whatever God has given us? It would have cost him nothing to have a heart-to-heart talk with me. If he had simply told me: Benia, here's my bank balance, wait a couple of days, let me have a breather. . . . What would I have answered? Swine wouldn't meet swine, but man can meet man. Mughinstein, you understand me?'

'Yes, I understand you,' Mughinstein answered, untruthfully, because he did not see at all why the 'Jew-and-a-half', a respectable wealthy man and the first tradesman in the town, should have gone on a tram to drink vodka with the family of the carter Mendel Creak.

"But meanwhile, misfortune was roaming outside the door like a beggar at sunrise. Misfortune burst into the office with a great noise. It burst in under the image of a Jew called Savka Butzis, and it was as drunk as a water-carrier.

'Ho-ho-ho,' shouted the Jew Savka, 'forgive me, Benchik, I'm late,' and he began to stamp his feet and brandish his arms. Then he fired his revolver, and the bullet hit Mughinstein in the stomach.

"Are words needed? There had been a man, and he ceased to be. There lived an innocent bachelor, like a bird on a branch—and he perished through silliness, through nothing. . . . A Jew came, a Jew who looked like a sailor, and fired not at some bottle with a bangle inside it, but at a live man. Are words needed?

'Leave the office at once,' shouted Benia, and ran out after the others. But before leaving, he had time to tell Butzis:

'I swear by my mother's grave, Savka, you'll lie beside him! . . .'

"Now tell me, young man, who cuts the coupons off other people's shares, what would you have done if you had been in Benia Creak's place? You don't know what you would have done. But he did know. That's why he's King, while you and I sit on the wall of the Jewish cemetery and hold our hands against our faces to protect them from the sun.

"The unfortunate son of Aunt Pessia did not die at once. An hour after he had been brought to the hospital, Benia put in an appearance. He demanded to see the Chief Surgeon and the Matron, and told them, without taking his hands out of the pockets of his cream-coloured trousers:

'I have an interest,' he said, 'in that your patient Joseph Mughinstein should recover. I might just as well introduce myself—Bencion Creak. Camphor, bags of oxygen, a private ward—he must have all that. If not, then remember that no doctor, be he even a doctor of philosophy, needs more than three yards of soil. . . ."

"Still, Mughinstein died the same night. And only then the 'Jew-and-a-half' started such a row that the whole of Odessa could hear him.

'Where do the police begin and where does Benia end?' he screamed.

'The police end where Benia begins,' reasonable people told him, but Tartakovsky wouldn't calm down, and he finished by getting what he asked for. A red motor-car with a musical box played the first march from the opera *Pagliacci* in the Seredinsky Square. In broad daylight the car flew up to the little house where Aunt Pessia lived.

"The car spat out smoke, back-fired, shone with its metal parts, stank of petrol, and played arias on its horn. A man jumped out of it, went into the house and through to the kitchen where little Aunt Pessia was having a fit on the earthen floor. The 'Jew-and-a-half' was sitting on a chair and gesticulating violently.

'A hooligan's snout!' he cried when he saw the visitor. 'Bandit! I wish the earth would spit you out. You're doing fine—killing live men!'

'Monsieur Tartakovsky,' Benia Creak answered him in a quiet voice, 'it's the second day that I've been grieving about the deceased as if he were my own brother. But I know you don't care a damn for my young tears. Shame, Monsieur Tartakovsky—in what safe have you locked up your shame? You had the heart to send the mother of our late Joseph a miserable hundred roubles! My brain rose in my head together with my hair when I heard the news.'

"Here Benia paused for a moment. He had on a chocolate-coloured jacket, cream-white trousers, and magenta shoes.

'Ten thousand at once,' he roared, 'ten thousand at once, and a pension for the rest of her life, even if she lives a hundred and twenty years. If not, then we shall go out of this apartment, Monsieur Tartakovsky, and get into my motor-car.'

"Then they argued and quarrelled with each other. The 'Jew-and-a-half' argued with Benia. I wasn't present at that quarrel. But those, who were there, remember. They compromised on five thousand roubles to be paid on the spot and on fifty roubles to be paid monthly.

'Aunt Pessia,' Benia then said to the dishevelled little woman, who was still rolling on the floor, 'if you need my life, you can have it, but every one makes mistakes, even God. Listen to me with

74

your ears, Aunt Pessia. You have five thousand roubles in ready money and fifty roubles a month until your death. I hope you will live to be a hundred and twenty. Joseph's funeral will be first-rate: six horses like six lions, two hearses with wreaths, a choir from the Brodskaia synagogue, the singer Minkovsky himself will come to sing at your son's funeral.'

"The funeral took place on the following morning. You ask the beggars who sit beside the cemetery about this funeral. Ask the servants from the synagogue about it, ask the tradesmen who sell cosher poultry, or the old women from alms-houses. Odessa had never seen such a funeral. The world will never see another such. Policemen put on their string gloves that day. Inside the synagogues, decorated with garlands of green, their doors wide open, electric lights were blazing. On the heads of white horses which drew the hearse, swung bunches of black ostrich feathers. A choir of sixty persons walked at the head of the procession. The singers were boys, but they sang with the voices of women. The elders of the synagogue, which was endowed by the dealers in cosher poultry, led Aunt Pessia, supporting her under the arms. The elders were followed by members of the Society of Jewish shop-assistants, and following them, came lawyers and barristers, doctors of medicine and trained midwives. On one side of Aunt Pessia walked the women who sold poultry in the Old Market, and on the other side the highly honoured women who sell milk on the Bugaevka, wrapped in their orange-coloured shawls. They stamped their feet like gendarmes on parade, and from their wide hips spread the smell of milk and of the sea. Behind every one slouched along the employees of Roovim Tartakovsky. There were a hundred of them, or five hundred, or two thousand, perhaps. All wore long black coats with satin revers, and new boots which squeaked like sucking-pigs in sacks.

"I will speak now as Jehovah spoke from the burning bush on the Mount of Sinai. Put my words into your ears. All I saw I saw with my own eyes, sitting here on the wall of the Second Jewish Cemetery, beside the stutterer Moiseika and Shimson from the funeral office. I saw all of it, I, Arie-Leib, the proud Jew who lives near the dead.

"The hearse drove up to the cemetery synagogue. The coffin was placed upon the steps. Aunt Pessia trembled like a little bird. The cantor climbed out of his carriage and began the funeral service. The voices of sixty choir-boys accompanied him. And at that moment the red motor-car flew out from round a corner. It played

'Laugh, Pagliaccio,' and stopped. The people were as silent as if they were dead. The trees were silent, so were the choir-boys, so were the beggars. Four men came out of the red car and, walking slowly, carried to the coffin a wreath of undreamed-of roses. And when the funeral service ended, four men propped the coffin with their steel-like shoulders, and with their eyes burning and their chests stuck out, strode along beside the members of the Society of Jewish shop-assistants.

"In front walked Benia Creak whom no one yet called King. He was the first to reach the grave. He mounted the pile of earth and stretched out his hand.

"An employee of the funeral company ran up to him.

'What do you wish to do, young man?'

'I want to make a speech.' Every one who wanted to hear, heard it. I, too, heard it, I, Arie-Leib, and the stutterer Moiseika, who sat on the wall beside me.

'Gentlemen and ladies,' said Benia Creak, 'gentlemen and ladies,' he said, and the sun stood above his head like a sentinel with a rifle. 'You came here to pay your last duties to an honest wage-earner, who perished for a brass farthing. In my own name and in the name of all those who aren't present here, I thank you, gentlemen and ladies. What has our dear Joseph seen in his life? He's seen a couple of trifles. What did he do in life? He counted money which belonged to another. What did he die for? He died for all the wage-earning class. There are people who are already doomed to die, and there are people who haven't yet begun to live. And a bullet which should have pierced a doomed breast, went and pierced our Joseph, who has seen nothing in his life except a couple of trifles. There are people who know how to drink vodka, and there are others who don't know how to drink it, yet drink it all the same. The former get their pleasure, both from grief and from joy, while the latter suffer for all those who drink vodka without knowing how to do it. For that reason, gentlemen and ladies, after we have prayed for the soul of our poor Joseph, I will beg you to accompany to his grave the unknown to you and now dead Savka Butzis.'

"Having made this speech, Benia came off the mound. The men the trees, and the beggars were all silent. Two grave-diggers carried a coffin of unpainted deal to the neighbouring grave. The cantor finished his prayers, stammering. Benia threw the first spadeful of earth upon the body of Joseph, then walked over to Savka's. A

76

the barristers and ladies with brooches followed him like sheep. He ordered the cantor to read a complete funeral service over Savka, and sixty choir-boys accompanied the cantor. Savka never dreamed of such a funeral service—believe the word of Arie-Leib, a very old man.

"They say that on that day the 'Jew-and-a-half' decided to close down his business. I wasn't there when he decided it. But that neither the cantor, nor the choir, nor the funeral company asked to be paid for their services—that I saw with the eyes of Arie-Leib. Arie-Leib is my name. And I could see nothing more, because the people who left Savka's grave at a quiet pace, started to run as if from a fire. They rushed off in their carriages, in carts, and on foot. And only those four, who had come in a red car, went away in it. The musical box played its march, the machine quivered and flew away.

'A King,' said the stutterer Moiseika, the same who always pinches from me the best seat on the wall.

"Now you know everything. You know who was the first to say the word 'King.' It was Moiseika. You know why he did not call thus either the one-eyed Grach or the madman Kolka. You know everything. But what is the use of it to you if you still have spectacles on your nose and autumn in your heart?"

HONORE DE BALZAC

HONORÉ DE BALZAC (French, 1799-1850). One of France's greatest and most prolific novelists, and founder of the French realistic school. Under general title of *La Comédie Humaine*, his novels give an exhaustive picture of his time. Best-known single works: *Le Père Goriot, Eugénie Grandet, Lost Illusions*. His life noteworthy for its poverty, emotional crises, and phenomenal productivity, including 85 novels.

DOOMED TO LIVE

THE clock of the little town of Menda had just struck midnight. At this moment a young French officer was leaning on the parapet of a long terrace which bounded the gardens of the castle. He seemed plunged in the deepest thought—a circumstance unusual amid the thoughtlessness of military life; but it must be owned that never were the hour, the night, and the place more propitious to meditation. The beautiful Spanish sky stretched out its azure dome above his head. The glittering stars and the soft moonlight lit up a charming valley that unfolded all its beauties at his feet. Leaning against a blossoming orange tree he could see, a hundred feet below him, the town of Menda, which seemed to have been placed for shelter from the north winds at the foot of the rock on which the castle was built. As he turned his head he could see the sea, framing the landscape with a broad silver sheet of glistening water. The castle was a blaze of light. The mirth and movement of a ball, the music of the orchestra, the laughter of the officers and their partners in the dance, were borne to him mingled with the distant murmur of the waves. The freshness of the night imparted a sort of energy to his limbs, weary with the heat of the day. Above all, the gardens were planted with trees so aromatic, and flowers so fragrant, that the young man stood plunged, as it were, in a bath of perfumes.

The castle of Menda belonged to a Spanish grandee, then living there with his family. During the whole of the evening his eldest daughter had looked at the officer with an interest so tinged with sadness that the sentiment of compassion thus expressed by the Spaniard might well call up a reverie in the Frenchman's mind.

Clara was beautiful, and although she had three brothers and a sister, the wealth of the Marques de Leganes seemed great enough for Victor Marchand to believe that the young lady would have a rich dowry. But how dare he hope that the most bigoted old hidalgo in all Spain would ever give his daughter to the son of a Parisian grocer? Besides, the French were hated. The Marques was suspected by General Gautier, who governed the province, of planning a revolt in favor of Ferdinand VII. For this reason the battalion commanded by Victor Marchand had been cantoned in the little town of Menda, to hold the neighboring hamlets, which were dependent on the Marques, in check. Recent dispatches from Marshal Ney had given ground for fear that the English would shortly land on the coast, and had indicated the Marques as a man who carried on communication with the cabinet of London.

In spite, therefore, of the welcome which the Spaniard had given him and his soldiers, the young officer Victor Marchand remained constantly on his guard. As he was directing his steps towards the terrace whither he had come to examine the state of the town and the country districts intrusted to his care, he debated how he ought to interpret the friendliness which the Marques had unceasingly shown him, and how the tranquillity of the country could be reconciled with his General's uneasiness. But in one moment these thoughts were driven from his mind by a feeling of caution and well-grounded curiosity. He had just perceived a considerable number of lights in the town. In spite of the day being the Feast of St. James, he had given orders, that very morning, that all lights should be extinguished at the hour prescribed by his regulations; the castle alone being excepted from his order. He could plainly see, here and there, the gleam of his soldiers' bayonets at their accustomed posts; but there was a solemnity in the silence, and nothing to suggest that the Spaniards were a prey to the excitement of a festival. After having sought to explain the offense of which the inhabitants were guilty, the mystery appeared all the more unaccountable to him because he had left officers in charge of the night police and the rounds. With all the impetuosity of youth, he was just about to leap through a breach and descend the rocks in haste, and thus arrive more quickly than by the ordinary road at a small outpost placed at the entrance of the town nearest to the castle, when a faint sound stopped him. He thought he heard the light footfall of a woman upon the gravel walk. He turned his head and saw nothing; but his gaze was arrested by the extraordinary brightness of the sea. All of a sudden he beheld a sight so portentous that he stood dumfounded; he thought that his senses deceived him. In the far distance he could distinguish sails gleaming white in the moonlight. He trembled and tried to convince himself that this vision was an optical illusion, merely the fantastic effect of the moon on the waves. At this moment a hoarse voice pronounced his name. He looked towards the breach, and saw slowly rising above it the head of the soldier whom he had ordered to accompany him to the castle.

"Is that you, Commandant?"

"Yes; what do you want?" replied the young man, in a low voice. A sort of presentiment warned him to be cautious.

"Those rascals down there are stirring like worms. I have hurried, with your leave, to tell you my own little observations."

"Go on," said Victor Marchand.

"I have just followed a man from the castle who came in this direction with a lantern in his hand. A lantern's a frightfully suspicious thing. I don't fancy it was tapers my fine Catholic was going to light at this time of night. 'They want to eat us body and bones!' says I to myself; so I went on his track to reconnoiter. There, on a ledge of rock, not three paces from here, I discovered a great heap of fagots."

Suddenly a terrible shriek rang through the town, and cut the soldier short. At the same instant a gleam of light flashed before the Commandant. The poor grenadier received a ball in the head and fell. A fire of straw and dry wood burst into flame like a house on fire, not ten paces from the young man. The sound of the instruments and the laughter ceased in the ballroom. The silence of death, broken only by groans, had suddenly succeeded to the noises and music of the feast. The fire of a cannon roared over the surface of the sea. Cold sweat trickled down the young officer's forehead; he had no sword. He understood that his men had been slaughtered, and the English were about to disembark. If he lived he saw himself dishonored, summoned before a council of war. Then he measured with his eyes the depth of the valley. He sprang forward, when just at that moment his hand was seized by the hand of Clara.

"Fly!" said she; "my brothers are following to kill you. Down yonder at the foot of the rock you will find Juanito's Andalusian. Quick!"

The young man looked at her for a moment, stupefied. She pushed him on; then, obeying the instinct of self-preservation which never forsakes even the bravest man, he rushed down the park in the direction she had indicated. He leapt from rock to rock, where only the goats had ever trod before; he heard Clara crying out to her brothers to pursue him; he heard the footsteps of the assassins; he heard the balls of several discharges whistle about his ears; but he reached the valley, he found the horse, mounted, and disappeared swift as lightning. In a few hours he arrived at the quarters occupied by General Gautier. He found him at dinner with his staff.

"I bring you my life in my hand!" cried the Commandant, his face pale and haggard.

He sat down and related the horrible disaster. A dreadful silence greeted his story.

"You appear to me to be more unfortunate than criminal," said the terrible General at last. "You are not accountable for the crime of the Spaniards, and unless the Marshal decides otherwise, I acquit you."

These words could give the unfortunate officer but slight consolation.

"But when the Emperor hears of it!" he exclaimed.

"He will want to have you shot," said the General. "However——But we will talk no more about it," he added severely, "except how we are to take such a revenge as will strike wholesome fear upon this country, where they carry on war like savages."

One hour afterwards, a whole regiment, a detachment of cavalry, and a convoy of artillery were on the road. The General and Victor marched at the head of the column. The soldiers, informed of the massacre of their comrades, were filled with extraordinary fury. The distance which separated the town of Menda from the general quarters was passed with marvelous rapidity. On the road the General found whole villages under arms. Each of these wretched townships was surrounded and their inhabitants decimated.

By some inexplicable fatality, the English ships stood off instead of advancing. It was known afterwards that these vessels had outstript the rest of the transports and only carried artillery. Thus the town of Menda, deprived of the defenders she was expecting, and which the sight of the English vessels had seemed to assure, was surrounded by the French troops almost without striking a blow. The inhabitants, seized with terror, offered to surrender at discretion. Then followed one of those instances of devotion not rare in the peninsula. The assassins of the French, foreseeing, from the cruelty of the General, that Menda would probably be given over to the flames and the whole population put to the sword, offered to denounce themselves. The General accepted this offer, inserting as a condition that the inhabitants of the castle, from the lowest valet to the Marques himself, should be placed in his hands. This capitulation agreed upon, the General promised to pardon the rest of the population and to prevent his soldiers from pillaging or setting fire to the town. An enormous contribution was exacted, and the richest inhabitants gave themselves up as hostages to guarantee the payment, which was to be accomplished within twenty-four hours.

The General took all precautions necessary for the safety of his troops, provided for the defense of the country, and refused to lodge his men in the houses. After having formed a camp, he went up and took military possession of the castle. The members of the family of Leganes and the servants were gagged, and shut up in the great hall where the ball had taken place, and closely watched. The windows of the apartment afforded a full view of the terrace which commanded the town. The staff was established in a neighboring gallery, and the General procceded at once to hold a council of war on the measures to be taken for opposing the debarkation. After having dispatched an aid-de-camp to Marshal Ney, with orders to plant batteries along the coast, the General and his staff turned their attention to the prisoners. Two hundred Spaniards, whom the inhabitants had surrendered, were shot down then and there upon the terrace. After this military execution, the General ordered as many gallows to be erected on the terrace as there were prisoners in the hall of the castle, and the town executioner to be brought. Victor Marchand made use of the time from then until dinner to go and visit the prisoners. He soon returned to the General.

"I have come," said he, in a voice broken with emotion, "to ask you a favor."

"You?" said the General, in a tone of bitter irony.

"Alas!" replied Victor, "it is but a melancholy errand that I am come on. The Marques has seen the gallows being erected, and expresses a hope that you will change the mode of execution for his family; he entreats you to have the nobles beheaded."

"So be it!" said the General.

"They further ask you to allow them the last consolations of religion, and to take off their bonds; they promise not to attempt to escape."

"I consent," said the General; "but you must be answerable for them."

"The old man also offers you the whole of his fortune if you will pardon his young son."

"Really!" said the General. "His goods already belong to King Joseph; he is under arrest." His brow contracted scornfully, then he added: "I will go beyond what they ask. I understand now the importance of the last request. Well, let him buy the eternity of his name, but Spain shall remember forever his treachery and its punishment. I give up the fortune and his life to whichever of his sons will fulfill the office of executioner. Go, and do not speak to me of it again."

Dinner was ready, and the officers sat down to table to satisfy appetites sharpened by fatigue.

One of them only, Victor Marchand, was not present at the banquet. He hesitated for a long time before he entered the room. The haughty family of Leganes were in their agony. He glanced sadly at the scene before him; in this very room, only the night before, he had watched the fair heads of those two young girls and those three youths as they circled in the excitement of the dance. He shuddered when he thought how soon they must fall, struck off by the sword of the headsman. Fastened to their gilded chairs, the father and mother, their three sons, and their two young daughters, sat absolutely motionless. Eight serving men stood upright before them, their hands bound behind their backs. These fifteen persons looked at each other gravely, their eyes scarcely betraying the thoughts that surged within them. Only profound resignation and regret for the failure of their enterprise left any mark upon the features of some of them. The soldiers stood likewise motionless, looking at them, and respecting the affliction of their cruel enemies. An expression of curiosity lit up their faces when Victor appeared. He gave the order to unbind the condemned, and went himself to loose the cords which fastened Clara to her chair. She smiled sadly. He could not refrain from touching her arm, and looking with admiring eyes at her black locks and graceful figure. She was a true Spaniard; she had the Spanish complexion and the Spanish eyes, with their long curled lashes and pupils blacker than the raven's wing.

"Have you been successful?" she said, smiling upon him mournfully with somewhat of the charm of girlhood still lingering in her eyes.

Victor could not suppress a groan. He looked one after the other at Clara and her three brothers. One, the eldest, was aged thirty; he was small, even somewhat ill made, with a proud disdainful look, but there was a certain nobleness in his bearing; he seemed no stranger to that delicacy of feeling which elsewhere has rendered the chivalry of Spain so famous. His name was Juanito. The second, Felipe, was aged about twenty; he was like Clara. The youngest was eight, Manuel; a painter would have found in his features a trace of that Roman steadfastness which David has given to children's faces in his episodes of the Republic. The old Marques, his head still covered with white locks, seemed to have come forth from a picture of Murillo. The young officer shook his head. When he looked at them, he was hopeless that he would ever see the bargain proposed by the General accepted by either of the four; nevertheless he ventured to impart it to Clara. At first she shuddered, Spaniard though she was; then, immediately recovering her calm demeanor, she went and knelt down before her father.

"Father," she said, "make Juanito swear to obey faithfully any orders that you give him, and we shall be content."

The Marquesa trembled with hope; but when she leant towards her husband, and heard—she who was a mother—the horrible confidence whispered by Clara, she swooned away. Juanito understood all; he leapt up like a lion in its cage. After obtaining an assurance of perfect submission from the Marques, Victor took upon himself to send away the soldiers. The servants were led out, handed over to the executioner, and hanged. When the family had no guard but Victor to watch them, the old father rose and said, "Juanito."

Juanito made no answer, except by a movement of the head, equivalent to a refusal; then he fell back in his seat, and stared at his parents with eyes dry and terrible to look upon. Clara went and sat on his knee, put her arm round his neck, and kissed his eyelids.

"My dear Juanito," she said gayly, "if thou didst only know how sweet death would be to me if it were given by thee, I should not have to endure the odious touch of the headsman's hands. Thou wilt cure me of the woes that were in store for me—and, dear Juanito, thou couldst not bear to see me belong to another, well——" Her soft eyes cast one look of fire at Victor, as if to awaken in Juanito's heart his horror of the French.

"Have courage," said his brother Felipe, "or else our race, that has almost given kings to Spain, will be extinct."

Suddenly Clara rose, the group which had formed round Juanito separated, and this son, dutiful in his disobedience, saw his aged father standing before him, and heard him cry in a solemn voice, "Juanito, I command thee."

The young Count remained motionless. His father fell on his knees before him; Clara, Manuel, and Felipe did the same instinctively. They all stretched out their hands to him as to one who was to save their family from oblivion; they seemed to repeat their father's words— "My son, hast thou lost the energy, the true chivalry of Spain? How long wilt thou leave thy father on his knees? What right hast thou to think of thine own life and its suffering? Madam, is this a son of mine?" continued the old man, turning to his wife.

"He consents," cried she in despair. She saw a movement in Juanito's eyelids, and she alone understood its meaning.

Mariquita, the second daughter, still knelt on her knees, and clasped her mother in her fragile arms; her little brother Manuel, seeing her weeping hot tears, began to chide her. At this moment

84

the almoner of the castle came in; he was immediately surrounded by the rest of the family and brought to Juanito. Victor could bear this scene no longer; he made a sign to Clara, and hastened away to make one last effort with the General. He found him in high good humor in the middle of the banquet, drinking with his officers; they were beginning to make merry.

An hour later a hundred of the principal inhabitants of Menda came up to the terrace, in obedience to the General's orders, to witness the execution of the family of Leganes. A detachment of soldiers was drawn up to keep back these Spanish burghers who were ranged under the gallows on which the servants of the Marques still hung. The feet of these martyrs almost touched their heads. Thirty yards from them a block had been set up, and by it gleamed a scimiter. The headsman also was present, in case of Juanito's refusal. Presently, in the midst of the profoundest silence, the Spaniards heard the footsteps of several persons approaching, the measured tread of a company of soldiers, and the faint clinking of their muskets. These diverse sounds were mingled with the merriment of the officers' banquet,—just as before it was the music of the dance which had concealed preparations for a treacherous massacre. All eyes were turned towards the castle; the noble family was seen advancing with incredible dignity. Every face was calm and serene; one man only leant, pale and haggard, on the arm of the Priest. Upon this man he lavished all the consolations of religion —upon the only one of them doomed to live. The executioner understood, as did all the rest, that for that day Juanito had undertaken the office himself. The aged Marques and his wife, Clara, Mariquita, and their two brothers, came and knelt down a few steps from the fatal spot. Juanito was led thither by the Priest. As he approached the block the executioner touched him by the sleeve and drew him aside, probably to give him certain instructions.

The Confessor placed the victims in such a position that they could not see the executioner; but like true Spaniards, they knelt erect without a sign of emotion.

Clara was the first to spring forward to her brother. "Juanito," she said, "have pity on my faint-heartedness; begin with me."

At that moment they heard the footsteps of a man running at full speed, and Victor arrived on the tragic scene. Clara was already on her knees, already her white neck seemed to invite the edge of the scimiter. A deadly pallor fell upon the officer, but he still found strength to run on.

"The General grants thee thy life if thou wilt marry me." he said to her in a low voice.

The Spaniard cast a look of proud disdain on the officer. "Strike, Juanito," she said, in a voice of profound meaning.

Her head rolled at Victor's feet. When the Marquesa heard the sound a convulsive start escaped her; this was the only sign of her affliction.

"Am I placed right so, dear Juanito?" little Manuel asked his brother.

"Ah, thou weepest, Mariquita!" said Juanito to his sister.

"Yes," answered the girl; "I was thinking of thee, my poor Juanito; thou wilt be so unhappy without us."

At length the noble figure of the Marques appeared. He looked at the blood of his children; then he turned to the spectators, who stood mute and motionless before him. He stretched out his hands to Juanito, and said in a firm voice: "Spaniards, I give my son a father's blessing. Now, *Marques*, strike without fear, as thou art without fault."

But when Juanito saw his mother approach, supported by the Confessor, he groaned aloud, "She fed me at her own breast." His cry seemed to tear a shout of horror from the lips of the crowd. At this terrible sound the noise of the banquet and the laughter and merrymaking of the officers died away. The Marquesa comprehended that Juanito's courage was exhausted. With one leap she had thrown herself over the balustrade, and her head was dashed to pieces against the rocks below. A shout of admiration burst forth. Juanito fell to the ground in a swoon.

"Marchand has just been telling me something about this execution," said a half-drunken officer. "I'll warrant, General, it wasn't by your orders that——"

"Have you forgotten, Messieurs," cried General Gautier, "that during the next month there will be five hundred French families in tears, and that we are in Spain? Do you wish to leave your bones here?"

After this speech there was not a man, not even a sublieutenant, who dared to empty his glass.

In spite of the respect with which he is surrounded—in spite of the title of El Verdugo (the executioner), bestowed upon him as a title of nobility by the King of Spain—the Marques de Leganes is a prey to melancholy. He lives in solitude, and is rarely seen. Overwhelmed with the load of his glorious crime, he seems only to await the birth of a second son, impatient to seek again the company of those Shades who are about his path continually.

JAMES MATTHEW BARRIE

JAMES MATTHEW BARRIE (English, 1860-1937). Scottish-born playwright and novelist, admired today for such plays as *The Admirable Crichton* and *What Every Woman Knows,* and the children's classic, *Peter Pan.* A consummate master of stagecraft, though works sometimes marred by sentimentality. At his unrivaled best in fantasy, combining humor, pathos and whimsey.

COURTSHIPS

WITH the severe Auld Lichts the Sabbath began at six o'clock on Saturday evening. By that time the gleaming shuttle was at rest, Davie Haggart had strolled into the village from his pile of stones on the Whunny road; Hendry Robb, the "dummy," had sold his last barrowful of "rozetty (resiny) roots" for firewood; and the people, having tranquilly supped and soused their faces in their water pails, slowly donned their Sunday clothes. This ceremony was common to all; but here divergence set in. The gray Auld Licht, to whom love was not even a name, sat in his high-backed armchair by the hearth, Bible or "Pilgrim's Progress" in hand, occasionally lapsing into slumber. But—though, when they got the chance, they went willingly three times to the kirk—there were young men in the community so flighty that, instead of dozing at home on Saturday night, they dandered casually into the square, and, forming into knots at the corners, talked solemnly and mysteriously of women.

Not even on the night preceding his wedding was an Auld Licht ever known to stay out after ten o'clock. So weekly conclaves at street corners came to an end at a comparatively early hour, one Coelebs after another shuffling silently from the square until it echoed, deserted, to the townhouse clock. The last of the gallants, gradually discovering that he was alone, would look around him musingly, and, taking in the situation, slowly wend his way home. On no other night of the week was frivolous talk about the softer sex indulged in, the Auld Lichts being creatures of habit who never thought of smiling on a Monday. Long before they reached their teens they were earning their keep as herds in the surrounding glens or filling "pirns" for their parents; but they were generally on the brink of twenty before they thought seriously of matrimony. Up to that time they only trifled with the other sex's affections at a distance—filling a maid's water pails, perhaps, when no one was looking or carrying her wob; at the recollection of which they would slap their knees almost jovially on Saturday night. A wife was expected to assist at the loom as well as to be cunning in the making of marmalade and the firing of bannocks, and there was consequently some heartburning among the lads for maids of skill and muscle. The Auld Licht, however, who meant marriage seldom loitered in the streets. By and by there came a time when the clock looked down through its cracked glass upon the hemmed-in square and saw him not. His companions, gazing at each other's boots, felt that something was going on, but made no remark.

A month ago, passing through the shabby familiar square, I brushed against a withered old man tottering down the street under a load of yarn. It was piled on a wheelbarrow, which his feeble hands could not have raised but for the rope of yarn that supported it from his shoulders; and though Auld Licht was written on his patient eyes, I did not immediately recognize Jamie Whamond. Years ago Jamie was a sturdy weaver and fervent lover whom I had the right to call my friend. Turn back the century a few decades, and we are together on a moonlight night, taking a short cut through the fields from the farm of Craigiebuckle. Buxom were Craigiebuckle's "dochters," and Jamie was Janet's accepted suitor. It was a muddy road through damp grass, and we picked our way silently over its ruts and pools. "I'm thinkin'," Jamie said at last, a little wistfully, " that I micht hae been as weel wi' Christy."

Christy was Janet's sister, and Jamie had first thought of her. Craigiebuckle, however, strongly advised him to take Janet instead, and he consented. Alack! heavy wobs have taken all the grace from Janet's shoulders this many a year, though she and Jamie go bravely down the hill together. Unless they pass the allotted span of life, the "poors-house" will never know them. As for bonny Christy, she proved a flighty thing, and married a deacon in the Established Church. The Auld Licht groaned over her fall, Craigiebuckle hung his head, and the minister told her sternly to go her way. But a few weeks afterwards Lang Tammas, the chief elder, was observed talking with her for an hour in Gowrie's close; and the very next

Sabbath Christy pushed her husband in triumph into her father's pew. The minister, though completely taken by surprise, at once referred to the stranger, in a prayer of great length, as a brand that might yet be plucked from the burning. Changing his text, he preached at him; Lang Tammas, the precentor, and the whole congregation (Christy included), sang at him; and before he exactly realized his position he had become an Auld Licht for life. Christy's triumph was complete when, next week, in broad daylight, too, the minister's wife called, and (in the presence of Betsy Munn, who vouches for the truth of the story) graciously asked her to come up to the manse on Thursday, at 4 P.M., and drink a dish of tea. Christy, who knew her position, of course begged modestly to be excused; but a coolness arose over the invitation between her and Janet—who felt slighted—that was only made up at the laying-out of Christy's father-in-law, to which Janet was pleasantly invited.

When they had red up the house, the Auld Licht lassies sat in the gloaming at their doors on three-legged stools, patiently knitting stockings. To them came stiff-limbed youths who, with a "Blawy nicht, Jeanie" (to which the inevitable answer was, "It is so Charles"), rested their shoulders on the door-post and silently followed with their eyes the flashing needles. Thus the courtship began—often to ripen promptly into marriage, at other times to go no further. The smooth-haired maids, neat in their simple wrappers, knew they were on their trial and that it behooved them to be wary. They had not compassed twenty winters without knowing that Marget Todd lost Davie Haggart because she "fittit" a black stocking with brown worsted, and that Finny's grieve turned from Bell Whamond on account of the frivolous flowers in her bonnet; and yet Bell's prospects, as I happen to know, at one time looked bright and promising. Sitting over her father's peat fire one night gossiping with him about fishing flies and tackle, I noticed the grieve, who had dropped in by appointment with some ducks' eggs on which Bell's clockin hen was to sit, performing some slight-of-hand trick with his coat sleeve. Craftily he jerked and twisted it, till his own photograph (a black smudge on white) gradually appeared to view. This he gravely slipped into the hands of the maid of his choice, and then took his departure, apparently much relieved. Had not Bell's light-headedness driven him away, the grieve would have soon followed up his gift with an offer of his hand. Some night Bell would have "seen him to the door," and they would have stared sheepishly at each other before saying good night. The parting salutation given, the grieve would still have stood his ground, and Bell would have waited with him. At last "Will ye hae 's Bell?" would have dropped from his half-reluctant lips; and Bell would have mumbled, "Ay," with her thumb in her mouth. "Guid nicht to ye, Bell," would be the next remark— "Guid nicht to ye, Jeames," the answer; the humble door would close softly, and Bell and her lad would have been engaged. But, as it was, their attachment never got beyond the silhouette stage, from which, in the ethics of the Auld Lichts, a man can draw back in certain circumstances without loss of honor. The only really tender thing I ever heard an Auld Licht lover say to his sweetheart was when Gowrie's brother looked softly into Easie Tamson's eyes and whispered, "Dou you swite (sweat)?" Even then the effect was produced more by the loving cast in Gowrie's eye that by the tenderness of the words themselves.

The courtships were sometimes of long duration, but as soon as the young man realized that he was courting he proposed. Cases were not wanting in which he realized this for himself, but as a rule he had to be told of it.

There were a few instances of weddings among the Auld Lichts that did not take place on Friday. Betsy Munn's brother thought to assert his two coal carts, about which he was sinfully puffed up, by getting married early in the week; but he was a pragmatical feckless body, Jamie. The foreigner from York that Finny's grieve after disappointing Jinny Whamond, took, sought to sow the seeds of strife by urging that Friday was an unlucky day; and I remember how the minister, who was always great in a crisis, nipped the bickering in the bud by adducing the conclusive fact that he had been married on the sixth day of the week himself. It was a judicious policy on Mr. Dishart's part to take vigorous action at once and insist on the solemnization of the marriage on a Friday or not at all, for he best kept superstition out of the congregation by branding it as heresy. Perhaps the Auld Lichts were only ignorant of the grieve's lass' theory because they had not thought of it. Friday's claims, too, were incontrovertible; for the Saturday's being a slack day gave the couple an opportunity to put their but and ben in order, and on Sabbath they had a gay day of it, three times at the kirk. The honeymoon over, the racket of the loom began again on the Monday.

The natural politeness of the Allardice family gave me my invitation to Tibbie's wedding. I was taking tea and cheese early one

wintry afternoon with the smith and his wife, when little Joey
Todd in his Sabbath clothes peered in at the passage, and then
knocked primly at the door. Andra forgot himself, and called out
to him to come in by; but Jess frowned him into silence, and
hastily donning her black mutch, received Willie on the threshold.
Both halves of the door were open, and the visitor had looked us
over carefully before knocking; but he had come with the compli-
ments of Tibbie's mother, requesting the pleasure of Jess and her
man that evening to the lassie's marriage with Sam'l Todd, and
the knocking at the door was part of the ceremony. Five minutes
afterward Joey returned to beg a moment of me in the passage;
when I, too, got my invitation. The lad had just received, with
an expression of polite surprise, though he knew he could claim
it as his right, a slice of crumbling shortbread, and taken his staid
departure, when Jess cleared the tea things off the table, remarking
simply that it was a mercy we had not got beyond the first cup. We
then retired to dress.

About six o'clock, the time announced for the ceremony, I
elbowed my way through the expectant throng of men, women and
children that already besieged the smith's door. Shrill demands of
"toss, toss!" rent the air every time Jess' head showed on the
window blind, and Andra hoped, as I pushed open the door, "that
I hadna forgotten my bawbees." Weddings were celebrated among
the Auld Lichts by showers of ha-pence, and the guests on their
way to the bride's house had to scatter to the hungry rabble like
housewives feeding poultry. Willie Todd, the best man, who had
never come out so strong in his life before, slipped through the
back window, while the crowd, led on by Kitty McQueen, seethed
in front, and making a bolt for it to the "Sosh," was back in a
moment with a handful of small change. "Dinna toss ower lavishly
at first," the smith whispered to me nervously, as we followed Jess
and Willie into the darkening yard.

The guests were packed hot and solemn in Johnny Allardice'
"room": the men anxious to surrender their seat to the ladies
who happened to be standing but too bashful to propose it, the
ham and the fish frizzling noisily side by side and hissing out
every now and then to let all whom it might concern know
that Janet Craik was adding more water to the gravy. A better
woman never lived; but oh! the hypocrisy of the face that beamed
greeting to the guests as if it had nothing to do but politely show
them in, and gasped next moment with upraised arms, over what

was nearly a fall in crockery. When Janet sped to the door her "spleet new" merion dress fell, to the pulling of a string, over her home-made petticoat, like the drop scene in a theater, and rose as promptly when she returned to slice the bacon. The murmur of admiration that filled the room when she entered with the minister was an involuntary tribute to the spotlessness of her wrapper, and a great triumph for Janet. If there is an impression that the dress of the Auld Lichts was on all occasions as somber as their faces, let it be known that the bride was but one of several in "whites," and that Mag Munn had only at the last moment been dissuaded from wearing flowers. The minister, the Auld Lichts congratulated themselves, disapproved of all such decking of the person and bowing of the head to idols; but on such an occasion he was not expected to observe it. Bell Whamond, however, has reason for knowing that, marriages or no marriages, he drew the line at curls.

By and by Sam'l Todd, looking a little dazed, was pushed into the middle of the room to Tibbie's side, and the minister raised his voice in prayer. All eyes closed reverently, except perhaps the bridegroom's, which seemed glazed and vacant. It was an open question in the community whether Mr. Dishart did not mis his chance at weddings, the men shaking their heads over the comparative brevity of the ceremony, the women worshipping him (though he never hesitated to rebuke them when they showed it too openly) for the urbanity of his manners. At that time, however, only a minister of such experience as Mr. Dishart's predecessor could lead up to a marriage in prayer without inadvertently joining the couple; and the catechizing was mercifully brief. Another prayer followed the union; the minister waived his right to kiss the bride; every one looked at every other one, as if he had for the moment forgotten what he was on the point of saying and found it very annoying; and Janet signed frantically to Willie Todd, who nodded intelligently in reply, but evidently had no idea what she meant. In time Johnny Allardice, our host, who became more and more doited as the night proceeded, remembered his instructions, and led the way to the kitchen, where the guests, having politely informed their hostess that they were not hungry, partook of a hearty tea. Mr. Dishart presided, with the bride and bridegroom near him; but though he tried to give an agreeable turn to the conversation by describing the extensions at the cemetery, his personality oppressed us, and we only breathed freely when he rose to go. Yet we marvelled at his versatility. In shaking hands with

92

the newly married couple the minister reminded them that it was leap year, and wished them "three hundred and sixty-six happy and God-fearing days."

Sam'l' station being too high for it, Tibbie did not have a penny wedding, which her thrifty mother bewailed, penny weddings starting a couple in life. I can recall nothing more characteristic of the nation from which the Auld Lichts sprung than the penny wedding, where the only revellers that were not out of pocket by it were the couple who gave the entertainment. The more the guests ate and drank the better, pecuniarily, for their hosts. The charge for admission to the penny wedding (practically to the feast that followed it) varied in different districts, but with us it was generally a shilling. Perhaps the penny extra to the fiddler accounts for the name penny wedding. The ceremony having been gone through in the bride's house, there was an adjournment to a barn or other convenient place of meeting, where was held the nuptial feast. Long white boards from Rob Angus' sawmill, supported on trestles, stood in lieu of tables; and those of the company who could not find a seat waited patiently against the wall for a vacancy. The shilling gave every guest the free run of the groaning board; but though fowls were plentiful, and even white bread, too, little had been spent on them. The farmers of the neighborhood, who looked forward to providing the young couple with drills of potatoes for the coming winter, made a bid for their custom by sending them a fowl gratis for the marriage supper. It was popularly understood to be the oldest cock of the farmyard, but for all that it made a brave appearance in a shallow sea of soup. The fowls were always boiled —without exception, so far as my memory carries me—the guidwife never having the heart to roast them, and so lose the broth. One round of whisky and water was all the drink to which his shilling entitled the guest. If he wanted more he had to pay for it. There was much revelry, with song and dance, that no stranger could have thought those stiff-limbed weavers capable of; and the more they shouted and whirled through the barn, the more their host smiled and rubbed his hands. He presided at the bar improvised for the occasion, and if the thing was conducted with spirit, his bride flung an apron over her gown and helped him. I remember one elderly bride-groom, who, having married a blind woman, had to do double work at his penny wedding. It was a sight to see him flitting about the torch-lit barn, with a kettle of hot water in one hand and a besom to sweep up crumbs in the other.

Though Sam'l had no penny wedding, however, we made a night of it at his marriage.

Wedding chariots were not in those days, though I know of Auld Lichts being conveyed to marriages nowadays by horses with white ears. The tea over, we formed in couples, and—the best man with the bride, the bridegroom with the best maid, leading the way —marched in slow procession in the moonlight night to Tibbie's new home, between lines of hoarse and eager onlookers. An attempt was made by an itinerant musician to head the company with his fiddle; but instrumental music, even in the streets, was abhorrent to sound Auld Lichts, and the minister had spoken privately to Willie Todd on the subject. As a consequence, Peter was driven from the ranks. The last thing I saw that night, as we filed, bare-headed and solemn, into the newly married couple's house, was Kitty McQueen's vigorous arm, in a dishevelled sleeve, pounding a pair of urchins who had got between her and a muddy ha'penny.

That night there was revelry and boisterous mirth (or what the Auld Lichts took for such) in Tibbie's kitchen. At eleven o'clock Davit Lunan cracked a joke. Davie Haggart, in reply to Bell Dundas' request, gave a song of distinctly secular tendencies. The bride (who had carefully taken off her wedding gown on getting home and donned a wrapper) coquettishly let the bridegroom's father hold her hand. In Auld Licht circles, when one of the company was offered whisky and refused it, the others, as if pained at the offer, pushed it from them as a thing abhorred. But Davie Haggart set another example on this occasion, and no one had the courage to refuse to follow it. We sat late round the dying fire, and it was only Willie Todd's scandalous assertion (he was but a boy) about his being able to dance that induced us to think of moving. In the community, I understand, this marriage is still memorable as the occasion on which Bell Whamond laughed in the minister's face.

BASHO

BASHO (Matsuo Munefusa, Japanese, 1644-1694). Master of the *Hokku* School of Japanese poetry (the *hokku*: a poem of seventeen syllables in three lines). Of samurai family, left feudal service to travel extensively and become a hermit, taking up Zen Buddhism. Works: *Fuyu no hi* and *Haru no hi* (anthologies) ; *Nozarashi kikō* and *Oku no hosomichi* (travel diaries).

NEW YEAR'S DAY

Ah, the New Year's Day reminds me
  Of a lonely autumn evening.

CROWS ON A SNOWY MORNING

The usually hateful crow—
How lovely on the morn of snow!

THE RUINS OF TAKADACHI FORT

The summer grass!
'Tis all that's left
Of ancient warriors' dreams.

VIOLETS

Beside a mountain path,
A graceful find
Is a tiny violet!

A CROW ON A BARE BRANCH

The autumn gloaming deepens into night;
Black 'gainst the slowly-fading orange light,
On withered bough a lonely crow is sitting.

THE OLD POND

A lonely pond in age-old stillness sleeps....
  Apart unstirred by sound or motion....till
Suddenly into it a lithe frog leaps.

A VERSE COMPOSED ON HORSEBACK

The roadside thistle, eager
To see the travellers pass
Was eaten by the passing ass.

THE MILKY WAY

O rough sea! Waves on waves do darkling rise,
The galaxy reaching down where Sado lies.

THE FIREFLY SEEN BY DAYLIGHT

Alas! the firefly seen by daylight
Is nothing but a red-necked insect.

95

THE FIRST SNOW

The first snow—just enough
To bend the jonquil leaves.

THE MOGAMI RIVER

Behold! the Mogami has sunk
The burning sun into the sea.

CHARLES BAUDELAIRE

CHARLES BAUDELAIRE (French, 1821-1867). Highly original 19th century
poet, whose masterpiece, *Les Fleurs du Mal*, created scandal on publication,
exerted greatest single influence on French modernists. Work falters between
blasphemy and bigotry. Travels to Africa and the East developed exotic taste.
Other major accomplishment was translation of Poe into French.

From SAD MADRIGAL

What care I that you be wise?
Be beautiful! Be sad! For tears
Add a charm unto your eyes,
As streams to meadows where they rise;
With the storm the bloom appears.

CORRESPONDENCES

Nature is a temple whose living spires
Send mingled words at times upon the air;
Man journeys through a wood of symbols there
That kindle, as he goes, with friendly fires.

As long-drawn echoes in a far-off bond
Blend in a deep and shadowed unity,
Vast as the night and as vast clarity,
Color and sound and fragrance correspond.

Some perfumes are as fresh as the cheek of a child,
Sweet as the hautboy, as the meadow green,
Others are triumphant, rich, defiled,

With all the expansion of infinite things,
Of amber, incense, musk, and benzoin,
Where the transport of the soul and the senses sings.

THE ALBATROSS

Often, in idle hours, men of the crew
Capture an albatross, great bird of the sea
That follows the vessel gliding through
The briny gulfs in indolent company.

No sooner are these sky-bound kings
Placed on the deck than dumb shame soars;
Piteously they droop their great white wings
To drag on either side of them like oars.

The winged adventurer, how dull and weak!
This handsome fellow wears a clownish guise!
One takes his stubby pipe to poke its beak,
One, limping, mimics how the cripple flies!

The poet resembles this prince of the clouds
Who soars with the tempest and mocks the bow:
Exiled on earth amid roaring crowds
His giant wings are weights to keep him low.

STEPHEN VINCENT BENET

STEPHEN VINCENT BENÉT (American, 1898-1943). Modern American
poet, who combined folksy wholesomeness with new classicism. Most famous
work, *John Brown's Body*, epic narrative of Civil War, won Pulitzer Prize in
1929. Also wrote five novels, two short operas (including *The Devil and Daniel
Webster*), many short stories. Benét celebrated exclusively the folk or epic
aspects of American life.

FREEDOM'S A HARD-BOUGHT THING

A LONG time ago, in times gone by, in slavery times, there was a
man named Cue. I want you to think about him. I've got a reason.
He got born like the cotton in the boll or the rabbit in the pea
patch. There wasn't any fine doings when he got born, but his

mammy was glad to have him. Yes. He didn't get born in the Big House, or the overseer's house, or anyplace where the bearing was easy or the work light. No, Lord. He came out of his mammy in a field hand's cabin one sharp winter, and about the first thing he remembered was his mammy's face and the taste of a piece of bacon rind and the light and shine of the pitch-pine fire up the chimney. Well, now, he got born and there he was.

His daddy worked in the fields and his mammy worked in the fields when she wasn't bearing. They were slaves; they chopped the cotton and hoed the corn. They heard the horn blow before the light came and the horn blow that meant the day's work was done. His daddy was a strong man—strong in his back and his arms. The white folks called him Cuffee. His mammy was a good woman, yes, Lord. The white folks called her Sarah, and she was gentle with her hands and gentle with her voice. She had a voice like the river going by in the night, and at night when she wasn't too tired she'd sing songs to little Cue. Some had foreign words in them—African words. She couldn't remember what some of them meant, but they'd come to her down out of time.

Now, how am I going to describe and explain about that time when that time's gone? The white folks lived in the Big House and they had many to tend on them. Old Marster, he lived there like Pharaoh and Solomon, mighty splendid and fine. He had his flocks and his herds, his butler and his baker; his fields ran from the river to the woods and back again. He'd ride around the fields each day on his big horse, Black Billy, just like thunder and lightning, and evenings he'd sit at his table and drink his wine. Man, that was a sight to see, with all the silver knives and the silver forks, the glass decanters, and the gentlemen and ladies from all over. It was a sight to see. When Cue was young, it seemed to him that Old Master must own the whole world, right up to the edge of the sky. You can't blame him for thinking that.

There were things that changed on the plantation, but it didn't change. There were bad times and good times. There was the time young Marse Edward got bit by the snake, and the time Big Rambo ran away and they caught him with the dogs and brought him back. There was a swivel-eyed overseer that beat folks too much, and then there was Mr. Wade, and he wasn't so bad. There was hog-killing time and Christmas and springtime and summertime. Cue didn't wonder about it or why things happened that way; he didn't expect it to be different. A bee in a hive don't ask you how there come to be a hive in the beginning. Cue grew up strong; he grew up smart with his hands. They put him in the blacksmith shop to help Daddy Jake; he didn't like it, at first, because Daddy Jake was mighty cross-tempered. Then he got to like the work; he learned to forge iron and shape it; he learned to shoe a horse and tire a wagon wheel, and everything a blacksmith does. One time they let him shoe Black Billy, and he shod him light and tight and Old Marster praised him in front of Mr. Wade. He was strong; he was black as night; he was proud of his back and his arms.

Now, he might have stayed that way—yes, he might. He heard freedom talk, now and then, but he didn't pay much mind to it. He wasn't a talker or a preacher; he was Cue and he worked in the blacksmith shop. He didn't want to be a field hand, but he didn't want to be a house servant either. He'd rather be Cue than poor white trash or owned by poor white trash. That's the way he felt; I'm obliged to tell the truth about that way.

Then there was a sickness came and his mammy and his daddy died of it. Old Miss got the doctor for them, but they died just the same. After that, Cue felt lonesome.

He felt lonesome and troubled in his mind. He'd seen his daddy and his mammy put in the ground and new slaves come to take their cabin. He didn't repine about that, because he knew things had to be that way. But when he went to bed at night, in the loft over the blacksmith shop, he'd keep thinking about his mammy and his daddy—how strong his daddy was and the songs that his mammy sang. They'd worked all their lives and had children. though he was the only one left, but the only place of their own they had was the place in the burying ground. And yet they'd been good and faithful servants, because Old Marster said so, with his hat off, when he buried them. The Big House stayed, and the cotton and the corn, but Cue's mammy and daddy were gone like last year's crop. It made Cue wonder and trouble.

He began to take notice of things he'd never noticed. When the horn blew in the morning for the hands to go to the fields, he'd wonder who started blowing that horn, in the first place. It wasn't like thunder and lightning; somebody had started it. When he heard Old Marster say, when he was talking to a friend, "This damned epidemic! It's cost me eight prime field hands and the best-trained butler in the state. I'd rather have lost the Flyaway colt than Old Isaac," Cue put that down in his mind and pondered it. Old Marster didn't mean it mean, and he'd sat up with Old Isaac all night before he died. But Isaac and Cue and the Flyaway colt, they all belonged to Old Marster and he owned them, hide and hair. He owned them, like money in his pockets. Well, Cue had known that all his life, but because he was troubled now, it gave him a queer feeling.

Well, now, he was shoeing a horse for young Marster Shepley one day, and he shod it light and tight. And when he was through, he made a stirrup for young Marster Shepley, and young Marster Shepley mounted and threw him a silver bit, with a laughing word. That shouldn't have bothered Cue, because gentlemen sometimes did that. And Old Marster wasn't mean; he didn't object. But all night Cue kept feeling the print of young Marster Shepley's heel in his hands. And yet he liked young Marster Shepley. He couldn't explain it at all.

Finally, Cue decided he must be conjured. He didn't know who had done it or why they'd done it. But he knew what he had to do. He had to go see Aunt Rachel.

Aunt Rachel was an old, old woman, and she lived in a cabin by herself, with her granddaughter, Sukey. She'd seen Old Marster's father and his father, and the tale went she'd seen George Washington with his hair all white, and General Lafayette in his gold-plated suit of clothes that the King of France gave him to fight in. Some folks said she was a conjure and some folks said she wasn't but everybody on the plantation treated her mighty respectful, because, if she put her eye on you, she mightn't take it off. Well, his mammy had been friends with Aunt Rachel, so Cue went to see her.

She was sitting alone in her cabin by the low light of a fire. There was a pot on the fire, and now and then you could hear it bubble and chunk, like a bullfrog chunking in the swamp, but that was the only sound. Cue made his obleegances to her and asked her about the misery in her back. Then he gave her a chicken he happened to bring along. It was a black rooster, and she seemed pleased to get it. She took it in her thin black hands and it fluttered and clucked a minute. So she drew a chalk line along a board and then it stayed still and frozen. Well, Cue had seen that trick before. But it was different, seeing it done in Aunt Rachel's cabin, with the big pot chunking on the fire. It made him feel uneasy and he jingled the bit in his pocket for company.

After a while the old woman spoke. "Well, Son Cue," said she, "that's a fine young rooster you've brought me. What else did you bring me, Son Cue?"

"I brought you trouble," said Cue, in a husky voice, because that was all he could think of to say.

She nodded her head as if she'd expected that. "They mostly brings me trouble," she said. "They mostly brings trouble to Aunt Rachel. What kind of trouble, Son Cue? Man trouble or woman trouble?"

"It's my trouble," said Cue, and he told her the best way he could. When he'd finished, the pot on the fire gave a bubble and a croak, and the old woman took a long spoon and stirred it.

"Well, Son Cue, son of Cuffee, son of Shango," she said, "you've got a big trouble, for sure."

"Is it going to kill me dead?" said Cue.

"I can't tell you right about that," said Aunt Rachel. "I could give you lies and prescriptions. Maybe I would, to some folks. But your Grandaddy Shango was a powerful man. It took three men to put irons on him, and I saw the irons break his heart. I won't lie to you, Son Cue. You've got a sickness."

"Is it a bad sickness?" said Cue.

"It's a sickness in your blood," said Aunt Rachel. "It's a sickness in your liver and your veins. Your daddy never had it that I knows of—he took after his mammy's side. But his daddy was a Corromantee, and they is bold and free, and you takes after him. It's the freedom sickness, Son Cue."

"The freedom sickness?" said Cue.

"The freedom sickness," said the old woman, and her little eyes glittered like sparks. "Some they break and some they tame down," she said, "and some is neither to be tamed or broken. Don't I know the signs and the sorrow—me, that come through the middle passage on the slavery ship and seen my folks scattered like sand? Ain't I seen it coming, Lord—O Lord, ain't I seen it coming?"

"What's coming?" said Cue.

"A darkness in the sky and a cloud with a sword in it," said the old woman, stirring the pot, "because they hold our people and they hold our people."

Cue began to tremble. "I don't want to get whipped," he said. "I never been whipped—not hard."

"They whipped your Grandaddy Shango till the blood ran twinkling down his back," said the old woman, "but some you can't break or tame."

"I don't want to be chased by dogs," said Cue. "I don't want to hear the dogs belling and the paterollers after me."

The old woman stirred the pot.

"Old Marster, he's a good marster," said Cue. "I don't want to do him no harm. I don't want no trouble or projecting to get me into trouble."

The old woman stirred the pot and stirred the pot.

"O God, I want to be free," said Cue. "I just ache and hone to be free. How am I going to be free, Aunt Rachel?"

"There's a road that runs underground," said the old woman. "I never seen it, but I knows of it. There's a railroad train that runs, sparking and snorting, underground through the earth. At least that's what they tell me. But I wouldn't know for sure," and she looked at Cue.

Cue looked back at her bold enough, for he'd heard about the Underground Railroad himself—just mentions and whispers. But he knew there wasn't any use asking the old woman what she wouldn't tell.

"How I going to find that road, Aunt Rachel?" he said.

"You look at the rabbit in the briar and you see what he do," said the old woman. "You look at the owl in the woods and you see what he do. You look at the star in the sky and you see what she do. Then you come back and talk to me. Now I'm going to eat, because I'm hungry."

That was all the words she'd say to him that night; but when Cue went back to his loft, her words kept boiling around in his mind. All night he could hear that train of railroad cars, snorting and sparking underground through the earth. So, next morning, he ran away.

He didn't run far or fast. How could he? He'd never been more than twenty miles from the plantation in his life; he didn't know the roads or the ways. He ran off before the horn, and Mr. Wade caught him before sundown. Now, wasn't he a stupid man, that Cue?

When they brought him back, Mr. Wade let him off light, because he was a good boy and never ran away before. All the same, he got ten, and ten laid over the ten. Yellow Joe, the head driver, laid them on. The first time the whip cut into him, it was just like a fire on Cue's skin, and he didn't see how he could stand it. Then he got to a place where he could.

After it was over, Aunt Rachel crope up to his loft and had her granddaughter, Sukey, put salve on his back. Sukey, she was sixteen, and golden-skinned and pretty as a peach on a peach tree. She worked in the Big House and he never expected her to do a thing like that.

"I'm mighty obliged," he said, though he kept thinking it was Aunt Rachel got him into trouble and he didn't feel as obliged as he might.

"Is that all you've got to say to me, Son Cue?" said Aunt Rachel, looking down on him. "I told you to watch three things. Did you watch them?"

"No'm," said Cue. "I run off in the woods just like I was a wild turkey. I won't never do that no more."

"You're right, Son Cue," said the old woman. "Freedom's a hard-bought thing. So, now you've been whipped, I reckon you'll give it up."

"I been whipped," said Cue, "but there's a road running underground. You told me so. I been whipped, but I ain't beaten."

"Now you're learning a thing to remember," said Aunt Rachel, and went away. But Sukey stayed behind for a while and cooked Cue's supper. He never expected her to do a thing like that, but he liked it when she did.

When his back got healed, they put him back with the field gang for a while. But then there was blacksmith work that needed to be done and they put him back in the blacksmith shop. And things went on for a long time just the way they had before. But there was a difference in Cue. It was like he'd lived up till now with his ears and his eyes sealed over. And now he began to open his eyes and his ears.

He looked at the rabbit in the briar and he saw it could hide. He looked at the owl in the woods and he saw it went soft through the night. He looked at the star in the sky and he saw she pointed north. Then he began to figure.

He couldn't figure things fast, so he had to figure things slow. He figure the owl and the rabbit got wisdom the white folks don't know about. But he figure the white folks got wisdom he don't know about. They got reading and writing wisdom, and it seem mighty powerful. He ask Aunt Rachel if that's so, and she say it's so.

That's how come he learned to read and write. He ain't supposed to. But Sukey, she learned some of that wisdom, along with the young misses, and she teach him out of a little book she tote from the Big House. The little book, it's all about bats and rats and cats, and Cue figure whoever wrote it must be sort of touched in the head not to write about things folk would want to know, instead of all those trifling animals. But he put himself to it and he learn. It almost bust his head, but he learn. It's a proud day for him when he write his name, "Cue," in the dust with the end of a stick and Sukey tell him that's right.

Now he began to hear the first rumblings of that train running underground—that train that's the Underground Railroad. Oh, Children, remember the names of Levi Coffin and John Hansen! Remember the Quaker saints that hid the fugitive! Remember the names of all those that helped set our people free!

There's a word dropped here and a word dropped there and a word that's passed around. Nobody know where the word come from or where it goes, but it's there. There's many a word spoken in the quarters that the Big House never hears about. There's a heap said in front of the fire that never flies up the chimney. There's a name you tell to the grapevine that the grapevine don't tell back.

There was a white man, one day came by, selling maps and pictures. The quality folks, they looked at his maps and pictures and he talked with them mighty pleasant and respectful. But while Cue was tightening a bolt on his wagon, he dropped a word and a word. The word he said made that underground train come nearer.

Cue meet that man one night, all alone, in the woods. He's a quiet man with a thin face. He hold his life in his hands every day he walk about, but he don't make nothing of that. Cue's seen bold folks and bodacious folks, but it's the first time he's seen a man bold that way. It made him proud to be a man. The man ask Cue questions and Cue give him answers. While he's seeing that man, Cue don't just think about himself any more. He think about all his people that's in trouble.

The man say something to him; he say, "No man own the earth. It's too big for one man." He say, "No man own another man; that's too big a thing too." Cue think about those words and ponder them. But when he gets back to his loft, the courage drains out of him and he sits on his straw tick, staring at the wall. That's the time the darkness comes to him and the shadow falls on him.

He aches and he hones for freedom, but he aches and he hones for Sukey too. And Long Ti's cabin is empty, and it's a good cabin. All he's got to do is to go to Old Marster and take Sukey with him. Old Marster don't approve to mix the field hand with the house servant, but Cue's different; Cue's a blacksmith. He can

104

see the way Sukey would look, coming back to her in the evening. He can see all that. It ain't freedom, but it's what he's used to. And the other way's long and hard and lonesome and strange.

"O Lord, why you put this burden on a man like me?" say Cue. Then he listen a long time for the Lord to tell him, and it seem to him, at last, that he get an answer. The answer ain't in any words, but it's a feeling in his heart.

So when the time come and the plan ripe and they get to the boat on the river and they see there's one too many for the boat, Cue know the answer. He don't have to hear the quiet white man say, "There's one too many for the boat." He just pitch Sukey into it before he can think too hard. He don't say a word or a groan. He know it's that way and there's bound to be a reason for it. He stand on the bank in the dark and see the boat pull away, like Israel's children. Then he hear the shouts and the shot. He know what he's bound to do then, and the reason for it. He knows it's the paterollers, and he show himself. When he get back to the plantation, he's worn and tired. But the paterollers, they've chased him, instead of the boat.

He creep by Aunt Rachel's cabin and he see the fire at her window. So he scratch at the door and go in. And there she is, sitting by the fire, all hunched up and little.

"You looks poorly, Son Cue," she say, when he come in, though she don't take her eye off the pot.

"I'm poorly, Aunt Rachel," he say. "I'm sick and sorry and distressed."

"What's the mud on your jeans, Son Cue?" she say, and the pot, it bubble and croak.

"That's the mud of the swamp where I hid from the paterollers," he say.

"What's the hole in your leg, Son Cue?" she say, and the pot, it croak and bubble.

"That's the hole from the shot they shot at me," say Cue. "The blood most nearly dried, but it make me lame. But Israel's children, they's safe."

"They's across the river?" say the old woman.

"They's across the river," say Cue. "They ain't room for no more in the boat. But Sukey, she's across."

"And what will you do now, Son Cue?" say the old woman. "For that was your chance and your time, and you give it up for another. And tomorrow morning, Mr. Wade, he'll see that hole in your leg and he'll ask questions. It's a heavy burden you've laid on yourself, Son Cue."

"It's a heavy burden," say Cue, "and I wish I was shut of it. I never asked to take no such burden. But freedom's a hard-bought thing."

The old woman stand up sudden, and for once she look straight and tall. "Now bless the Lord!" she say. "Bless the Lord and praise him! I come with my mammy in the slavery ship—I come through the middle passage. There ain't many that remember that, these days, or care about it. There ain't many that remember the red flag that witched us on board or how we used to be free. Many thousands gone, and the thousands of many thousands that lived and died in slavery. But I remember. I remember them all. Then they took me into the Big House—me that was a Mandingo and a witch woman—and the way I live in the Big House, that's between me and my Lord. If I done wrong, I done paid for it—I paid for it with weeping and sorrow. That's before Old Miss' time and I help raise up Old Miss. They sell my daughter to the South and my son to the West, but I raise up Old Miss and tend on her. I ain't going to repine of that. I count the hairs on Old Miss' head when she's young, and she turn to me, weak and helpless. And for that there'll be a kindness between me and the Big House—a kindness that folks will remember. But my children's children shall be free."

"You do this to me," say Cue, and he look at her, and he look at her, and he look dangerous. "You do this to me, old woman," he say, and his breath come harsh in his throat, and his hands twitch.

"Yes," she say, and look him straight in the eyes. "I do to you what I never even do for my own. I do it for your Grandaddy Shango, that never turn to me in the light of the fire. He turn to that soft Eboe woman, and I have to see it. He roar like a lion in the chains, and I have to see that. So, when you come, I try you and test you, to see if you fit to follow after him. And because you fit to follow after him, I put freedom in your heart, Son Cue."

"I never going to be free," say Cue, and look at his hands. "I done broke all the rules. They bound to sell me now."

"You'll be sold and sold again," say the old woman. "You'll know the chains and the whip. I can't help that. You'll suffer for your people and with your people. But while one man's got freedom in his heart, his children bound to know the tale."

She put the lid on the pot and it stop bubbling.

106

"Now I come to the end of my road," she say, "but the tale don't stop there. The tale go backward to Africa and it go forward, like clouds and fire. It go, laughing and grieving forever, through the earth and the air and the waters—my people's tale."

Then she drop her hands in her lap and Cue creep out of the cabin. He know then he's bound to be a witness, and it make him feel cold and hot. He know then he's bound to be a witness and tell that tale. O Lord, it's hard to be a witness, and Cue know that. But it help him in the days to come.

Now, when he get sold, that's when Cue feel the iron in his heart. Before that, and all his life, he despise bad servants and bad masters. He live where the marster's good; he don't take much mind of other places. He's a slave, but he's Cue, the blacksmith, and Old Marster and Old Miss, they tend to him. Now he know the iron in his heart and what it's like to be a slave.

He know that on the rice fields in the hot sun. He know that, working all day for a handful of corn. He know the bad marsters and the cruel overseers. He know the bite of the whip and the gall of the iron on the ankle. Yes, Lord, he know tribulation. He know his own tribulation and the tribulation of his people. But all the time, somehow, he keep freedom in his heart. Freedom mighty hard to root out when it's in the heart.

He don't know the day or the year, and he forget, half the time, there ever was a gal named Sukey. All he don't forget is the noise of the train in his ears, the train snorting and sparking underground. He think about it at nights till he dream it carry him away. Then he wake up with the horn. He feel ready to die then, but he don't die. He live through the whip and the chain; he live through the iron and the fire. And finally he get away.

When he get away, he ain't like the Cue he used to be—not even back at Old Marster's place. He hide in the woods like a rabbit, he slip through the night like an owl. He go cold and hungry, but the star keep shining over him and he keep his eyes on the star. They set the dogs after him and he hear the dogs belling and yipping through the woods.

He's scared when he hear the dogs, but he ain't scared like he used to be. He ain't more scared than any man. He kill the big dog in the clearing—the big dog with the big voice—and he do it with his naked hands. He cross water three times after that to kill the scent, and he go on.

He got nothing to help him—no, Lord—but he got a star. The

107

star shine in the sky and the star shine—the star point north with its shining. You put that star in the sky, O Lord; you put it for the prisoned and the humble. You put it there—you ain't never going to blink it out.

He hungry and he eat green corn and cowpeas. He thirsty and he drink swamp water. One time he lie two days in the swamp, too puny to get up on his feet, and he know they hunting around him. He think that's the end of Cue. But after two days he lift his head and his hand. He kill a snake with a stone, and after he's cut out the poison bag, he eat the snake to strengthen him, and go on.

He don't know what the day is when he come to the wide, cold river. The river yellow and foaming, and Cue can't swim. But he hide like a crawdad on the bank; he make himself a little raft with two logs. He know this time's the last time and he's obliged to drown. But he put out on the raft and it drift him to the freedom side. He mighty weak by then.

He mighty weak, but he careful. He know tales of Billy Shea, the slave catcher; he remember those tales. He slide into the town by night, like a shadow, like a ghost. He beg broken victuals at a door; the woman give them to him, but she look at him suspicious. He make up a tale to tell her, but he don't think she believe the tale. In the gutter he find a newspaper; he pick it up and look at the notices. There's a notice about a runaway man named Cue. He look at it and it make the heart beat in his breast.

He patient; he mighty careful. He leave that town behind. He got the name of another town, Cincinnati, and a man's name in that town. He don't know where it is, he have to ask his way, but he do it mighty careful. One time he ask a yellow man directions; he don't like the look on the yellow man's face. He remember Aunt Rachel; he tell the yellow man he conjure his liver out if the yellow man tell him wrong. The yellow man scared and tell him right. He don't hurt the yellow man; he don't blame him for not wanting trouble. But he made the yellow man change pants with him, because his pants mighty ragged.

He patient; he very careful. When he get to the place he been told about, he look all about that place. It's a big house; it don't look right. He creep around to the back—he creep and he crawl. He look in a window; he see white folks eating their supper. They just look like any white folks. He expect them to look different. He feel mighty bad. All the same, he rap at the window the way he

108

been told. They don't nobody pay attention and he just about to go away. Then the white man get up from the table and open the back door a crack. Cue breathe in the darkness.

"God bless the stranger the Lord sends us," say the white man in a low, clear voice, and Cue run to him and stumble, and the white man catch him. He look up and it's a white man, but he ain't like thunder and lightning.

He take Cue and wash his wounds and bind them up. He feed him and hide him under the floor of the house. He ask him his name and where he's from. Then he send him on. O Lord, remember thy tried servant, Asaph Brown! Remember his name!

They send him from there in a wagon and he's hidden in the straw at the bottom. They send him from the next place in a closed cart with six others, and they can't say a word all night. One time a tollkeeper ask them what's in the wagon, and the driver say, "Southern calico," and the tollkeeper laugh. Cue always recollect that.

One time they get to big water—so big it look like the ocean. They cross that water in a boat; they get to the other side. When they get to the other side, they sing and pray, and white folks look on, curious. But Cue don't even feel happy; he just feel he want to sleep.

He sleep like he never sleep before—not for days and years. When he awake up, he wonder; he hardly recollects where he is. He lying in the loft of a barn. Ain't nobody around him. He get up and go out in the air. It's a fine sunny day.

He get up and go out. He say to himself, *I'm free,* but it don't take hold yet. He say to himself, *This is Canada and I'm free,* but it don't take hold. Then he start to walk down the street.

The first white man he meet on the street he scrunch up in himself and start to run across the street. But the white man don't pay him any mind. Then he know.

He say to himself in his mind, *I'm free. My name's Cue—John H. Cue. I got a strong back and strong arms. I got freedom in my heart. I got a first name and a last name and a middle name. I never had them all before.*

He say to himself, *My name's Cue—John H. Cue. I got a name to tell. I got a hammer to swing. I got a tale to tell my people. I got recollection. I call my first son "John Freedom Cue." I call my first daughter "Come-Out-of-the-Lion's-Mouth."*

Then he walk down the street, and he pass a blacksmith shop. The blacksmith, he's an old man and he lift the hammer heavy. Cue look in that shop and smile.

He pass on; he go his way. And soon enough he see a girl like a peach tree—a girl named Sukey—walking free down the street.

PIERRE JEAN DE BERANGER

PIERRE JEAN DE BÉRANGER (French, 1780-1857). Songwriter and poet, who was the great bohemian of early 19th century. A clerk who broke with his father and began writing in a garret. Two imprisonments for his poetry helped make him idol of Parisian working and middle classes. Several collections of poems and an autobiography published during lifetime. His work, sometimes sentimental, sometimes licentious, still moving.

FIFTY YEARS

(Cinquante Ans)

Wherefore these flowers? floral applause?
   Ah, no, these blossoms came to say
That I am growing old, because
   I number fifty years to-day.
O rapid, ever-fleeting day!
   O moments lost, I know not how!
O wrinkled cheek and hair grown gray!
   Alas, for I am fifty now!

Sad age, when we pursue no more—
   Fruit dies upon the withering tree:
Hark! some one rapped upon my door.
   Nay, open not. 'Tis not for me—
Or else the doctor calls. Not yet
   Must I expect his studious bow.
Once I'd have called, "Come in, Lizzette"—
   Alas, for I am fifty now!

In age what aches and pains abound:
  The torturing gout racks us awhile;
Blindness, a prison dark, profound;
  Or deafness that provokes a smile.
Then Reason's lamp grows faint and dim
  With flickering ray. Children, allow
Old Age the honor due to him—
  Alas, for I am fifty now!

Ah, heaven! the voice of Death I know,
  Who rubs his hands in joyous mood;
The sexton knocks and I must go,—
  Farewell, my friends the human brood!
Below are famine, plague, and strife;
  Above, new heavens my soul endow:
Since God remains, begin, new life!
  Alas, for I am fifty now!

But no, 'tis you, sweetheart, whose youth,
  Tempting my soul with dainty ways,
Shall hide from it the somber truth,
  This incubus of evil days.
Springtime is yours, and flowers; come then,
  Scatter your roses on my brow,
And let me dream of youth again—
  Alas, for I am fifty now!

THE OLD TRAMP

(*Le Vieux Vagabond*)

Here in this gutter let me die;
  Weary and sick and old, I've done.
"He's drunk," will say the passers-by;
  All right, I want no pity,—none.
I see the heads that turn away,
  While others glance and toss me sous.
"Off to your junket! go," I say:
Old tramp—to die I need no help from you.

111

Yes, of old age I'm dying now—
  Of hunger people never die.
I hoped some almshouse might allow
  A refuge when the end was nigh;
But all retreats are overflowed,
  Such crowds are suffering and forlorn.
My nurse, alas! has been the road:
Old tramp—let me die here where I was born.

When young, it used to be my prayer
  To craftsmen, "Let me learn your trade:"
"Clear out—we've got no work to spare;
  Go beg," was all reply they made.
You rich, who bade me work, I've fed
  With relish on the bones you threw;
Made of your straw an easy bed:
Old tramp—I have no curse to vent on you.

Poor wretch, how easy 'twas to steal!
  But no, I'd rather beg my bread.
At most I've thieved a wayside meal
  Of apples ripening overhead.
Yet twenty times have I been thrown
  In prison,—'twas the King's decree;
Robbed of the only thing I own:
Old tramp—at least the sun belongs to me.

The poor—is any country his?
  What are to me your grain, your wine,
Your glory and your industries,
  Your orators? They are not mine.
And when a foreign foe waxed fat
  Within your undefended walls,
I shed my tears, poor fool, at that:
Old tramp—his hand was open to my calls.

Why, like the venomous bug you kill,
  Did you not crush me when you could?
Or, better yet, have taught me skill
  To labor for the common good?

The grub a useful ant may end
  If sheltered from the blast and fed;
And so might I have been your friend:
  Old tramp—I die your enemy instead.

THE PEOPLE'S REMINISCENCES

(*Les Souvenirs du Peuple*)

Ah, many a day the straw-thatched cot
  Shall echo with his glory!
The humblest shed, these fifty years,
  Shall know no other story.
There shall the idle villagers
  To some old dame resort,
And beg her with those good old tales
  To make their evenings short.
"What though they say he did us harm?
  Our love this cannot dim:
Come, granny, talk of him to us;
  Come, granny, talk of him."

"Well, children—with a train of kings
  Once he passed by this spot;
'Twas long ago; I had but just
  Begun to boil the pot.
On foot he climbed the hill, whereon
  I watched him on his way;
He wore a small three-cornered hat;
  His overcoat was gray.
I was half frightened till he said
  'Good-day, my dear!' to me."——
"O granny, granny! did he speak?
  What, granny! you and he?"

"Next year, as I, poor soul, by chance
  Through Paris strolled one day,
I saw him taking, with his Court,
  To Notre Dame his way.

113

The crowd were charmed with such a show;
    Their hearts were filled with pride;
'What splendid weather for the fête!
    Heaven favors him!' they cried.
Softly he smiled, for God had given
    To his fond arms a boy."——
"Oh, how much joy you must have felt!
    O granny, how much joy!"

"But when at length our poor Champagne
    By foes was overrun,
He seemed alone to hold his ground;
    Nor dangers would he shun.
One night—as might be now—I heard
    A knock—the door unbarred—
And saw—good God!—'twas he, himself,
    With but a scanty guard.
'Oh, what a war is this!' he cried,
    Talking this very chair"——
"What! granny, granny, there he sat?
    What! granny, he sat there?"

" 'I'm hungry,' said he: quick I served
    Thin wine and hard brown bread;
He dried his clothes, and by the fire
    In sleep dropped down his head.
Waking, he saw my tears—'Cheer up,
    Good dame,' says he, 'I go
'Neath Paris' walls to strike for France
    One last avenging blow.'
He went; but on the cup he used,
    Such value did I set
It has been treasured——" "What! till now?
    You have it, granny, yet?"

"Here 'tis; but 'twas the hero's fate
    To ruin to be led;
He whom a Pope had crowned, alas!
    In a lone isle lies dead.

'Twas long denied: 'No, no,' said they,
  'Soon shall he reappear!
O'er ocean comes he, and the foe
  Shall find his master here.'
Ah, what a bitter pang I felt,
  When forced to own 'twas true!"——
"Poor granny! Heaven for this will look—
  Will kindly look on you."

BHARTRIHARI

BHARTRIHARI (Sanskrit, —— -651). Distinguished Sanskrit grammarian
and lyric poet, compared with Horace. His three *satakas* or "centuries" of
verse are *Sringāra Sataka* (*Century of Love*), *Nīti Sataka* (*Century of Worldly
Life*), and *Vairāgyra Sataka* (*Century of Renunciation*).

LOVE, THE FISHER

Love, the fisher, casts his woman-hook
  Into the sea of lust and fond desire,
And just as soon as greedy men-fish look
  And snap the red bait, lips so sweet, so dire:
Then he is quick to catch them and to cook
  The hungry wretches over passion's fire.

STRUGGLING FANCIES

It is my body leaves my love, not I;
  My body moves away, but not my mind;
For back to her my struggling fancies fly
  Like silken banners borne against the wind.

THE WISE MISOGYNIST

The wise misogynist, poor soul,
  To self-deceit is given;
For heaven rewards his self-control,
  And women swarm in heaven.

DIGNITY

The dog will roll, and wag his tail, and fawn,
　　Show mouth and belly, just to get some meat;
The majestic elephant gazes gravely on;
　　Till coaxed a hundred times, he will not eat.

FLAMING BANNERS

Learning and dignity,
　　Wisdom and manners
Last till the god of love
　　Plants flaming banners.

BETTER IN THE WILD

Better to dwell in mountains wild
　　With beasts of prey
Than in the palaces of gods
　　With fools to stay.

THE BETTER PART

Is there no splendid Himalayan height,
　　Cooled by the spray from Ganges' holy springs
With rocks where fairies now and then alight,
　　That men should fawn upon contemptuous kings?

ARROWS OF LOVE

Where are you going, winsome maid,
Through deepest, darkest night? (he said.)
I go to him whom love has made
Dearer to me than life (she said.)
Ah, girl, and are you not afraid,
For you are all alone? (he said.)
The god of love shall be mine aid,
Arrows of love fly true (she said).

LOVE GROWS BY WHAT IT FEEDS ON

When she is far, I only want to see her;
　　When she is seen, I only want to kiss her;
When she is kissed, I never want to flee her;
　　I know that I could never bear to miss her.

116

WHEN I KNEW A LITTLE BIT

When I knew a little bit,
Then my silly, blinded wit,
Mad as elephants in rut,
Thought it was omniscient; but
When I learned a little more
From the scholar's hoarded store,
Madness' fever soon grew cool,
And I knew I was a fool.

SWEET AND BITTER

Sweet are the moonbeams, sweet the grass-grown wood,
Sweet is the peaceful converse of the good,
The poet's song is sweet, the maiden's face
When angry tear-drops lend a sudden grace:
All would be sweet if human fate were fitter;
The thought of death turns all the sweet to bitter.

WHY MY POEMS DIED

The critics all were jealous,
    The patrons full of pride,
The public had no judgment;
    And so my poems died.

WOMEN'S EYES

The world is full of women's eyes,
Defiant, filled with shy surprise,
Demure, a little overfree,
Or simply sparkling roguishly;
It seems a gorgeous lily-bed,
Whichever way I turn my head.

BHASA

BHĀSA (Sanskrit, *ca.* A.D. 350). Legendary dramatist, author of thirteen Sanskrit plays discovered in Malabar in 1912. The most important is *Svapnavāsavadatta (The Dream af Vāsavadattā)*.

TRUE LOVE

[Scene where the King and his friend, the Court Jester, meet and talk. Padmavati, the newly espoused princess, hears the conversation from behind. Vasavadatta, the former Queen of the King, reported as dead, is in disguise in Padmavati's place and acts as her companion. A maid-servant also attends on them.]

Vidusaka:	Friend, there is none here in the garden. Let me crave of you an answer to a question of mine.
King:	As you please.
Vidusaka:	Whom do you love the more of the two, Vasavadatta, who is no more, or Padmavati, who is alive?
King:	Why do you place me in a dilemma?
Padmavati:	(From her hiding-place) Dear friend! What a mischievous fellow he is for causing this perplexing situation for the King!
Vasavadatta:	(To herself) Indeed, I am equally in a fix.
Vidusaka:	Reveal yourself to me without fear. For the one is no longer alive and the other nowhere within our hearing.
King:	I cannot, I cannot give it out. You are a regular chatterbox.
Padmavati:	Why, the King by this vacillation has almost said it.
Vidusaka:	Upon my honour, I will tell none. See, I have already closed my mouth so tightly that the teeth have bitten off the tip of my tongue.
King:	No, I dare not say it out.
Padmavati:	Look at the Court Jester! Still he is dense and understands not the King's meaning.
Vidusaka:	Please do tell me. I swear upon our lasting friendship that I shall never communicate it to any one else.
King:	Well, you are obstinate and I feel no escape. Please listen.

118

	However worthy of me Padmavati may be by her beauty, her character and her sweet amiability, My love for Vasavadatta remains unshaken and refuses to be lured away by her.
Vasavadatta:	(To herself) I have at last my reward for waiting. Indeed, my presence here *incognito* has its own advantages.
Maid-servant:	Madam, the King lacks grace.
Padmavati:	Why girl, do not say so. The King is gracious enough; for he cherishes still his old love, Vasavadatta.

SERENITY

[Scene: Rama in the company of Sita in his palace. He is informed of Dasaratha's unconscious state in Kaikeyi's palace.]

(*Enter Chamberlain.*)

Chamberlain:	Help, Oh help, Prince!
Rama:	Who wants help?
Chamberlain:	The great King, thy sire.
Rama:	What my father? Well, it is like saying the entire world asks for help. Who is the cause of this sudden mishap?
Chamberlain:	From his nearest the King has received this blow.
Rama:	What! from his own near and dear? Alas, then how can there be consolation.
	The enemy aims his blow only at the body; but relatives aim at the heart.
	Well, Oh! who can be that whose claim to kinship with me thus makes me so much ashamed?
Chamberlain:	Who else but Queen Kaikeyi herself?
Rama:	Ah! Do you mouth Kaikeyi's name? She cannot labour but for ultimate good, I know.
Chamberlain:	How, Prince?
Rama:	Listen to me,
	What could be there for her to covet for which she should perpetrate a wrong?
	How can she require wants when she has for a husband one equal to Indra and for a son one like me?

Chamberlain:	Ah, do not expect the same sense of fairness in women, who cannot be trusted. Know, it was she who prevented your anointment as king.
Rama:	Am I not then lucky?
Chamberlain:	How could you justify her for demanding Bharata's coronation unasked? Is it not avaricious?
Rama:	Your partiality towards me makes you blind to the good that is concealed within that prayer.

BHAVABHUTI

BHAVABHUTI (Sanskrit, *ca.* A.D. 730). Leading Sanskrit dramatist, of the 8th century. Author of three dramas: *Mālatī Mādhava (Stolen Marriage)*, *Mahāvīracharita (Story of the Great Hero)*, and *Uttara Rāmacharita (Later Story of Rama)*.

THE RESCUE OF MALĀTĪ

Persons: Madhava, *the lover;* Malati, *the heroine;* Kapala-Kundala, *priestess of the fearful goddess* Chamunda; Aghoraghanta, *priest of the same.*

SCENE: *Inside of the Temple of Chamunda.*—Aghoraghanta, *dancing and invoking the goddess, is about to sacrifice Malati.*

Malati [dressed as a victim]—
Unpitying sire, thy hapless daughter dies!
Mother beloved, remorseless fate consigns
Thy gentle heart to agony. Revered
And holy dame, who lived but for thy Malati,
Whose every thought was for her happiness,
Thy love will teach thee long and bitter anguish.
Ah, my dear friend, Lavangika, to thee
But in thy dreams I henceforth shall appear!
Madhava [enters behind]—
My fears were true—'tis she! but still she lives.
　　　　　　　[*Listens to Aghoraghanta's invocation.*
What luckless chance is this, that such a maid,

120

With crimson garb and garland like a victim
Adorned for sacrifice, should be the captive
Of impious wretches, like a timid fawn
Begirt by ravenous wolves: that she, the child
Of the all-powerful minister, should lie
Thus in the jaws of death? Ah, cruel destiny,
How ruthless are thy purposes!

Kapala-Kundala—

Fair maid,
Think upon him whom thou in life hast loved,
For pitiless death is near thee.

Malati—

Ah, Madhava,
Lord of my heart! Oh may I after death
Live in thy memory! They do not die,
Whom love embalms in long and fond embrace.

Kapala-Kundala—

Poor child, her heart is Madhava's.

Aghoraghanta [*raising his sword*]—

No matter—
Come what come may, we must delay no longer.
This offering vowed to thee, divine Chamunda,
Deign to accept.

Madhava [*rushing forward and snatching Malati up in his arms*]

Vile wretch, forbear!

Kapala-Kundala—

The term profane is thine.

Malati—

Oh, save me, save me! [*Embraces Madhave.*]

Madhava—

Princess, do not fear.
A faithful friend, who in the hour of death
Finds courage to declare his love, is near thee.
Be of good courage—on this impious wretch
The retribution of his crimes descends.

Aghoraghanta—

What sinful youth is this that interrupts
Our solemn rite?

Kapala-Kundala—

The lover of the maiden,
The pupil of Kamandaki, who treads

121

These precincts for unholy purposes,
And vends the flesh of man.

Madhava—

Inform me, princess,
How has this chanced?

Malati—

I know not. I reposed
At eve upon the terrace. When I woke
I found myself a prisoner.—But what led
Your steps to this retreat?

Madhava [*ashamed*]—

By passion urged,
Incited by the hope my life might be
Yet blest by this fair hand, I hither came
To invoke the unclean spirits of the dead.
Your cries I heard, and instant hurried here.

Malati—

And wert thou thus regardless of thyself,
And wandering here for me?

Madhava—

Blest was the chance
That snatched my love from the uplifted swords
Like the pale moon from Rahu's ravenous jaws.
My mind is yet with various passions tossed,
And terror, pity, wonder, joy, and rage,
By turns possess my soul.

Aghoraghanta—

Rash Brahman boy,
Thou seek'st thy fate. The pitying stag defies
The tiger in the rescue of his doe,
And both are made the forest monarch's prey.
So shalt thou perish, who darest hope to save
The victim of my sacrifice. Thy blood,
As flies the severed head before my scymetar,
Shall stream an offering to the mighty mother
Of all created beings.

Madhava—

Wretch accursed,
Impious and vile! Couldst thou raise thy sword
Against this delicate frame, that timid shrunk
Even from the flowers her fond companions cast

122

In sportive mood upon her—but my arm
Like Yama's mace now falls upon thy head.

Malati—

Lord of my life, refrain from violence:
His crime is baffled, let him be. Avoid
All needless peril.

Kapala-Kundala—

Holy sir, be firm;
Destroy the culprit.

*Madhava and Aghoraghanta [to the women, each concerning the
  other]*—

Banish your alarms:
The villain dies. What other chance should wait
The issue of the conflict, when the lion,
Whose talons light upon the elephant's brow,
As falls the thunderbolt upon the mountain,
Raises their might against the feeble deer.

[*Noise behind.*]

What, ho! Ye who are now in search of **Malati**,
The venerable priestess whose commands
Are ever wise, enjoins ye to surround
The temple of Karala. This can be
The act of none but him who ministers
To the terrific goddess, and the princess
Can be an offering for no other shrine.

Kapala-Kundala—

We are surrounded!

Aghoraghanta—

Greater is the need
Of manly resolution.

Malati—

My dear father!
My venerable mistress!

Madhava—

I will place
The princess out of peril with her friends,
Then swift return for vengeance.

[*He carries Malati off and returns confronting Aghoraghanta.*]

Now let the falchion piecemeal hew thy form,
Ring on thy bones, and cleave thy sinewy joints,
Sport in the yielding marrow, and divide,

123

Resistless in its fury, limb from limb.
[Exeunt fighting.

THE STORY OF THE RAMAYANA

[Rama meeting his twin sons Lava and Kusa without knowing their identity.]

Lava: Sir! What is this? Thy face so full of benediction for mankind is so suddenly transformed, sorrow-laden with tears even as a white lotus bloom bathed in dew.

Kusa: How can Raghupati remain unaffected by grief without his own Sita? The world to one bereft of one's own dearest will be a wilderness enough. Such is his love for his Queen; and his grief is unending. Why then this question of yours, as if you were not aware of the story of the *Ramayana?*

Rama: (To himself) Indeed, a most impartial opinion! (Aloud) Boys, we hear of the *Ramayana* often and are told that poetry flowed from Valmiki's lips and that the glory of the Solar race is sung. Let me hear it from you.

Kusa: We know the entire *Ramayana.* But we can just now recollect for you two verses only from the earlier portion of it.

Rama: Do sing for me, please.

Kusa: (Singing):
Sita was naturally drawn to the great Rama. His love grew more even as Sita's looks and qualities increased with his knowledge of her.
Similarly Rama became dearer to Sita than her own life.
Indeed their hearts alone can plumb the depths of true love between them.

Rama: Alas! these words pierce me more to the heart.
The many recollections of Sita have awakened me to a procession of emotions.
My unbearable grief has become alive again.

Lava: Another verse, let me sing, which brings out Rama's words to Sita on the Citra-kuta, encircled by the Mandakini River.
(Sings):

124

This slab of a seat looking as one arranged for you
Has been covered all over with flowers from the overhanging Kesara branches.

Rama: (With shame, pleasure, sorrow and love in his feelings)
These boys are innocent to a fault, especially because
they are forest-bred.
Ha, Love! Do you remember those delightful incidents?

HAYYIM NAHMAN BIALIK

HAYYIM NAHMAN BIALIK (Hebrew, 1873-1934). Outstanding Hebrew
poet. Born in Russia, died in Israel, where he was leader of cultural life and
shaper of Zionism. The poet of both the vanishing ghetto and the new
nationalism. In Israel, wrote stories, fairy tales and essays, and last great
poem, *Yatmut*. Also collected legends of the Talmud and Midrash in
Sefer Ha'agada.

WHERE ARE YOU?

Out of your hiding place, heart of my being,
Come forth, come quickly to my side.
If I may find salvation, come and save me;
Come, be my master and my guide.
Bring back for but a day the stolen boy;
Let me perish in the springtide of my joy.
At your lips let my soul succumb,
Between your breasts let me bury my hours,
As a butterfly droops when night has come,
Among the scented flowers.

Where are you?

Before I had known you, heart of my being,
Your name was atremble on my lips.
At night I tossed sleepless, crushed my pillow,
My flesh dissolved, my heart was in eclipse.
And all day long, in the Talmud scroll,
In a ray of light, in the form of a white cloud,
When thoughts concern me, or when prayers console,
Lifted on joyous visions, in deepest sorrow bowed,
My soul sought one end, one desire knew,
You, you, you.

HER EYES

She walked like a fawn unafraid among the trees;
She came upon my sight.
   The last rays of the sun spangled the rustling leaves,
Strewing ducats of light.
   She walked alone. . . Light splashed upon her face,
Fell pattering to the ground.
   Two circles of sunlight caught and held her eyes.
She stood, with never a sound.
   Two glittering coals flamed fiercely in the dark:
Lord, hearken to my prayer!
   Two adders darted forth and found my heart
And poured their poison there.
   Two dragons of fire devoured my flaming heart:
Lord, I am Lilith's prize!
   I watched her turn, watched her twinkling heels depart. . .
But I lie drowned in her eyes.

*

The dark is a shroud over living.
Stars die after the spark.
Look! Everywhere—and within me,
Dark, my friend, dark.

Dreams are a shadow that lengthens.
Hearts blossom, and blow.
Look! Everywhere—and within me,
Woe, my friend, woe.

"Light!" is the prayer all are breathing;
A prayer that will not be heard.
Long is the murmur, and weary
The word, the only word.

The night is too worn to pass swiftly.
The moon is pallid and gray,
And yawns, overspent and weary
For day, for the sleep of day.

*

Tuck me in under your wing.
Be a mother and sister to me.
Let your bosom my refuge be,
Where my lorn prayers cling.

Hearken, and hear my grief,
At dusk, in an hour of truth:
They say there is youth in the world;
Where is my youth?

Bear one more mystery
I am burned in the fire of:
They say there is love in the world;
What—what is love?

I dreamed, and the stars betrayed
My eager call;
And now there is naught for me in the world,
Nothing at all.

Tuck me in under your wing,
Be a mother and sister to me.
Let your bosom my refuge be,
Where my lorn prayers cling.

BILHANA

BILHANA (Kashmiri, *ca.* A.D. 1100). Kashmir historian and poet. His works:
Vikramānkadeva Charita (*The History of King Vikramānka*), and
Saurīsuratapanchāsikā (*Fifty Poems of Stolen Love*).

AN INDIAN LOVE-LAMENT

I

I am to die! yet I remember, dying,
　My Soul's delight—my sweet unequalled, love,
Like a fresh champak's golden blossom lying,
　Her smile its opening leaves; and, bright above,
Over her sleepful brow those lustrous tresses
Dark-winding down, tangled with love's caresses.

II

I die, but I remember! How it thrilled me
　The first glad seeing of her glorious face
Clear-carven like the moon; and how it filled me
　With tremors, drinking in the tender grace

Which, like a fine air, clothed her; and the rise
Of her twinned breast-hills, and the strange surprise

III

Of love's new rapture! Dying I recall
   Each marvel of her beauty in its blossom;
The large deep lotos-eyes, whence dew did fall
   Of jewelled tears; the swelling maiden bosom—
Heavy to bear—the long smooth arms; the lips
Where, like the Bee, Desire still clings and sips:

IV

I die, yet well I mind, after embracing,
   When hands relaxed, and gentle strife relented,
And—loosened from the gem-strings interlacing
   Their night-black threads—some wandering locks, rich-scented,
Strayed o'er her chin and cheek, how she would hide
Delicious flush of love, with arms close-tied

V

Over her happy eyes. Dear eyes! I see you
   Shining like stars out of the shade made so,
Tearful for joy. Bright stars of morning be you
   For ever to this heart! Then would she go—
Her sweet head somewhat drooping—to her bath,
With such royal glory as the Queen-swan hath.

VI

Ah, dying—dying—I remember! Let me
   But once again behold her so—behold
Those jet brows, like black crescent-moons, once get me
   So close that love might soothe with comforts cold
The fever of her burning breast—that minute
Would have a changeless, endless Heaven in it.

VII

Yet now, this but abides, to picture surely
   How in the palace-dance foremost she paced;
Her glancing feet and light limbs swayed demurely
   Moonlike, amid their cloudy robes; moon-faced,
With hips majestic under slender waist,
And hair with gold and blooms banded and laced.

VIII

'Tis to mock Death to think how, where she lay,
  What tender odours drifted from the sheets—
Sandal and musk—such as when pilgrims pray
  Rise for the Gods to savour—subtle sweets
Of her rose-flesh; and, gazing in her eyes,
The love-sick *chakur* had the same deep dyes.

XI

And sometimes, I remember, when we dipped
  Our joys in wine, how her fine blood would flush
Ruddier, to mouth and limb; and how she tripped
  With livelier steps, while saffron-flower's blush
And Kashmir gums, and hill-deer's bag, made sweeting
For breath too sweet, and pearl-teeth—idly eating

X

Honies and betel. How the spell re-grows
  Strong in my soul of that dear face divine,
Hooded in scarlet silk, which, opening, shews
  The brow dew-pearled from haste, dark orbs that shine
With tremulous light of love; as when the Moon
Escapes from Rahu, round and splendent soon.

IX

Ah, my pale Moon eclipsed! How may I bear
  To think on that ill hour of severing
When, in the ear of the King's Daughter dear,
  (So close my mouth touched its warm gems that swing)
I murmured "jivit mangal"—"Fairest! be
Healthful and happy! I will fare to thee!"

BJORNSTJERNE BJORNSON

BJÖRNSTJERNE BJÖRNSON (Norwegian, 1832-1910). One of founders of
modern Norwegian literature. As dramatist, poet, novelist, orator, was political
mentor of his country. Wrote national anthem, was great traveler, and edited
many newspapers and periodicals. His peasant stories outstanding. Best-
known works: *Sigurd Slembe, A Bankruptcy, Beyond Human Power, Paul
Lange and Tora Parsberg*. Nobel Prize, 1903.

THE man whose story is here to be told was the wealthiest and most influential person in his parish; his name was Thord Overaas. He appeared in the priest's study one day, tall and earnest.

"I have gotten a son," said he, "and I wish to present him for baptism."

"What shall his name be?"

"Finn—after my father."

"And the sponsors?"

They were mentioned, and proved to be the best men and women of Thord's relations in the parish.

"Is there anything else?" inquired the priest, and looked up.

The peasant hesitated a little.

"I should like very much to have him baptized by himself," said he, finally.

"That is to say on a week-day?"

"Next Saturday, at twelve o'clock noon."

"Is there anything else?" inquired the priest.

"There is nothing else;" and the peasant twirled his cap, as though he were about to go.

Then the priest rose. "There is yet this, however," said he, and walking toward Thord, he took him by the hand and looked gravely into his eyes: "God grant that the child may become a blessing to you!"

One day sixteen years later, Thord stood once more in the priest's study.

"Really, you carry your age astonishingly well, Thord," said the priest; for he saw no change whatever in the man.

"That is because I have no troubles," replied Thord.

To this the priest said nothing, but after a while he asked: "What is your pleasure this evening?"

"I have come this evening about that son of mine who is to be confirmed to-morrow."

"He is a bright boy."

"I did not wish to pay the priest until I heard what number the boy would have when he takes his place in church to-morrow."

"He will stand number one."

"So I have heard; and here are ten dollars for the priest."

"Is there anything else I can do for you?" inquired the priest, fixing his eyes on Thord.

"There is nothing else."

Thord went out.

Eight years more rolled by, and then one day a noise was heard outside of the priest's study, for many men were approaching, and at their head was Thord, who entered first.

The priest looked up and recognized him.

"You come well attended this evening, Thord," said he.

"I am here to request that the banns may be published for my son; he is about to marry Karen Storliden, daughter of Gudmund, who stands here beside me."

"Why, that is the richest girl in the parish."

"So they say," replied the peasant, stroking back his hair with one hand.

The priest sat a while as if in deep thought, then entered the names in his book, without making any comments, and the men wrote their signatures underneath. Thord laid three dollars on the table.

"One is all I am to have," said the priest.

"I know that very well; but he is my only child, I want to do it handsomely."

The priest took the money.

"This is now the third time, Thord, that you have come here on your son's account."

"But now I am through with him," said Thord, and folding up his pocket-book he said farewell and walked away.

The men slowly followed him.

A fortnight later, the father and son were rowing across the lake, one calm, still day, to Storliden to make arrangements for the wedding.

"This thwart is not secure," said the son, and stood up to straighten the seat on which he was sitting.

At the same moment the board he was standing on slipped from under him; he threw out his arms, uttered a shriek, and fell overboard.

"Take hold of the oar!" shouted the father, springing to his feet and holding out the oar.

But when the son had made a couple of efforts he grew stiff.

"Wait a moment!" cried the father, and began to row toward his son. Then the son rolled over on his back, gave his father one long look, and sank.

Thord could scarcely believe it; he held the boat still, and stared at the spot where his son had gone down, as though he must surely come to the surface again. There rose some bubbles, then some more, and finally one large one that burst; and the lake lay there as smooth and bright as a mirror again.

For three days and three nights people saw the father rowing round and round the spot, without taking either food or sleep; he was dragging the lake for the body of his son. And toward morning of the third day he found it, and carried it in his arms up over the hills to his gard.

It might have been about a year from that day, when the priest, late one autumn evening, heard someone in the passage outside of the door carefully trying to find the latch. The priest opened the door, and in walked a tall, thin man, with bowed form and white hair. The priest looked long at him before he recognized him. It was Thord.

"Are you out walking so late?" said the priest, and stood still in front of him.

"Ah yes! it is late," said Thord, and took a seat.

The priest sat down also, as though waiting. A long, long silence followed. At last Thord said:

"I have something with me that I should like to give to the poor; I want it to be invested as a legacy in my son's name."

He rose, laid some money on the table, and sat down again. The priest counted it.

"It is a great deal of money," said he.

"It is half the price of my gard. I sold it to-day."

The priest sat long in silence. At last he asked, but gently:

"What do you propose to do now, Thord?"

"Something better."

They sat there for a while, Thord with downcast eyes, the priest with his eyes fixed on Thord. Presently the priest said, slowly and softly:

"I think your son has at last brought you a true blessing."

"Yes, I think so myself," said Thord, looking up, while two big tears coursed slowly down his cheeks.

GIOVANNI BOCCACCIO

GIOVANNI BOCCACCIO (Italian, 1313-1375). Earliest prose writer in Italian, thus called "father of Italian prose." Most celebrated work, the *Decameron*, a collection of 100 novelle—witty, realistic licentious, often imitated. Author of lesser-known novels (*Fiammetta*), poems (*Il Filostrato*), and biographies (*Life of Dante*). A precursor of the Renaissance, profound influence on later literature.

GRISELDA

IT is a long time ago, that, amongst the marquisses of Saluzzo the principal or head of the family was a youth, called Gualtieri, who, as he was a bachelor, spent his whole time in hawking and hunting, without any thought of ever being encumbered with a wife and children; in which respect, no doubt, he was very wise. But this being disagreeable to his subjects, they often pressed him to marry, to the end that he might neither die without an heir, nor they be left without a lord; offering themselves to provide such a lady for him, and of such a family, that they should have great hopes from her, and he reason enough to be satisfied. "Worthy friends," he replied, "you urge me to do a thing which I was fully resolved against, considering what a difficult matter it is to find a person of suitable temper, with the great abundance everywhere of such as are otherwise, and how miserable also the man's life must be who is tied to a disagreeable woman. As to your getting at a woman's temper from her family, and so choosing one to please me, that seems quite a ridiculous fancy; for, besides the uncertainty with regard to their true fathers, how many daughters do we see resembling neither father nor mother? Nevertheless, as you are so fond of having me noosed, I will agree to be so. Therefore, that I may have no body to blame but myself, should it happen amiss, I will make my own choice; and I protest, let me marry who I will, that, unless you show her the respect that is due to her as my lady, you shall know, to your cost, how grievous it is to me to have taken a wife at your request, contrary to my own inclination." The honest men replied, that they were well satisfied, provided he would but make the trial. Now, he had taken a fancy some time before to the behaviour of a poor country girl, who lived in a village not far from his palace; and thinking that he might live comfortably enough with her, he determined, without seeking any farther, to marry her. Accordingly, he sent for her father, who was a very poor man, and acquainted him with it. Afterwards he summoned all his subjects together, and said to them, "Gentlemen, it was and is your desire that I take a wife; I do it rather to please you, than out of any liking I have to matrimony. You know that you promised me to be satisfied, and to pay her due honour, whoever she is that I shall make choice of. The time is now come when I shall fulfil my promise to you, and I expect you to do the like to me: I have found a young woman in the neighbourhood after my own heart, whom I intend to espouse and bring home in a very few days. Let it be your care, then, to do honour to my nuptials, and to respect her as your sovereign lady: so that I may be satisfied with the performance of your promise, even as you are with that of mine." The people all declared themselves pleased, and promised to regard her in all things as their mistress. Afterwards they made preparations for a most noble feast, and the like did the prince, inviting all his relations, and the great lords in all parts and provinces about him: he had also most rich and costly robes made shaped by a person that seemed to be of the same size with his intended spouse; and provided a girdle, ring, and fine coronet, with everything requisite for a bride. And when the day appointed was come, about the third hour he mounted his horse, attended by all his friends and vassals; and having everything in readiness, he said, "My lords and gentlemen, it is now time to go for my new spouse." So on they rode to the village, and when he was come near the father's house, he saw her carrying some water from the well, in great haste, to go afterwards with some of her acquaintance to see the new marchioness; when he called her by name, which was Griselda, and inquired where her father was. She modestly replied, "My gracious lord, he is in the house." He then alighted from his horse, commanding them all to wait for him, and went alone into the cottage, where he found the father, who was called Giannucolo, and said to him, "Honest man, I am come to espouse thy daughter, but would first ask her some questions before thee." He then inquired, whether she would make it her study to please him, and not be uneasy at any time, whatever he should do or say; and whether she would always be obedient; with more to that purpose. To which she answered, "Yes." He then led her out by the hand, and made her strip before them all; and, ordering the rich apparel to be brought which he had provided, he had her clothed completely, and a coronet set upon her head, all disordered as her hair was;

after which, every one being in amaze, he said, "Behold, this is the person whom I intend for my wife, provided she will accept of me for her husband." Then, turning towards her, who stood quite abashed, "Will you," said he, "have me for your husband?" She replied, "Yes, if it so please your lordship."—"Well," he replied; "and I take you for my wife." So he espoused her in that public manner, and, mounting her on a palfrey, conducted her honourably to his palace, celebrating the nuptials with as much pomp and grandeur as though he had been married to the daughter of the king of France; and the young bride showed apparently that with her garments she had changed both her mind and behaviour. She had a most agreeable person, and was so amiable, and so good-natured withal, that she seemed rather a lord's daughter than that of a poor shepherd; at which every one that knew her before was greatly surprised. She was, too, so obedient to her husband, and so obliging in all respects, that he thought himself the happiest man in the world; and to her subjects likewise so gracious and condescending, that they all honoured and loved her as their own lives, praying for her health and prosperity, and declaring, contrary to their former opinion, that Gualtieri was the most prudent and sharp-sighted prince in the whole world; for that no one could have discerned such virtues under a mean habit, and a country disguise, but himself. In a very short time her discreet behaviour and good works were the common subject of discourse, not in the country only, but everywhere else; and what had been objected to the prince, with regard to his marrying her, now took a contrary turn. They had not lived long together before she proved with child, and at length brought forth a daughter, for which he made great rejoicings. But soon afterwards a new fancy came into his head, and that was, to make trial of her patience by long and intolerable sufferings: so he began wtih harsh words, and an appearance of great uneasiness; telling her, that his subjects were greatly displeased with her for her mean parentage, especially as they saw she bore children; and that they did nothing but murmur at the daughter already born. Which, when she heard, without changing countenance, or her resolution, in any respect, she replied, "My lord, pray dispose of me as you think most for your honour and happiness: I shall entirely acquiesce, knowing myself to be meaner than the meanest of the people, and that I was altogether unworthy of that dignity to which your favour was pleased to advance me." This was very agreeable to the prince, seeing that she was no way elevated with the honour he had conferred upon her. Afterwards, having often told her, in general terms, that his subjects could not bear with the daughter that was born of her, he sent one of his servants, whom he had instructed what to do, who, with a very sorrowful countenance, said to her, "Madam, I must either lose my own life, or obey my lord's commands; now he has ordered me take your daughter, and" —without saying anything more. She, hearing these words, and noting the fellow's looks, remembering also what she had heard before from her lord, concluded that he had orders to destroy the child. So she took it out of the cradle, kissed it, and gave it her blessing; when, without changing countenance, though her heart throbbed with maternal affection, she tenderly laid it in the servant's arms, and said, "Take it, and do what thy lord and mine has commanded; but prythee leave it not to be devoured by the fowls, or wild beasts, unless that be his will." Taking the child, he acquainted the prince with what she said, who was greatly surprised at her constancy, and he sent the same person with it to a relation at Bologna, desiring her, without revealing whose child it was, to see it carefully brought up and educated. Afterwards the lady became with child a second time, and was delivered of a son, at which he was extremely pleased. But, not satisfied with what he had already done, he began to grieve and persecute her still more; saying one day to her, seemingly much out of temper, "Since thou hast brought me this son, I am able to live no longer with my people; for they mutiny to that degree, that, unless I would run the risk of being driven out of my dominions, I must be obliged to dispose of this child as I did the other; and then to send thee away, in order to take a wife more suitable to me." She heard this with a great deal of resignation, making only this reply: "My lord, study only your own ease and happiness, without the least care for me; for nothing is agreeable to me but what is pleasing to yourself." Not many days after, he sent for the son in the same manner as he had done for the daughter; and, seeming also as if he had procured him to be destroyed, had him conveyed to Bologna, to be taken care of with the daughter. This she bore with the same resolution as before, at which the prince wondered greatly, declaring to himself, that no other woman was capable of doing the like. And, were it not that he had observed her extremely fond of her children, whilst that was agreeable to him, he should have thought it want of affection in her: but he saw it was only her entire obedience and condescension. The people, imagining the children were both put to

136

death, blamed him to the last degree, thinking him the most cruel and worst of men, and showing great compassion for the lady; who, whenever she was in company with the ladies of her acquaintance, and they condoled with her for her loss, she would only say, "It was not my will, but his who begot them." But more years being now passed, and he resolving to make the last trial of her patience, declared, before many people, that he could no longer bear to keep Griselda as his wife, owning that he had done very foolishly and like a young man in marrying her, and that he meant to solicit the Pope for a dispensation to take another, and send her away; for which he was much blamed by many worthy persons: but he said nothing in return, only that it should be so. She, hearing this, and expecting to go home to her father, and possibly tend the cattle as she had done before, whilst she saw some other lady possessed of him whom she dearly loved and honoured, was perhaps secretly grieved; but, as she had withstood other strokes of fortune, so she determined resolutely to do now. Soon afterwards Gualtieri had counterfeit letters come to him, as from Rome, acquainting all his people that his holiness thereby dispensed with his marrying another, and turning away Griselda. He had her brought before them, when he said, "Woman, by the Pope's leave I may dispose of thee, and take another wife. As my ancestors, then, have been all sovereign princes of this country, and thine only peasants, I intend to keep thee no longer, but to send thee back to thy father's cottage, with the same portion that thou broughtest me, and afterwards to make choice of one more suitable in quality to myself." It was with the utmost difficulty she could now refrain from tears; and she replied, "My lord, I was always sensible that my servile condition would no way accord with your high rank and descent. For what I have been I own myself indebted to Providence and you; I considered it as a favour lent me: you are now pleased to demand it back; I therefore willingly restore it. Behold the ring with which you espoused me: I deliver it to you. You bid me take the dowry back which I brought you: you will have no need for a teller to count it, nor I for a purse to put it in, much less a sumpter-horse to carry it away; for I have not forgotten that you took me naked: and if you think it decent to expose that body, which has borne you two children, in that manner, I am contented; but I would entreat you, as recompense for my virginity, which I brought you and do not carry away, that you would please to let me have one shift over and above my dowry." He, though ready to weep, yet put on a stern

137

countenance, and said, "Thou shalt have one only then." And, notwithstanding the people all desired that she might have an old gown, to keep her body from shame who had been his wife thirteen years and upwards, yet it was all in vain; so she left his palace in that manner, and returned weeping to her father's, to the great grief of all who saw her. The poor man, never supposing that the prince would keep her long as his wife, and expecting this thing to happen every day, had safely laid up the garments of which she had been despoiled the day he espoused her. He now brought them to her, and she put them on, and went as usual about her father's little household affairs, bearing this fierce trial of adverse fortune with the greatest courage imaginable. The prince then gave it out that he was to espouse a daughter of one of the counts of Panago; and, seeming as if he had made great preparations for his nuptials, he sent for Griselda to come to him, and said to her, "I am going to bring this lady home whom I have just married, and intend to show her all possible respect at her first coming: thou knowest that I have no women with me able to set out the rooms, and do many things which are requisite on so solemn an occasion. As, therefore, thou art best acquainted with the state of the house, I would have thee make such provision as thou shalt judge proper, and invite what ladies thou wilt, even as though thou wert mistress of the house, and, when the marriage is ended, return thee home to thy father's again." Though these words pierced like daggers to the heart of Griselda, who was unable to part with her love for the prince so easily as she had done her great fortune, yet she replied, "My lord, I am ready to fulfil all your commands." She then went into the palace, in her coarse attire, from whence she had just departed in her shift, and with her own hands did she begin to sweep, and set all the rooms to rights, cleaning the stools and benches in the hall like the meanest servant, and directing what was to be done in the kitchen, never giving over till everything was in order and as it ought to be. After this was done, she invited, in the prince's name, all the ladies in the country to come to the feast. And on the day appointed for the marriage, meanly clad as she was, she received them in the most genteel and cheerful mannr imaginable. Now Gualtieri, who had his children carefully brought up at Bologna, (the girl being about twelve years old, and one of the prettiest creatures that ever was seen, and the boy six,) had sent to his kinswoman there, to desire she would bring them, with an honourable retinue, to Saluzzo, giving it out, all the way she came, that she was bringing the young lady to be married to him, without letting any one know to the contrary. Accordingly they all three set forwards, attended by a goodly train of gentry, and, after some day's travelling, reached Saluzzo about dinner-time, when they found the whole country assembled, waiting to see their new lady. The young lady was most graciously received by all the women present, and being come into the hall where the tables were all covered, Griselda, meanly dressed as she was, went cheerfully to meet her, saying, "Your ladyship is most kindly welcome." The ladies, who had greatly importuned the prince, though to no purpose, to let Griselda be in a room by herself, or else that she might have some of her own clothes, and not appear before strangers in that manner, were now seated, and going to be served round, whilst the young lady was universally admired, and every one said that the prince had made a good change; but Griselda in particular highly commended both her and her brother. The marquis now thinking that he had seen enough with regard to his wife's patience, and perceiving that in all her trials she was still the same, being persuaded likewise that this proceeded from no want of understanding in her, because he knew her to be singularly prudent, he thought it time to take her from that anguish which he supposed she might conceal under her firm and constant deportment. So, making her come before all the company, he said, with a smile, "What thinkest thou, Griselda, of my bride?"—"My lord," she replied, "I like her extremely well; and if she be as prudent as she is fair, you may be the happiest man in the world with her; but I most humbly beg you would not take those heart-breaking measures with this lady as you did with your last wife, because she is young, and has been tenderly educated, whereas the other was inured to hardships from a child."

Gualtieri perceiving, that though Griselda thought that person was to be his wife, that she nevertheless answered him with great humility and sweetness of temper, he made her sit down by him, and said, "Griselda, it is now time for you to reap the fruit of your long patience, and that they who have reputed me to be cruel, unjust, and a monster in nature, may know that what I have done has been all along with a view to teach you how to behave as a wife; and, lastly, to secure my own ease and quiet as long as we live together, which I was apprehensive might have been endangered by my marrying. Therefore I had a mind to prove you by harsh and injurious treatment; and not being sensible that you have ever transgressed my will, either in word or deed, I now seem to have met with that happiness I desired. I intend, then, to restore in one hour what I have taken away from you in many, and to make you the sweetest recompense for the many bitter pangs I have caused you to suffer. Accept, therefore, this young lady, whom you thought my spouse, and her brother, as your children and mine. They are the same which you and many others believed that I had been the means of cruelly murdering: and I am your husband, who love and value you above all things; assuring myself that no person in the world can be happier in a wife than I am." With this he embraced her most affectionately, when, rising up together, she weeping for joy, they went where their daughter was sitting, quite astonished with these things, and tenderly saluted both her and her brother, undeceiving them and the whole company. At this the women all arose, overjoyed, from the tables, and taking Griselda into the chamber, they clothed her with her own noble apparel, and as a marchioness, resembling such an one even in rags, and brought her into the hall. And being extremely rejoiced with her son and daughter, and every one expressing the utmost satisfaction at what had come to pass, the feasting was prolonged many days. The marquis was judged a very wise man, though abundantly too severe, and the trial of his lady most intolerable; but as for Griselda, she was beyond compare. In a few days the Count de Panago returned to Bologna, and the marquis took Giannucolo from his drudgery and maintained him as his father-in-law, and so he lived very comfortably to a good old age. Gualtieri afterwards married his daughter to one of equal nobility, continuing the rest of his life with Griselda, and showing her all the respect and honour that was possible. What can we say, then, but that divine spirits may descend from heaven into the meanest cottages, while royal palaces shall produce such as seem rather adapted to have the care of hogs than the government of men?

CHARLOTTE BRONTË

CHARLOTTE BRONTE (English, 1816-1855). Eldest of three talented literary sisters, who lived entire lives in Yorkshire parsonage, died of tuberculosis. Charlotte worked for time as governess. *Jane Eyre*, published under pseudonym of Currer Bell, became Victorian classic. Other novels: *Shirley, Villette, The Professor*. All her books reflect life of sorrow, struggle and gloom.

From *JANE EYRE*

SOPHIE came at seven to dress me; she was very long indeed in accomplishing her task, so long that Mr. Rochester, grown, I suppose, impatient of my delay, sent up to ask why I did not come. She was just fastening my veil (the plain square of blonde after all) to my hair with a brooch; I hurried from under her hands as soon as I could.

"Stop!" she cried in French. "Look at yourself in the mirror; you have not taken one peep."

So I turned at the door: I saw a robed and veiled figure, so unlike my usual self that it seemed almost the image of a stranger.

"Jane!" called a voice, and I hastened down. I was received at the foot of the stairs by Mr. Rochester.

"Lingerer," he said, "my brain is on fire with impatience, and you tarry so long!"

He took me into the dining-room, surveyed me keenly all over, pronounced me "fair as a lily, and not only the pride of his life, but the desire of his eyes," and then telling me he would give me but ten minutes to eat some breakfast, he rung the bell. One of his lately hired servants, a footman, answered it.

"Is John getting the carriage ready?"

"Yes, sir."

"Is the luggage brought down?"

"They are bringing it down now, sir."

"Go you to the church: see if Mr. Wood (the clergyman) and the clerk are there; return and tell me."

The church, as the reader knows, was just beyond the gates. The footman soon returned.

"Mr. Wood is in the vestry, sir, putting on his surplice."

"And the carriage?"

"The horses are harnessing."

"We shall not want it to go to church, but it must be ready the moment we return; all the boxes and luggage arranged and strapped on, and the coachman in his seat."

"Yes, sir."

"Jane, are you ready?"

I rose. There were no groomsmen, no bridesmaids, no relatives to wait for or marshal; none but Mr. Rochester and I. Mrs. Fairfax stood in the hall as we passed. I would fain have spoken to her, but my hand was held by a grasp of iron; I was hurried along by a stride I could hardly follow; and to look at Mr. Rochester's face was to feel that not a second of delay would be tolerated for any purpose. I wonder what other bridegroom ever looked as he did— so bent up to a purpose, so grimly resolute; or who, under such steadfast brows, ever revealed such flaming and flashing eyes.

I know not whether the day was fair or foul; in descending the drive I gazed neither on sky nor earth: my heart was with my eyes, and both seemed migrated into Mr. Rochester's frame. I wanted to see the invisible thing on which, as we went along, he appeared to fasten a glance fierce and fell. I wanted to feel the thoughts whose force he seemed breasting and resisting.

At the churchyard wicket he stopped; he discovered I was quite out of breath. "Am I cruel in my love?" he said. "Delay an instant; lean on me, Jane."

And now I can recall the picture of the gray old house of God rising calm before me, of a rook wheeling round the steeple, of a ruddy morning sky beyond. I remember something, too, of the green grave-mounds; and I have not forgotten, either, two figures of strangers, straying among the low hillocks, and reading the mementos graven on the few mossy headstones. I noticed them because, as they saw us, they passed round to the back of the church; and I doubted not they were going to enter by the side-aisle door, and witness the ceremony. By Mr. Rochester they were not observed; he was earnestly looking at my face, from which the blood had, I dare say, momentarily fled; for I felt my forehead dewy, and my cheeks and lips cold. When I rallied, which I soon did, he walked gently with me up the path to the porch.

We entered the quiet and humble temple; the priest waited in his white surplice at the lowly altar, the clerk beside him. All was still; two shadows only moved in a remote corner. My conjecture had been correct; the strangers had slipped in before us, and they now stood by the vault of the Rochesters, their backs toward us, viewing through the rails the old, time-stained, marble tomb, where a kneeling angel guarded the remains of Damon de Rochester, slain at Marston Moor, in the time of the civil wars, and of Elizabeth, his wife.

Our place was taken at the communion-rails. Hearing a cautious step behind me, I glanced over my shoulder; one of the strangers —a gentleman, evidently—was advancing up the chancel. The service began. The explanation of the intent of matrimony was gone through;

and then the clergyman came a step further forward, and, bending slightly toward Mr. Rochester, went on.

"I require and charge you both (as ye will answer at the dreadful day of judgment, when the secrets of all hearts shall be disclosed) that if either of you know any impediment why ye may not be lawfully joined together in matrimony, ye do now confess it; for be ye well assured that so many as are coupled together otherwise than God's Word doth allow, are not joined together by God, neither is their matrimony lawful."

He paused, as the custom is. When is the pause after that sentence ever broken by reply? Not, perhaps, once in a hundred years. And the clergyman, who had not lifted his eyes from his book, and had held his breath but for a moment, was proceeding, his hand was already stretched toward Mr. Rochester, as his lips unclosed to ask, "Wilt thou have this woman for thy wedded wife?" when a distinct and near voice said,—

"The marriage cannot go on; I declare the existence of an impediment."

The clergyman looked up at the speaker, and stood mute; the clerk did the same; Mr. Rochester moved slightly, as if an earthquake had rolled under his feet: taking a firmer footing, and not turning his head or eyes, he said, "Proceed."

Profound silence fell when he had uttered that word, with deep but low intonation. Presently Mr. Wood said:

"I cannot proceed without some investigation into what has been asserted, and evidence of its truth or falsehood."

"The ceremony is quite broken off," subjoined the voice behind us. "I am in a condition to prove my allegation; an insuperable impediment to this marriage exists."

Mr. Rochester heard, but heeded not; he stood stubborn and rigid, making no movement but to possess himself of my hand. What a hot and strong grasp he had!—and how like quarried marble was his pale, firm, massive front at this moment! How his eyes shone, still watchful, and yet mild beneath!

Mr. Wood seemed at a loss. "What is the nature of the impediment?" he asked. "Perhaps it may be got over—explained away?"

"Hardly," was the answer. "I have called it insuperable, and I speak advisedly."

The speaker came forward, and leaned on the rails. He continued, uttering each word distinctly, calmly, steadily, but not loudly,—

143

"It simply consists in the existence of a previous marriage; Mr. Rochester has a wife now living."

READER, I married him. A quiet wedding we had; he and I, the parson and clerk, were alone present. When we got back from church, I went into the kitchen of the manor-house, where Mary was cooking the dinner, and John cleaning the knives, and I said,— "Mary, I have been married to Mr. Rochester this morning." The housekeeper and her husband were both of that decent phlegmatic order of people, to whom one may at any time safely communicate a remarkable piece of news without incurring the danger of having one's ears pierced by some shrill ejaculation, and subsequently stunned by a torrent of wordy wonderment. Mary did look up, and she did stare at me; the ladle with which she was basting a pair of chickens roasting at the fire, did for some three minutes hang suspended in air; and for the same space of time John's knives also had rested from the polishing process; but Mary, bending again over the roast, said only,—

"Have you, miss? Well, for sure!"

ELIZABETH BARRETT BROWNING

ELIZABETH BARRETT BROWNING (English, 1806-1861). Wife of Robert Browning, excellent poet in own right. A semi-invalid, lived in Wimpole Street with clergyman father. Her flight to Italy with Browning became famous romantic episode. Most moving work: *Sonnets from the Portuguese*. Others: *The Cry of the Children, Aurora Leigh*.

THE SLEEP
"He giveth His beloved sleep."—Psalm cxxvii, 2

Of all the thoughts of God that are
   Borne inward unto souls afar
   Along the Psalmist's music deep,
Now tell me if that any is
For gift or grace surpassing this,—
"He giveth His beloved sleep"?

What would we give to our beloved?
The hero's heart to be unmoved,
 The poet's star-tuned harp to sweep,
The patriot's voice to teach and rouse,
The monarch's crown to light the brows?
 "He giveth *His* beloved sleep."

What do we give to our beloved?
A little faith all undisproved,
 A little dust to overweep,
And bitter memories to make
The whole earth blasted for our sake.
 "He giveth *His* beloved sleep."

"Sleep soft, beloved!" we sometimes say,
But have no tune to charm away
 Sad dreams that through the eyelids creep.
But never doleful dream again
Shall break the happy slumber when
 "He giveth *His* beloved sleep."

O earth, so full of dreary noises!
O men, with wailing in your voices!
 O delvèd gold, the wailers heap!
O strife, O curse, that o'er it fall!
God strikes a silence through you all,
 And "giveth His beloved sleep."

His dews drop mutely on the hill,
His cloud above it saileth still,
 Though on its slope men sow and reap.
More softly than the dew is shed,
Or cloud is floated overhead,
 "He giveth His beloved sleep."

Ay, men may wonder while they scan
A living, thinking, feeling man,
 Confirm'd in such a rest to keep;
But angels say—and through the word
I think their happy smile is *heard*—
 "He giveth His beloved sleep."

For me, my heart, that erst did go
Most like a tired child at a show,
  That sees through tears the mummers leap,
Would now its weary vision close,
Would childlike on His love repose
  Who "giveth His beloved sleep!"

And, friends, dear friends, when it shall be
That this low breath is gone from me,
  And round my bier ye come to weep,
Let one, most loving of you all,
Say, "Not a tear must o'er her fall,—
  He giveth His beloved sleep."

MY HEART AND I

I

Enough! we're tired, my heart and I.
  We sit beside the headstone thus,
  And wish that name were carved for us.
The moss reprints more tenderly
  The hard types of the mason's knife,
  As heaven's sweet life renews earth's life
With which we're tired, my heart and I.

II

You see we're tired, my heart and I.
  We dealt with books, we trusted men,
  And in our own blood drenched the pen,
As if such colors could not fly.
  We walked too straight for fortune's end,
  We loved too true to keep a friend;
At last we're tired, my heart and I.

III

How tired we feel, my heart and I!
  We seem of no use in the world;
  Our fancies hang gray and uncurled
About men's eyes indifferently;
  Our voice which thrilled you so, will let
  You sleep; our tears are only wet:
What do we hear, my heart and I?

IV

So tired, so tired, my heart and I!
  It was not thus in that old time
  When Ralph sat with me neath the lime
To watch the sunset from the sky.
  "Dear love, you're looking tired," he said;
  I, smiling at him, shook my head:
'Tis now we're tired, my heart and I.

V

So tired, so tired, my heart and I!
  Though now none takes me on his arm
  To fold me close and kiss me warm
Till each quick breath end in a sigh
  Of happy languor. Now, alone,
  We lean upon this graveyard stone,
Uncheered, unkissed, my heart and I.

VI

Tired out we are, my heart and I.
  Suppose the world brought diadems
  To tempt us, crusted with loose gems
Of powers and pleasures? Let it try.
  We scarcely care to look at even
  A pretty child, or God's blue heaven,
We feel so tired, my heart and I.

VII

Yet who complains? My heart and I?
  In this abundant earth no doubt
  Is little room for things worn out:
Disdain them, break them, throw them by!
  And if before the days grew rough
  We once were loved, used,—well enough,
I think, we've fared, my heart and I.

THE PET-NAME

I

I have a name, a little name,
  Uncadenced for the ear,
Unhonored by ancestral claim,
Unsanctified by prayer and psalm
  The solemn font anear.

II

It never did to pages wove
  For gay romance, belong.
It never dedicate did move
As "Sacharissa," unto love—
  "Orinda," unto song.

III

Though I write books, it will be read
  Upon the leaves of none,
And afterwards, when I am dead,
Will ne'er be graved for sight or tread
  Across my funeral stone.

IV

This name, whoever chance to call,
  Perhaps your smile may win.
Nay, do not smile! mine eyelids fall
Over mine eyes, and feel withal
  The sudden tears within.

V

Is there a leaf that greenly grows
  Where summer meadows bloom
But gathereth the winter snows,
And changeth to the hue of those,
  If lasting till they come?

VI

Is there a word, or jest, or game,
  But time encrusteth round
With sad associate thought the same?
And so to me my very name
  Assumes a mournful sound.

VII

My brother gave that name to me
  When we were children twain;
When names acquired baptismally
Were hard to utter as to see
  That life had any pain.

VIII

No shade was on us then, save one
    Of chestnuts from the hill—
And through the word our laugh did run
As part thereof. The mirth being done,
    He calls me by it still.

IX

Nay, do not smile! I hear in it
    What none of you can hear!
The talk upon the willow seat,
The bird and wind that did repeat
    Around, our human cheer.

X

I hear the birthday's noisy bliss,
    My sister's woodland glee,—
My father's praise, I did not miss,
When stooping down he cared to kiss
    The poet at his knees;—

XI

And voices, which to name me, aye
    Their tenderest tones were keeping!—
To some I never more can say
An answer, till God wipes away
    In heaven those drops of weeping.

XII

My name to me a sadness wears;
    No murmurs cross my mind;
Now God be thanked for these thick tears,
Which show, of those departed years,
    Sweet memories left behind!

XIII

Now God be thanked for years enwrought
    With love which softens yet!
Now God be thanked for every thought
Which is so tender it has caught
    Earth's guerdon of regret!

149

XIV

Earth saddens, never shall remove,
   Affections purely given;
And e'en that mortal grief shall prove
The immortality of love,
   And brighten it with Heaven.

A FALSE STEP

I

Sweet, thou hast trod on a heart.
   Pass! there's a world full of men;
And women as fair as thou art
   Must do such things now and then.

II

Thou only hast stepped unaware,—
   Malice, not one can impute;
And why should a heart have been there
   In the way of a fair woman's foot?

III

It was not a stone that could trip,
   Nor was it a thorn that could rend:
Put up thy proud underlip!
   'Twas merely the heart of a friend.

IV

And yet peradventure one day
   Thou, sitting alone at the glass,
Remarking the bloom gone away,
   Where the smile in its dimplement was,

V

And seeking around thee in vain
   From hundreds who flattered before,
Such a word as, "Oh, not in the main
   Do I hold thee less precious, but more!"
Thou'lt sigh, very like, on thy part,
   "Of all I have known or can know.
I wish I had only that Heart
   I trod upon ages ago!"

ROBERT BROWNING

ROBERT BROWNING (English, 1812-1889). One of major Victorian poets. A dramatist of thought and emotion rather than of action. Metaphysical content of later poems gave him reputation for obscurity. Most admired for dramatic monologues and the long narrative, *The Ring and the Book,* based on actual 17th century murder case. All his work marked by high moral tone of the Victorians.

THE LOST LEADER

Just for a handful of silver he left us,
    Just for a riband to stick in his coat—
Found the one gift of which fortune bereft us,
    Lost all the others she lets us devote;
They, with the gold to give, doled him out silver,
    So much was theirs who so little allowed:
How all our copper had gone for his service!
    Rags—were they purple, his heart had been proud!
We that had loved him so, followed him, honoured him,
    Lived in his mild and magnificent eye,
Learned his great language, caught his clear accents,
    Made him our pattern to live and to die!
Shakespeare was of us, Milton was for us,
    Burns, Shelley, were with us,—they watch from their
        graves!
He alone breaks from the van and the freemen,
    —He alone sinks to the rear and the slaves!
We shall march prospering,—not through his presence;
    Songs may inspirit us,—not from his lyre;
Deeds will be done,—while he boasts his quiescence,
    Still bidding crouch whom the rest bade aspire:
Blot out his name, then, record one lost soul more,
    One task more declined, one more footpath untrod,
One more devils'-triumph and sorrow for angels,
    One wrong more to man, one more insult to God!
Life's night begins: let him never come back to us!
    There would be doubt, hesitation and pain,
Forced praise on our part—the glimmer of twilight,
    Never glad confident morning again!

Best fight on well, for we taught him—strike gallantly,
    Menace our heart ere we master his own;
Then let him receive the new knowledge and wait us,
    Pardoned in heaven, the first by the throne!

INSTANS TYRANNUS

I

Of the million or two, more or less,
I rule and possess,
One man, for some cause undefined,
Was least to my mind.

II

I struck him, he grovelled of course—
For, what was his force?
I pinned him to earth with my weight
And persistence of hate:
And he lay, would not moan, would not curse,
As his lot might be worse.

III

"Were the object less mean, would he stand
At the swing of my hand!
For obscurity helps him and blots
The hole where he squats."
So, I set my five wits on the stretch
To inveigle the wretch.
All in vain! Gold and jewels I threw,
Still he couched there perdue;
I tempted his blood and his flesh,
Hid in roses my mesh,
Choicest cates and the flagon's best spilth:
Still he kept to his filth.
At the thought of his face,
The droop, the low cares of the mouth,
The trouble uncouth

To put out of its pain.
And, "no!" I admonished myself,
"Is one mocked by an elf,

IV

Had he kith now or kin, were access
To his heart, did I press:
Just a son or a mother to seize!
No such booty as these!
Were it simply a friend to pursue
'Mid my million or two,
Who could pay me in person or pelf
What he owes me himself!
No: I could not but smile through my chafe:
For the fellow lay safe
As his mates do, the midge and the nit,
—Through minuteness, to wit.

V

Then a humour more great took its place
At the thought of his face,
The droop, the low cares of the mouth,
The trouble uncouth
'Twixt the brows, all that air one is fain
To put out of its pain.
And, "no!" I admonished myself,
Is one baffled by toad or by rat?
The gravamen's in that!
How the lion, who crouches to suit
His back to my foot,
Would admire that I stand in debate!
But the Small turns the Great
If it vexes you,—that is the thing!
Toad or rat vex the King?
Though I waste half my realm to unearth
Toad or rat, 'tis well worth!

VI

So, I soberly laid my last plan
To extinguish the man.
Round his creep-hole, with never a break
Ran my fires for his sake;
Over-head, did my thunder combine
Till I looked from my labour content
To enjoy the event.

153

When sudden . . . how think ye, the end?
Did I say "without friend"?
Say rather, from marge to blue marge
The whole sky grew his targe
With the sun's self for visible boss,
While an Arm ran across
Which the earth heaved beneath like a breast
Where the wretch was safe prest!
Did you see? Just my vengeance complete.
The man sprang to his feet,
Stood erect, caught at God's skirts, and prayed!
—So, *I* was afraid!

KARL GEORG BÜCHNER

KARL GEORG BÜCHNER (German, 1813-1837). Forerunner of the modern drama. His reputation not established until a century after death. Student of medicine, went underground after writing revolutionary pamphlet. Author of three pessimistic plays: *Dantons Tod, Leonce und Lena,* and *Woyzeck* (the source of Alban Berg's opera). His psychology and realism are uncannily modern.

WOYZECK

The action apparently takes place in Leipzig, 1824.

1 AT THE CAPTAIN'S

The CAPTAIN *in a chair;* WOYZECK *shaving him.*

CAPTAIN. Easy, Woyzeck, take it easy. One thing after the other! You're making me dizzy. You'll finish up early and what'll I do with ten minutes on my hands? Use your head, Woyzeck. You've got thirty years to live. Thirty! That's three hundred sixty months. And days! Hours! Minutes! What are you going to do with that horrible stretch of time? Figure it out for yourself, Woyzeck!

WOYZECK. Yes sir, Captain.

CAPTAIN. *Touched, but condescending.*

Woyzeck, you're a good man, but

With dignity

you have no morals. Morals! That's what a man's got who behaves morally! Understand? It's a good word. You went and got yourself a child without the blessing of the Church, as our right reverend chaplain put it. "Without the blessing of the Church." Now, I didn't invent the phrase.

WOYZECK. Captain, the Good Lord's not going to be hard on the little worm, just because no one said Amen before they made him. The Lord said, "Suffer little children to come unto me." You see, Captain—with us poor people—it's money, money! If you don't have money . . . Well, you just can't have morals when you're bringing someone like yourself into the world. We're only flesh and blood. People like us can't be holy in this world—or the next. If we ever did get into heaven, they'd put us to work on the thunder.

CAPTAIN. Woyzeck, you have no virtue. You are not a virtuous man.

WOYZECK. Yes, Captain. Virtue. I don't have much of that. But you see, what happens to us ordinary people—that's just nature. Now, if I was a gentleman and wore a hat and a watch and a cane, and could talk smooth—well, I'd like to be virtuous too. It must be fine to be virtuous, Captain, but I'm just ordinary.

CAPTAIN. You're good, Woyzeck. You're a good man. But you think too much. It wears you out. You're always so moody. Well, this conversation has exhausted me too. You can go. But don't run. Take it easy, nice and easy, out into the street.

3   THE TOWN

MARIE *with her child at the window,* MARGRET. *The Retreat passes, the Drum-Major in front.*

MARIE, *dandling her child.* Hey, boy! Ta-ra-ra-ra! Hear them? Here they come!

MARGRET. What a man! Built like a tree.

MARIE. He handles himself like a lion.

The Drum Major salutes her.

MARGRET. Ooh, he's giving you the glad eye, neighbor. I hardly expected it of *you.*

MARIE, *singing.*

Oh, soldiers are such handsome guys.

155

MARGRET. Your eyes are still shining.

MARIE. Who cares? If you took yours to the pawnbroker's and had them polished up, maybe they'd shine enough to be sold for a couple of buttons.

MARGRET. What's that? Why, you! Listen, Mrs. Virginity, I'm at least respectable. But you, everyone knows you could stare your way through seven pairs of leather pants.

MARIE. You bitch!

Slams the window.

Come on, little fellow. What do people want, anyhow? Maybe you are just a poor whore's kid, but your illegitimate little face still brings joy to your mother. Da, da, dum.

A knock at the window.

Who's there? That you, Franz? Come on in.

WOYZECK. Can't. Got roll call.

MARIE. Get the wood cut for the Captain?

WOYZECK. Yes. Marie.

MARIE. What's the matter, Franz? You look upset.

WOYZECK. It followed me all the way into town. Something we can't understand, that drives you out of your senses. What's going to happen?

MARIE. Franz!

WOYZECK. I've got to go. See you tonight at the fair grounds. I saved something up.

MARIE. That man! He's seeing things. Didn't even notice his own child. He'll crack up with these ideas of his. Why so quiet, little fellow? Are you scared? It's getting so dark it's like going blind. Only that street light shining in. It gives me the creeps.

8 MARIE'S ROOM

MARIE, *the* DRUM-MAJOR.

DRUM-MAJOR. Marie!

MARIE. *Looking at him intently.* Stand up there!—A chest like a bull and a beard like a lion. In a class by himself—no woman is prouder than I am.

DRUM-MAJOR. But Sunday, when I'm wearing my white gloves and the hat with the plume in it, hot damn! The Prince always says, "By God, there's a real man!"

MARIE, *mockingly.* Does he?

Steps up before him.

A real man!

DRUM-MAJOR. And you're a real piece of woman, too. Hell's bells, let's raise a race of Drum-majors. Eh?

He embraces her.

MARIE, *moody.* Let me go!

DRUM-MAJOR. You wildcat!

MARIE, *violently.* Just touch me!

DRUM-MAJOR. You've got the devil in your eyes.

MARIE. What's the difference?

10 MARIE'S ROOM

MARIE, WOYZECK.

WOYZECK, *staring straight at her and shaking his head.* Hm! I can't see it. I can't see it. You should be able to. You should be able to hold it in your fist.

MARIE, *frightened.* What is it, Franz? You're raving, Franz.

WOYZECK. A sin, so big, and so wide. It should stink, until the angels are smoked out of heaven. You have a red mouth, Marie. No blisters on it? Marie, you're as beautiful as sin—but can mortal sin be so beautiful?

MARIE. Franz, you're talking like you had a fever.

WOYZECK. Hell! Did he stand there? Like this? Like this?

MARIE. The world is old and the day is long, so lots of people can stand in the same place, one after the other.

WOYZECK. I saw him!

MARIE. There's a lot you can see if you have two eyes, you're not blind, and the sun is shining.

WOYZECK. You whore!

He goes for her.

MARIE. Just touch me, Franz! I'd rather have a knife in my ribs than your hands on me. At ten, my father didn't dare touch me. I only had to look at him.

WOYZECK. Bitch! No, it should show on you. Each one of us is a precipice. You get dizzy when you look down.— There should be! She's innocence itself. All right, innocence. You bear the mark on you. Do I know it though? Do I know it? Who does?

12 AN INN

The windows open. Dancing. WOYZECK *posts himself by the window. Marie and the* DRUM-MAJOR *dance by, without noticing him.*

WOYZECK. Him and her! Damn it to hell!

MARIE, *dancing by.* Don't stop! Don't stop!

WOYZECK, *choking.* Don't stop!

He jumps up and falls back on the bench.

Don't stop! Don't stop!

Pounding his hands.

Turn around! Roll on! Why doesn't God blow out the sun so they can all roll on top of each other in filth? Male and Female! Man and Beast! They'll do it in broad daylight! They'll do it on your hands, like flies! Women! That woman is hot, hot! Don't stop!

That bastard! Look how he's feeling her up—all over her body! He's, he's got her—like I did at first.

He slumps down, bewildered.

FOOL. It smells.

WOYZECK. Yes, it smells! She had a red, red mouth. Is that what you smell?

FOOL. I smell blood.

WOYZECK. Blood! Everything's going red before my eyes. Like they were all rolling on top of each other in a sea of it!

14 A ROOM IN THE BARRACKS

Night. ANDRES *and* WOYZECK *in one bed.*

WOYZECK, *softly.* Andres!

ANDRES, *murmurs in his sleep.*

WOYZECK, *shaking* ANDRES. Hey, Andres! Andres!

ANDRES. What do you want?

WOYZECK. I can't sleep. When I close my eyes, everything turns around and I hear the fiddles saying: Don't stop! Don't stop! Then it comes out of the wall, too. Don't you hear anything?

ANDRES. Sure. Let them dance. A man gets tired. God bless us all. Amen.

WOYZECK. It keeps saying: Stab! Stab! And it pulls my eyes open, like a knife. A big, thick knife, lying on a counter in a dark narrow street, with an old man sitting behind it. That's the knife I keep seeing in front of my eyes.

ANDRES. Yon ought to drink some schnapps with a powder in it. That cuts the fever.

WOYZECK. Don't stop! Don't stop!

ANDRES. Go to sleep, you fool!

He goes to sleep.

WOYZECK, *the* JEW.

WOYZECK. The pistol's too much.

JEW. So, are you buying or not buying? Make up your mind!

WOYZECK. How much was the knife?

JEW. It's good and sharp. Going to cut your throat with it? Make up your mind. I'm giving it to you cheap as anybody. You can die cheap, but not for nothing.

WOYZECK. It'll cut more than bread . . .

JEW. Two groschen.

WOYZECK. Here!

Goes out.

JEW. Here! Like it was nothing. And it's good money! The pig!

19 MARIE'S ROOM

MARIE, *leafing through the bible.* "And no guile is found in his mouth." Lord God, Lord God, don't look at me!

Leafs again.

"And the scribes and the Pharisees brought unto him a woman taken in adultery, and set her in the midst . . . And Jesus said unto her, 'Neither do I condemn thee; go, and sin no more.'" Lord God, Lord God, I can't—Lord God, give me the strength to pray!

The child cuddles up to her.

The child stabs me to the heart.

Franz hasn't been here yesterday or today. It's getting hot in here.

She opens the window.

"And stood at his feet weeping, and began to wash his feet with tears, and did wipe them with the hairs of her head, and kissed his feet, and annointed them with ointment."

Beats her breast.

Everything's dead. Saviour, Saviour! If only I could annoint Thy feet!

22 A WOODLAND PATH BY A POND

MARIE *and* WOYZECK.

MARIE. The town's that way. It's dark.

WOYZECK. You're not going. Come on, sit down.

MARIE. But I have to go.

WOYZECK. Your feet will get sore running.

MARIE. You're so changed.

WOYZECK. Do you know how long it's been, Marie?

MARIE. Two years, Pentecost.

WOYZECK. Do you know how long it will last?

MARIE. I have to go and get supper.

WOYZECK. You're not freezing. Marie? No, you're warm. You've got hot lips. Hot! A hot whore's breath! And I'd still give heaven to kiss them again. Are you freezing? When your bones are cold, you don't freeze anymore. You won't freeze in the morning dew.

MARIE. What are you saying?

WOYZECK. Nothing.

Silence.

MARIE. The moon's rising. It's red.

WOYZECK. Like a sword with blood on it!

MARIE. What are you going to do, Franz? You're so pale.

He raises the knife.

Franz, stop! For Heaven's sake! Help! Help!

WOYZECK, *stabbing madly*. Take that, and that! Why can't you die? There! There! Ha! She's still twitching. Still can't? Still twitching?

Stabs again.

Now are you dead? Dead! Dead!

He drops the knife and runs away.

23 THE INN

WOYZECK. Dance, everyone dance! Don't stop! Sweat and stink! He'll get all of you in the end.

He dances.

Whew, Kathe! Sit down. I'm hot, hot!

He takes off his coat.

KATHE. But what's that on your hand?

WOYZECK. On me? Me?

KATHE. Red! Blood!

People gather round.

WOYZECK. Blood? Blood?

INNKEEPER. Ugh! Blood!

WOYZECK. I think, I cut myself. There, on my right hand.

INNEEPER. How come it's on your elbow?

WOYZECK. I wiped it off.

INNKEEPER. Wiped your right hand on your right elbow? You have talent!

160

FOOL. And the Giant said: I smell, I smell. What do I smell? A man, a man who's bound for Hell! Pah! it stinks already!

WOYZECK. What the devil do you all want? What business is it of yours? Out of my way, or the first one who . . . Hell, do you think I did away with someone? Am I a murderer? What are you gaping at? Gawk at yourselves! Get out of my way! *He runs off.*

24 AT THE POND

WOYZECK *alone.*

WOYZECK. The knife? Where's the knife? I left it here. It'll give me away. Nearer. Nearer yet. What place is this? What's that I hear? Something moving! No, it's quiet. Over there. Marie? Ha, Marie! You're quiet. Everything's quiet! What are you so white for, Marie? What's that red string around your neck? Who did your sins earn that necklace from? You were black with them, black! Did I bleach you white again? Why is your black hair hanging so wild? Didn't you braid your long braids today? Here's something! Cold and wet, and still. The knife! the knife! Got it? Get rid of it!

He runs into the water.

There! Down it goes.

He throws the knife in.

It dives down into the water like a stone. The moon's like a sword with blood on it! Is the whole world going to gab about it? No, it's lying too close. When they're swimming. . . .

He goes into the pond and throws it further.

There, that's it! But, in the summer, when they're diving for mussels? Bah! it'll be rusty. Who'd recognize it—I should have broken it. Am I still bloody? I better wash up. There's a spot and there's another.

Goes deeper into the water.

Time passes. People come.

FIRST PERSON. Wait up!

SECOND PERSON. You hear? Shh! Over there!

FIRST PERSON. Ugh! Over there. What a sound!

SECOND PERSON. It's the water, calling. It's been a long time since anyone was drowned. Let's go, it's not a pleasant thing to hear.

FIRST PERSON. Ugh! There it is again! Like a man, dying.

SECOND. It's eerie. So foggy, that gray mist everywhere, and the bugs humming like broken bells. Let's go!

FIRST. Wait! It's too clear, too loud. It's up there. Come on!

161

CHILDREN.

FIRST CHILD. Let's go look at Marie! *

SECOND CHILD. What for?

FIRST CHILD. Don't you know? Everybody's gone out there.

To Marie's Child.

Hey, your mother's dead.

MARIE'S CHILD, *playing horsey.* Giddyap, giddyap!

FIRST CHILD. On the path to the pond.

SECOND CHILD. Hurry up! Let's get there before they bring her back.

MARIE'S CHILD. Giddyap, giddyap!

IVAN BUNIN

IVAN BUNIN (Russian, 1870-1953). Russian poet and noted translator from the English. Lived in exile after 1919. His poetry, largely descriptive, based on experience and travels. Author of famous novel, *The Village,* and short stories, *The Gentleman from San Francisco,* which won him Nobel Prize in 1933. High technical skill has given him reputation as a "writers' writer."

SUNSTROKE

LEAVING the hot, brightly lighted dining saloon after dinner, they went on deck and stood near the rail. She closed her eyes, leant her cheek on the back of her hand, and laughed—a clear charming laugh—everything about this little woman was charming.

"I am quite drunk," she said. "In fact I have gone mad. Where did you come from? Three hours ago I did not know of your existence. I don't even know where you got on the boat. Was it Samara? But it doesn't matter, you're a dear. Am I dizzy, or is the boat really turning round?"

In front of them lay darkness and the light of lamps. A soft wind blew strongly against their faces and carried the light to one side. With the smartness characteristic of the Volga boats, the steamer was making a wide curve towards the small wharf.

The lieutenant took her hand and raised it to his lips. The firm little fragrant hand was tanned. His heart became faint with fear and ecstasy as he thought how strong and bronzed must be the body under the light linen dress after having basked in the South-

162

ern sun on the hot beach for a whole month. (She had told him that she was on her way from Anapi.)

"Let's get off," he murmured.

"Where?" she asked in surprise.

"At this wharf."

"What for?"

He was silent. She raised her hand to her hot cheek again.

"You are mad."

"Let's get off," he repeated stubbornly. "I implore you——"

"Oh, do as you like," she said, turning from him.

With its final impetus, the steamer bumped gently against the dimly lit wharf, and they nearly fell over each other. The end of a rope flew over their heads, the boat heaved back, there was a foam of churning waters, the gangways clattered. The lieutenant rushed away to collect their things.

A moment later they passed through the sleepy ticket office into the ankle-deep sand of the road, and silently got into a dusty open cab. The soft, sandy road sloping gradually uphill, lit by crooked lamp-posts at long intervals on either side, seemed unending, but they reached its top and clattered along a high-road until they came to a sort of square with municipal buildings and a watch-tower. It was all full of warmth and the smells peculiar to a hot night in a small provincial town. The cab drew up at a lighted portico, behind the door of which a steep old wooden stairway was visible, and an old unshaven waiter, in a pink shirt and black coat, reluctantly took their luggage, and led the way in his down-at-heel slippers. They entered a large room stuffy from the hot sun which had beaten on it all day, its white curtains drawn. On the toilet table were two unlit candles.

The instant the door closed on the waiter, the lieutenant sprang towards her with such impetuosity, and they were carried away by a breathless kiss of such passion, that they remembered it for many, many years. Neither of them had ever before experienced anything like it.

At ten o'clock next morning the little, nameless woman left. She never told him her name, and referred to herself jokingly as "the fair stranger." It was a hot, sunny morning. Church bells were ringing, and a market was in full swing in the square in front of the hotel. There were scents of hay and tar and all the odours characteristic of a Russian provincial town.

They had not slept much, but when she emerged from behind

163

the screen, where she had washed and dressed in five minutes, she was as fresh as a girl of seventeen. Was she embarrassed? Very little, if at all. She was as simple and gay as before, and —already rational. "No, no, dear," she said in reply to his request that they should continue the journey together. "No, you must wait for the next boat. If we go together, it will spoil it all. It would be very unpleasant for me. I give you my word of honour that I am not in the least what you may think I am. Nothing at all like this has ever happened to me before or will ever happen again. I seem to have been under a spell. Or, rather, we both seem to have had something like sunstroke."

The lieutenant readily agreed with her. In a bright, happy mood he drove her to the wharf—just before the pink steamer of the Samolet Line started. He kissed her openly on the deck, and had barely time to get ashore before the gangway was lowered. He returned to the hotel in the same care-free, easy mood. But something had changed. The room without her seemed quite different from what it had been with her. He was still full of her; he did not mind, but it was strange. The room still held the scent of her excellent English lavender water, her unfinished cup of tea still stood on the tray, but she was gone. . . . The lieutenant's heart was suddenly filled with such a rush of tenderness that he hurriedly lit a cigarette and began to pace the room, switching his topboots with his cane.

"A strange adventure," he said aloud, laughing and feeling tears well up in his eyes. " 'I give you my word of honour that I am not in the least what you think I am,' and she's gone. Absurd woman!"

The screen had been moved—the bed had not been made. He felt that he had not the strength to look at that bed. He put the screen in front of it, closed the window to shut out the creaking of the wheels and the noisy chatter of the market, drew the white billowing curtains, and sat down on the sofa. Yes, the roadside adventure was over. She was gone, and now, far away, she was probably sitting in the windowed saloon, or on the deck, gazing at the enormous river glittering in the sun, at the barges drifting down-stream, at the yellow shoals, at the shining horizon of sky and water, at the immeasurable sweep of the Volga. And it was good-bye for ever and ever. For where could they possibly meet again? "For," he thought, "I can hardly appear on the scene without any excuse, in the town where she lives her everyday life with her huband, her three-year-old daughter and all her family."

164

The town seemed to him a special, a forbidden town. He was aggravated and stunned by the thought that she would live her lonely life there, often perhaps remembering him, recalling their brief encounter, that he would never see her again. No, it was impossible. It would be too mad, too unnatural, too fantastic. He suffered and was overwhelmed by horror and despair in feeling that without her his whole life would be futile. "Damn it all!" he thought, as he got up and began to pace the room again, trying not to look at the bed behind the screen. "What in the world's the matter with me? It's not the first time, is it? And yet— Was there anything very special about her, or did anything very special happen? It really is like sunstroke. And how on earth am I to spend a whole day in this hole without her?"

He still remembered all of her, down to the minutest detail: her sunburn, her linen frock, her strong body, her unaffected, bright, gay voice. . . . The sense of ecstatic joy which her feminine charm had given him was still extraordinarily strong, but now a second feeling rose uppermost in his mind—a new, strange, incomprehensible feeling, which had not been there while they had been together, and of which he would not, the day before, have believed himself capable when he had started what he had thought to be the amusment of a passing acquaintance. And now there was no one, no one, whom he could tell. "And the point is," he thought, "that I never shall be able to tell anyone! And how am I to get through this endless day with these memories, this inexplicable agony, in this god-forsaken town on the banks of that same Volga along which the steamer is carrying her away?" He must do something to save himself, something to distract him, he must go somewhere. He put on his hat with an air of determination, took his stick and walked along the corridor with his spurs jingling, ran down the stairs and out on to the porch. But where should he go? A cab was drawn up in front of the hotel. A young, smartly-dressed driver sat on the box calmly smoking a cigar. He was obviously waiting for someone. The lieutenant stared at him, bewildered and astonished: How could anyone sit calmly on a box and smoke and in general be unmoved and indifferent? "I suppose that in the whole town there is no one so miserably unhappy as I am," he thought, as he went towards the market.

It was already breaking up. For some unknown reason he found himself making his way over fresh droppings, among carts, loads of cucumbers, stacks of pots and pans, and women seated on the ground who outdid each other in their efforts to attract his attention. They lifted basins and tapped them that he might hear how sound they were, while the men deafened him with cries of "First-class cucumbers, your honour." It was all so stupid, so ridiculous that he fled from the square. He went into the cathedral, where the choir was singing loudly, resolutely, as though conscious of fulfilling a duty; then he strolled aimlessly about a small, hot, unkempt garden on the edge of a cliff overhanging the silvery steel breadth of the river.

The epaulettes and buttons of his linen uniform were unbearably hot to the touch. The inside of his hat was wet, his face was burning. He returned to the hotel and was delighted to get into the large, empy, cool dining-room, delighted to take off his hat and seat himself at a small table near the open window. The heat penetrated from outside, but it was airy. He ordered iced soup.

Everything was all right in this unknown town, happiness and joy emanated from everything, from the heat and the market smells. Even this old provincial hotel seemed full of gladness, and yet his heart was being torn to pieces. He drank several glasses of vodka and ate a salted cucumber with parsley. He felt that he would unhesitatingly die tomorrow if, by some miracle, he could achieve her return and spend to-day, only this one day, with her, solely, solely in order that he might tell her and prove to her and convince her somehow of his agonising and exalted love for her. "Why prove? Why convince?" He did not know why, but it was more essential than life.

"My nerves have all gone to pieces," he said, pouring out his fifth glass of vodka. He drank the entire contents of the small decanter, hoping to stupefy, to benumb himself, hoping to get rid at last of this agonising and exalted feeling. But, instead, it increased. He pushed away the soup, ordered black coffee, and began to smoke and to think with intensity. What was he to do now, how was he to free himself from this sudden and unexpected love? To free himself—but he felt only too clearly that that was impossible. He rose abruptly, quickly, took his hat and his stick, asked the way to the post office and hurried off, the text of the telegram already composed in his mind: "Henceforth all my life, for all time till death, is yours, in your power." But on reaching the thick-walled old building which housed the post and telegraph, he stopped in dismay. He knew the name of her town, he knew that she had a husband and a child of three, but he knew neither her first name

166

nor her surname. Last night, while they were dining at the hotel, he had asked her several times, and each time she had answered with a laugh: "Why do you want to know who I am? I am Marie Marevna, the mysterious princess of the fairy story; or the fair stranger; isn't that enough for you?"

At the corner of the street, near the post office, was a photographer's window. He stared for a long time at the portrait of an officer in braided epaulettes, with protruding eyes, a low forehead, unusually luxuriant whiskers, and a very broad chest entirely covered with orders. How mad, how ridiculous, how terrifyingly ordinary, everyday things appear when the heart is struck—yes, *struck*, he understood it now, by the "sunstroke" of a love too great, a joy too immense. He looked at the picture of a bridal couple— a young man in a frock-coat and white tie, with closely-cropped hair, very erect, arm-in-arm with a girl in white tulle. His gaze wandered to a pretty piquant girl wearing a student's cap on the back of her head.

Then, filled with envy of all these unknown people who were not suffering, he stared fixedly down the street. "Where shall I go? What shall I do?" The difficult, unanswerable questions occupied both mind and soul.

The street was completely empty. All the houses were alike, middle-class, two-storied white houses with large gardens, but they were lifeless; the pavement was covered with thick white dust; it was all blinding, all bathed in hot, flaming, joyful sun which now somehow seemed futile. In the distance the street rose, humped and ran into the clear, cloudless, grey-mauve horizon. There was something southern about it; it reminded one of Sebastopol, Kerch— Anapi. This was more than he could bear. With eyes half closed and head bowed from the light, staring intently at the pavement, staggering, stumbling, catching one spur in the other, the lieutenant retraced his steps.

He returned to the hotel worn out with fatigue, as though he had done a long day's march in Turkestan or the Sahara. With a final effort he got to his large empty room. It had been "done." The last traces of her were gone except for one hairpin forgotten by her on the table. He took off his coat and looked at himself in the mirror. He saw reflected, skin bronzed and moustache bleached by the sun, the bluish whites of the eyes looking so much whiter on account of the tan, an ordinary enough officer's face, but now wild and excited. And about the whole figure standing there in the thin white shirt and stiff collar there was something pathetically young and terribly unhappy. He lay down on the bed, on his back, resting his dusty boots on the footrail. The windows were open, the blinds were lowered. From time to time a slight wind billowed them out, letting in the heat, the smell of hot roofs and of all the radiant, but now empty, silent, deserted Volga country-side. He lay there, his hands under his head, and stared into space. In his mind he had a vague picture of the far-away south: sun and sea, Anapi. Then arose something fantastic, a town unlike any other town—the town in which she lived, which she had probably already reached. The thought of suicide stubbornly persisted. He closed his eyes and felt hot, smarting tears well up under his eyelids. Then at last he fell asleep, and when he woke he could see by the reddish-yellow light of the sun that it was evening. The wind had died down, the room was as hot and dry as an oven. Yesterday and this morning both seemed ten years ago. Unhurriedly he rose, unhurriedly he washed, drew up the blinds and rang for a samovar and his bill, and for a long time sat there drinking tea with lemon. Then he ordered a cab to be called and his things to be carried down. As he got into the cab with its faded red seat, he gave the waiter five roubles. "I believe I brought you here last night, your honour," said the driver gaily as he gathered up the reins.

By the time they reached the wharf, the Volga was roofed by the blue of the summer night. Multitudes of many-tinted lights were dotted along the river, and bright lamps shone from the masts of the ships.

"I got you here in the nick of time," said the cabdriver ingratiatingly.

The lieutenant gave five roubles to him also, took his ticket and went to the landing-place. Just as it had done yesterday, the boat bumped gently as it touched the wharf, there was the same slight dizziness from the unsteadiness underfoot, the end of a rope was thrown, there was a sound of foaming and rushing water under the paddles as the steamer backed a little. . . .

The brightly lighted, crowded steamer, smelling of food, seemed unusually friendly and agreeable, and in a few minutes it was speeding forward up the river, whither in the morning she had been carried.

The last glimmer of summer twilight gradually faded on the far horizon; capriciously, lazily reflecting their varied hues in the river, making here and there bright patches on the rippling surface under

168

the dim dome of blue, the gleaming lights everywhere sprinkled in the darkness seemed to be swimming, swimming back.

Under an awning on deck sat the lieutenant. He felt older by ten years.

JOHN BUNYAN

JOHN BUNYAN (English, 1628-1688). Uneducated, a tinker by trade, thrown into jail for Baptist preaching. In prison began his great allegory, *The Pilgrim's Progress*, portraying man's journey through this world to the next. Simple, graphic prose has made it, next to Bible, most widely read book in English. Other works: *Grace Abounding, The Holy City*.

THE GOLDEN CITY

Now I saw in my dream that by this time the pilgrims were got over the Enchanted Ground, and entering into the country of Beulah, whose air was very sweet and pleasant, the way lying directly through it, they solaced them there for the season. Yea, here they heard continually the singing of birds, and saw every day the flowers appear in the earth, and heard the voice of the turtle in the land. In this country the sun shineth night and day; wherefore it was beyond the Valley of the Shadow of Death, and also out of the reach of Giant Despair; neither could they from this place so much as see Doubting Castle. Here they were within sight of the city they were going to; also here met them some of the inhabitants thereof; for in this land the shining ones commonly walked, because it was upon the borders of Heaven. In this land, also, the contract between the bride and bridegroom was renewed; yea, here, "as the bridegroom rejoiceth over the bride, so did their God rejoice over them." Here they had no want of corn and wine; for in this place they met abundance of what they had sought for in all their pilgrimage. Here they heard voices from out of the city—loud voices—saying: "Say ye to the daughter of Zion, behold, thy salvation cometh! Behold, his reward is with him!" Here all the inhabitants of the country called them "the holy people, the redeemed of the Lord, sought out," &c.

Now, as they walked in this land, they had more rejoicing than in parts more remote from the kingdom to which they were bound; and drawing nearer to the city yet, they had a more perfect view thereof: it was built of pearls and precious stones, also the streets thereof were paved with gold; so that, by reason of the natural glory of the city, and the reflection of the sunbeams upon it, Christian with desire fell sick; Hopeful also had a fit or two of the same disease: wherefore here they lay by it a while, crying out, because of their pangs: "If you see my Beloved, tell him that I am sick of love."

But being a little strengthened, and better able to bear their sickness, they walked on their way, and came yet nearer and nearer, where were orchards, vineyards and gardens, and their gates opened into the highway. Now, as they came up to these places, behold the gardener stood in the way, to whom the pilgrims said: "Whose goodly vineyards and gardens are these?" He answered:

"They are the King's, and are planted here for his own delight, and also for the solace of pilgrims."

So the gardener had them into the vineyards, and bid them refresh themselves with dainties; he also showed them there the King's walks and arbors, where he delighted to be; and here they tarried and slept.

Now, I beheld in my dream that they talked more in their sleep at this time than ever they did in all their journey; and being in a muse thereabout, the gardener said even to me: "Wherefore musest thou at the matter?" It is the nature of the fruit of the grapes of these vineyards to go down so sweetly as to cause the lips of them that are asleep to speak.

So I saw that when they awoke, they addressed themselves to go up to the city. But, as I said, the reflection of the sun upon the city—for the city was pure gold—was so extremely glorious that they could not as yet with open face behold it, but through an instrument made for that purpose. So I saw that, as they went on, there met them two men in raiment that shone like gold; also their faces shone as the light.

These men asked the pilgrims whence they came; and they told them. They also asked them where they had lodged, what difficulties and dangers, what comforts and pleasures, they had met with in their way; and they told them. Then said the men that met them: "You have but two difficulties more to meet with, and then you are in the city."

Christian and his companion then asked the men to go along

with them; so they told them that they would. But, said they, you must obtain it by your own faith. So I saw in my dream that they went on together till they came in sight of the gate.

Now, I further saw that betwixt them and the gate was a river, but there was no bridge to go over, and the river was very deep. At the sight, therefore, of this river, the pilgrims were much stunned; but the men that went with them said: "You must go through, or you cannot come to the gate."

The pilgrims then began to inquire if there was no other way to the gate; to which they answered: "Yes; but there hath not any, save two—to wit, Enoch and Elijah—been permitted to tread that path since the foundation of the world, nor shall, until the last trumpet shall sound. The pilgrims then—especially Christian—began to despond in their minds, and looked this way and that; but no way could be found by them by which they might escape the river. Then they asked the men if the waters were all of a depth. They said: "No; yet they could not help them in that case; for, said they, you shall find it deeper or shallower, as you believe in the King of the place."

They then addressed themselves to the water, and entering, Christian began to sink, and crying out to his good friend Hopeful, he said:

"I sink in deep waters: the billows go over my head; all the waters go over me. Selah."

Then said the other: "Be of good cheer, my brother; I feel the bottom, and it is good."

Then said Christian: "Ah! my friend, the sorrow of death hath encompassed me about: I shall not see the land that flows with milk and honey."

Then I saw in my dream that Christian was in a muse a while. To whom also, Hopeful added these words: "Be of good cheer; Jesus Christ maketh thee whole;" and with that Christian brake out with a loud voice—"Oh! I see him again; and he tells me: 'When thou passest through the waters, I will be with thee; and through the rivers, they shall not overflow thee.' " Then they both took courage, and the enemy was after that as still as a stone, until they were gone over. Christian, therefore, presently found ground to stand upon, and so it followed that the rest of the river was but shallow. Thus they got over. Now, upon the bank of the river on the other side, they saw the two shining men again, who there waited for them; wherefore, being come out of the river, they saluted them, saying: "We are ministering spirits, sent forth to minister to those that shall be heirs of salvation." Thus they went along toward the gate. Now, you must note that the city stood upon a mighty hill; but the pilgrims went up that hill with ease, because they had these two men to lead them up by the arms; they had likewise left their mortal garments behind them in the river; for though they went in with them, they came out without them. They therefore went up here with much agility and speed, though the foundation upon which the city was framed was higher than the clouds; they therefore went up through the region of the air, sweetly talking as they went, being comforted because they got safely over the river, and had such glorious companions to attend them.

Now, while they were thus drawing towards the gate, behold a company of the heavenly host came out to meet them; to whom it was said by the other two shining ones:

"These are the men who loved our Lord when they were in the world, and have left all for his holy name; and he hath sent us to fetch them, and we have brought them thus far on their desired journey, that they may go in and look their Redeemer in the face with joy." Then the heavenly host gave a great shout, saying: "Blessed are they that are called to the marriage-supper of the Lamb." There came also out at this time to meet them several of the King's trumpeters, clothed in white and shining raiment, who, with melodious and loud noises, made even the heavens to echo with their sound. These trumpeters saluted Christian and his fellow with ten thousand welcomes from the world; and this they did with shouting and sound of trumpet.

This done, they compassed them round about on every side; some went before, some behind, and some on the right hand, some on the left—as it were to guard them through the upper regions —continually sounding as they went, with melodious noise, in notes on high; so that the very sight was to them that could behold it as if heaven itself was come down to meet them. Thus, therefore, they walked on together; and as they walked, ever and anon these trumpeters, even with joyful sound, would, by mixing their music with looks and gestures, still signify to Christian and his brother how welcome they were into their company, and with what gladness they came to meet them; and now were these two men, as it were, in heaven before they came at it, being swallowed up with the sight of angels, and with hearing their melodious notes. Here, also, they had the city itself in view, and thought they heard all the bells therein to ring, to welcome thereto. But, above all, the warm and joyful thoughts that they had about their own dwelling here with such company, and that for ever and ever. Oh! by what tongue or pen can their glorious joy be expressed! Thus they came up to the gate.

Now, when they were come up to the gate, there were written over in letters of gold: "Blessed are they that do his commandments, that they may have a right to the tree of life, and may enter in through the gates into the city."

Then I saw in my dream that the shining men bid them call at the gate; the which, when they did, some from above looked over the gate, to wit: Enoch, Moses, Elijah, &c.: to whom it was said: These pilgrims are come from the City of Destruction, for the love that they bear to the King of this place; and then the pilgrims gave in unto them each man his certificate, which they had received in the beginning: those, therefore, were carried in to the King, who, when he had read them, said: "Where are the men?" To whom it was answered: They are standing without the gate. The King then commanded to open the gate, "That the righteous nation," said he, "that keepeth truth may enter in."

Now, I saw in my dream that these two men went in at the gate; and lo! as they entered, they were transfigured, and they had raiment put on that shone like gold. There were also that met them with harps to praise withal, and the crowns in token of honor. Then I heard in my dream that all the bells in the city rang again for joy, and that it was said unto them: "Enter ye into the joy of your Lord." I also heard the men themselves, that they sank with a loud voice, saying: "Blessing, honor, and glory, and power be to Him that sitteth upon the throne, and to the Lamb, for ever and ever."

Now, just as the gates were opened to let in the men, I looked in after them, and behold the city shone like the sun; the streets, also, were paved with gold, and in them walked many men with crowns on their heads, palms in their hands, and golden harps, to sing praises withal.

ROBERT BURNS

ROBERT BURNS (Scottish, 1759-1796). Leading Scottish poet of his day. An uneducated natural singer and dialect poet. Learned his trade from popular traditional poetry and balladry. Most notable for love lyrics and satires. Celebrates nature, robust humor, natural passions. Tumultuous private life.

THE TWA DOGS

In that fair part of Scotland's Isle
That bears the name of Old King Coil,
Upon a bonnie day in June,
And latish in the afternoon,
Two dogs, with naught to do at home,
Forgathered once upon a time.

    The first I'll name; they called him Caesar,
Kept by his Honour for his pleasure;
His coat, his ears, his mouth, his girth
Showed he was not of Scottish birth
But whelped in some place far abroad,
Where sailors go to fish for cod.
    His locked and lettered, fine brass collar
Proved him a gentleman and scholar;
But though he was of high degree
No trace of snobbish ways had he,
But would spend hours in field or ditch
With any gipsy's mongrel bitch.
At church or market, mill or smithy,
No matted cur, however nitty,
But he would hail, right glad to view him,
And wet a post in greeting to him.
    The other was a ploughman's collie,
A rhyming, ranting, silly billy
Who for his friend and comrade held him
And in a joke had Luath called him,
After some dog in Highland song
Made centuries since—Lord knows how long.

174

He was a shrewd and faithful tyke
As ever leapt a gate or dyke;
His honest, jolly, brindled face
Won him good friends in every place.
His breast was white, his shaggy back
Well clad with coat of glossy black;
His bushy tail, with upward curl,
Hung o'er his haunches in a swirl.

No doubt but each was fond of t'other
And warmly intimate together;
With social nose they ran and snuffed
For moles or mice at mound and tuft;
At times scoured off on long excursion,
Or rolled each other for diversion;
Until, with larking weary grown,
Upon a knoll they sat them down,
And there began a long digression
About the lords of the creation.

CAESAR

I've often wondered, honest Luath,
What sort of life poor dogs like you have;
And when the gentry's life I mark,
How fare the poor who live by work.
Our Laird gets in his rents and sums,
His coal, his produce, all his claims;
He rises when he thinks he will;
His flunkeys answer to his bell:
He calls his coach; he calls his horse;
He draws a well-filled silken purse
Long as my tail, where, through the stitches
I see his golden guinea riches.
From morn to night it's nought but toiling
At baking, roasting, frying, boiling,
And though the gentry cram and swill
Yet all the servants take their fill
Of sauce, ragouts and spicy hash
That's nothing more than wasteful trash.
Our lap-dog, that small withered wonder,
Eats bigger dinners, yes, by thunder!

175

Than any honest tenant eats
In all his Honour's wide estates.
What the poor cotters fill their paunch on
I own is past my comprehension.

LUATH

Caesar, you're right; they're tried enough;
A labourer digging hard and rough
In sodden ditch and stony dyke,
Laying bare quarries and suchlike;
He and his wife he just sustains,
Besides a troop of ragged bairns,
And nought but his strong hands to keep
Them right and tight in food and sleep.

And when they meet with black disaster,
Like loss of health, or lack of masters,
You'd almost think, a little longer
And they must starve of cold and hunger;
But yet—I never understand it!—
They're mostly wonderful contented;
And strapping lads and clever hussies
Are bred just such a way as this is.

CAESAR

But look, my friend, how you're neglected,
How huffed and cuffed and disrespected!
Lord, man! our gentry care so little
For ploughmen, ditchers and such cattle;
They go as scornful past a hedger
As I would by a stinking badger.

I've noticed, on our Laird's court-day,
And many a time with sore dismay,
Poor tenants, late with rents and dues,
Taking the factor's harsh abuse;
He'll stamp and threaten, curse and swear
He'll jail them and distrain their gear;
While they must stand with aspect humble,
And hear it all, and fear and tremble!
I see how folk live that have riches;
But surely poor folk must be wretches!

176

They're not so wretched as you'd think,
Though always on privation's brink:
They're so accustomed to the sight,
The view it gives them little fright.

Then chance and fortune are so guided
They're always more or less provided;
And though fatigued with close employment,
A spell of rest's a sweet enjoyment.

The dearest comfort of their lives,
Their thriving brood and faithful wives;
The prattling things are just their pride,
That sweeten board and fireside.

And then, twelvepenny-worth of ale
Will always over care prevail;
They lay aside their private cares
To canvass Church and State affairs:
They'll talk of patronage and priests
With kindling fury in their breasts;
Or tell what new taxation's coming,
And hear the news from London humming.

As bleak-faced Hallowmass returns
They hear the jolly rattling churns,
When rural life of every station
Unite in common recreation;
Love smiles, Wit sparkles, social Mirth
Forgets there's trouble on the earth.

That merry day the year begins
They bar the door on frosty winds;
The strong ale wreathes with mantling cream
And gives a heart-inspiring steam;
The treasured pipe and snuffbox full
Are handed round with right goodwill;
The cheerful elders talk and browse,
The young go romping through the house—
My heart has been so glad to see them
That I for joy ran barking with them.

Still, it's too true what you have said:
That game is far too often played.
There's many a creditable stock
Of decent, honest, kindly folk,

177

Are bundled out both root and branch,
Some rascal's greedy pride to quench,
Who thinks to knit himself the faster
In favour with his absent master,
Who, maybe, is a-parliamenting,
For Britain's good his soul indenting—

CAESAR

Faith, lad, you little know about it;
For Britain's good!—good faith! I doubt it!
Say rather, going as premiers lead him,
With Aye or No just as they bid him!
At operas and plays parading,
Mortgaging, gambling, masquerading.
Or maybe, in a frolic daft,
For Hague or Calais boards a craft.
To make a tour, by pleasure swirled,
To learn *bon ton* and see the world.
   There, at Vienna or Versailles,
He breaks his father's old entails,
Or to Madrid diverts his route
To strum guitars or fight with nought;
Or down Italian vistas hurtles,
Whore-hunting among groves of myrtles;
Then boozes muddy German water
To make himself look fair and fatter
And clear the consequential sorrows—
Love-gifts of carnival signoras.
For Britain's good!—for her destruction!
With dissipation, feud and faction!

LUATH

Well, well! dear sirs! is that the way
So many great estates decay?
Are we so goaded, cramped and pressed
For wealth to go that way at last?
   O, if they'd stay away from courts
And please themselves with country sports,
It would for everyone be better,
The laird, the tenant and the cotter!

For these wild, noisy, rambling sparks,
They're not ill-natured in their larks:
Except for stripping ancient glades,
Or speaking lightly of their jades,
Or shooting of a hare or moorcock,
They little harm the simple poor folk.

But will you tell me, Master Caesar,
Sure, great folks live a life of pleasure?
No cold nor hunger's grip can press them,
The very thought need not distress them.

CAESAR

Lord, man, you'd never envy them
If you were sometimes where I am.
It's true, they needn't starve or sweat
Through winter's cold or summer's heat;
They've no hard work to cramp their bones
And fill old age with aches and groans:
But human beings are such fools,
For all their colleges and schools,
That when no present ills perplex them
They make enough themselves to vex them;
The less they have to disconcert them
In like proportion less will hurt them.
A country fellow at the plough,
His acres tilled, his heart's aglow;
A country lassie at her wheel,
Her dozens done, she's fine and well;
But gentlemen, and ladies worst,
At dusk with idleness are cursed.
They loiter, lounging, lank and lazy;
Though nothing ails them, yet uneasy;
Their days insipid, dull and tasteless;
Their nights unquiet, long and restless.
And even sports, their balls and races,
Their galloping through public places,
Are such parades of pomp and art,
The joy can scarcely reach the heart.
The men fall out in party matches,
Then make it up in wild debauches:

One night they're mad with drink and whoring,
Next day their life is past enduring.
The ladies arm-in-arm, in clusters,
Are great and gracious all as sisters;
But hear their thoughts of one another,
They're downright devils all together.
And then, with eggshell cup and platie,
They sip the scandal-brew so pretty,
Or through long nights, with acid looks,
Pore on the devil's picture books;
Stake on a chance a farmer's stackyard,
And cheat like any unhanged blackguard.
    There are exceptions, man and woman;
But this is gentry's life in common.

    By this the sun was out of sight
And twilight darkening brought the night;
A beetle hummed with lazy drone,
The cows stood lowing in the lane;
When up they got with friendly shrugs,
Rejoiced they were not men but dogs;
And each took off his homeward way,
Resolved to meet some other day.

GEORGE GORDON BYRON

GEORGE GORDON BYRON (English, 1788-1824). The most gifted showman
of English Romanticism. Suffered handicap of clubfoot. *Childe Harold's
Pilgrimage* brought early fame and acclaim of English society, despite scandalous private life. Settled in Italy, where he wrote greatest work, the
satirical *Don Juan*. Joined Greek rebels in 1823, died of fever a year later.
    Poetry expresses the essence of romantic melancholy and pessimism.

SHE WALKS IN BEAUTY

SHE walks in beauty, like the night
    Of cloudless climes and starry skies;
And all that's best of dark and bright
    Meet in her aspect and her eyes:
Thus mellowed to that tender light
    Which heaven to gaudy day denies.

180

One shade the more, one ray the less,
　　Had half impaired the nameless grace
Which waves in every raven tress,
　　Or softly lightens o'er her face;
Where thoughts serenely sweet express
　　How pure, how dear their dwelling-place.

And on that cheek, and o'er that brow,
　　So soft, so calm, yet eloquent,
The smiles that win, the tints that glow,
　　But tell of days in goodness spent,
A mind at peace with all below,
　　A heart whose love is innocent!

SO, WE'LL GO NO MORE A-ROVING

So, we'll go no more a-roving
　　So late into the night,
Though the heart be still as loving,
　　And the moon be still as bright.

For the sword outwears its sheath,
　　And the soul wears out the breast,
And the heart must pause to breathe,
　　And Love itself have rest.

Though the night was made for loving,
　　And the day returns too soon,
Yet we'll go no more a-roving
　　By the light of the moon.

THE ISLES OF GREECE

The isles of Greece! the isles of Greece
　　Where burning Sappho loved and sung,
Where grew the arts of war and peace,
　　Where Delos rose, and Phœbus sprung!
Eternal summer gilds them yet,
But all, except their sun, is set.

The Scian and the Teian muse,
　　The hero's harp, the lover's lute,
Have found the fame your shores refuse;
　　Their place of birth alone is mute
To sounds which echo further west
Than your sires' "Islands of the Blest."

The mountains look on Marathon—
　　And Marathon looks on the sea;
And musing there an hour alone,
　　I dreamed that Greece might still be free;
For standing on the Persians' grave,
I could not deem myself a slave.

A king sate on the rocky brow
　　Which looks o'er sea-born Salamis;
And ships, by thousands, lay below,
　　And men in nations—all were his!
He counted them at break of day—
And when the sun set, where were they?

And where are they? and where art thou,
　　My country? On thy voiceless shore
The heroic lay is tuneless now—
　　The heroic bosom beats no more!
And must thy lyre, so long divine,
Degenerate into hands like mine?

'Tis something in the dearth of fame,
　　Though linked among a fettered race,
To feel at least a patriot's shame,
　　Even as I sing, suffuse my face;
For what is left the poet here?
For Greeks a blush—for Greece a tear.

Must *we* but weep o'er days more blest?
　　Must *we* but blush?—Our fathers bled.
Earth! render back from out thy breast
　　A remnant of our Spartan dead!
Of the three hundred grant but three,
To make a new Thermopylae!

What, silent still? and silent all?
    Ah! no— the voices of the dead
Sound like a distant torrent's fall,
    And answer, "Let one living head,
But one, arise—we come, we come!"
'Tis but the living who are dumb.

In vain—in vain; strike other chords;
    Fill high the cup with Samian wine!
Leave battles to the Turkish hordes,
    And shed the blood of Scio's vine!
Hark! rising to the ignoble call—
How answers each bold Bacchanal!

You have the Pyrric dance as yet;
    Where is the Pyrric phalanx gone?
Of two such lessons, why forget
    The nobler and the manlier one?
You have the letters Cadmus gave—
Think ye he meant them for a slave?

Fill high the bowl with Samian wine!
    We will not think of themes like these!
It made Anacreon's song divine.
    He served—but served Polycrates—
A tyrant; but our masters then
Were still, at least, our countrymen.

The tyrant of the Chersonese
    Was freedom's best and bravest friend;
That tyrant was Miltiades!
    O that the present hour would lend
Another despot of the kind!
Such chains as his were sure to bind.

Fill high the bowl with Samian wine!
    On Suli's rock, and Parga's shore,
Exists the remnant of a line
    Such as the Doric mothers bore;
And there, perhaps, some seed is sown,
The Heracleidan blood might own.

Trust not for freedom to the Franks—
  They have a king who buys and sells;
In native swords and native ranks
  The only hope of courage dwells.
But Turkish force and Latin fraud
Would break your shield, however broad.

Fill high the bowl with Samian wine!
  Our virgins dance beneath the shade—
I see their glorious black eyes shine;
  But gazing on each glowing maid,
My own the burning teardrop laves,
To think such breasts must suckle slaves.

Place me on Sunium's marbled steep,
  Where nothing, save the waves and I,
May hear our mutual murmurs sweep;
  There, swan-like, let me sing and die.
A land of slaves shall ne'er be mine—
Dash down yon cup of Samian wine!

WHEN WE TWO PARTED

When we two parted
  In silence and tears,
Half broken-hearted,
  To sever for years,
Pale grew thy cheek and cold,
  Colder thy kiss;
Truly that hour foretold
  Sorrow to this!

The dew of the morning
  Sunk chill on my brow;
It felt like the waning
  Of what I feel now.
Thy vows are all broken,
  And light is thy fame:
I hear thy name spoken
  And share in its shame.

They name thee before me,
    A knell to mine ear;
A shudder comes o'er me—
    Why wert thou so dear?
They knew not I knew thee
    Who knew thee too well:
Long, long shall I rue thee
    Too deeply to tell.

In secret we met:
    In silence I grieve
That thy heart could forget,
    Thy spirit deceive.
If I should meet thee
    After long years,
How should I greet thee?
    With silence and tears.

ELEGY ON THYRZA

And thou art dead, as young and fair
    As aught of mortal birth;
And form so soft and charms so rare
    Too soon return'd to Earth!
Though Earth received them in her bed,
And o'er the spot the crowd may tread
    In carelessness or mirth,
There is an eye which could not brook
A moment on that grave to look.

I will not ask where thou liest low,
    Nor gaze upon the spot;
There flowers or weeds at will may grow,
    So I behold them not:
It is enough for me to prove
That what I loved and long must love
    Like common earth can rot;
To me there needs no stone to tell
'Tis Nothing that I loved so well.

Yet did I love thee to the last,
   As fervently as thou,
Who didst not change through all the past
   And canst not alter now.
The love where Death has set his seal
Nor age can chill, nor rival steal,
   Nor falsehood disavow:
And, what were worse, thou canst not see
Or wrong, or change, or fault in me.

The better days of life were ours;
   The worst can be but mine:
The sun that cheers, the storm that lours,
   Shall never more be thine.
The silence of that dreamless sleep
I envy now too much to weep;
   Nor need I to repine
That all those charms have pass'd away
I might have watch'd through long decay.

The flower in ripen'd bloom unmatch'd
   Must fall the earliest prey;
Though by no hand untimely snatch'd,
   The leaves must drop away.
And yet it were a greater grief
To watch it withering, leaf by leaf,
   Than see it pluck'd to-day;
Since earthly eye but ill can bear
To trace the change to foul from fair.

I know not if I could have borne
   To see thy beauties fade;
The night that follow'd such a morn
   Had worn a deeper shade:
Thy day without a cloud hath past,
   And thou wert lovely to the last,
      Extinguish'd, not decay'd;
As stars that shoot along the sky
Shine brightest as they fall from high.

As once I wept, if I could weep,
  My tears might well be shed,
To think I was not near, to keep
  One vigil o'er thy bed:
To gaze, how fondly! on thy face,
To fold thee in a faint embrace,
  Uphold thy drooping head;
And show that love, however vain,
Nor thou nor I can feel again.

Yet how much less it were to gain,
  Though thou hast left me free,
The loveliest things that still remain
  Than thus remember thee!
The all of thine that cannot die
Through dark and dread Eternity
  Returns again to me,
And more thy buried love endears
Than aught except its living years.

C

PEDRO CALDERON DE LA BARCA

PEDRO CALDERON DE LA BARCA (Spanish, 1600-1681). Baroque and
Catholic playwright and poet. Won early fame as dramatist. After service in
Spanish army, became priest at 50. Wrote 120 plays, notable for elaborate
construction and philosophic content, and many *autos* (religious mysteries).
Among them: *La vida es sueño, El alcalde de Zalamea, El médico de Su
Honra.*

SEGISMUND'S DREAM

(The King of Poland, frightened by an omen at his son's birth,
which the soothsayers have interpreted to mean that the boy will
grow up a mere wild beast, bringing fire and slaughter on the
country if he succeeds to power, has imprisoned him in a tower till
he shall come of age, with a faithful officer for guard. He then has
him released—to see if the oracle has been mistaken!—and told
that all this confinement and misery has been a dream—as in the
"Induction" to the "Taming of the Shrew.")

   Segismund (*within*)—
Forbear! I stifle with your perfume! cease
Your crazy salutations! peace, I say—
Begone, or let me go, ere I go mad
With all this babble, mummery, and glare,
For I am growing dangerous—Air! room! air!—
   (*He rushes in. Music ceases.*)
Oh but to save the reeling brain from wreck
With its bewildered senses!—
   (*He covers his eyes for a while.*)
   (*After looking in the mirror.*)
What, this fantastic Segismund the same

Who last night, as for all his nights before,
Lay down to sleep in wolfskin on the ground
In a black turret which the wolf howled round.
And woke again upon a golden bed,
Round which as clouds about a rising sun,
In scarce less glittering caparison,
Gathered gay shapes that, underneath a breeze
Of music, handed him upon their knees
The wine of heaven in a cup of gold,
And still in soft melodious undersong
Hailing me Prince of Poland!—"Segismund,"
They said, "Our Prince! The Prince of Poland!" and
Again, "Oh, welcome, welcome, to his own
Our own Prince Segismund—"

If reason, sense, and self-identity
Obliterated from a worn-out brain,
Art thou not maddest striving to be sane,
And catching at that Self of yesterday
That, like a leper's rags, best flung away!
Or if not mad, then dreaming—dreaming?—well—
Dreaming then—Or, if self to self be true,
Not mocked by that, but as poor souls have been
By those who wronged them, to give wrong new relish?
Or have those stars indeed they told me of
As masters of my wretched life of old,
Into some happier constellation rolled,
And brought my better fortune out on earth
Clear as themselves in heav'n!—

(The great officers of state crowd around him with protestations of
fidelity; Clotaldo, his old warder, comes, and after attempts at
explaining and justifying the situation, Segismund in a fury attempts
to strike his head off; the Princess Estrella, betrothed to the Duke
of Muscovy, enters, and Segismund claims her for his own and
attempts to throttle the Duke; the King is called in, and after a
storm of reproaches which the King parries on the ground of good
intentions, Segismund closes as follows:)

Be assured your Savage, once let loose,
Will not be caged again so quickly; not
By threat or adulation to be tamed,

Till he have had his quarrel out with those
Who made him what he is.

    King—
Beware! Beware!
Subdue the kindled Tiger in your eye,
Nor dream that it was sheer necessity
Made me thus far relax the bond of fate,
And, with far more of terror than of hope
Threaten myself, my people, and the State.
Know that, if old, I yet have vigor left
To wield the sword as well as wear the crown;
And if my more immediate issue fail,
Not wanting scions of collateral blood,
Whose wholesome growth shall more than compensate
For all the loss of a distorted stem.

    Segismund—
That will I straightway bring to trial—Oh,
After a revelation such as this,
The Last Day shall have little left to show
Of righted wrong and villainy requited!
Nay, Judgment now beginning upon earth,
Myself, methinks, in right of all my wrongs,
Appointed heav'n's avenging minister,
Accuser, judge, and executioner,
Sword in hand, cite the guilty—First, as worst,
The usurper of his son's inheritance;
Him and his old accomplice, time and crime
Inveterate, and unable to repay
The golden years of life they stole away.
What, does he yet maintain his state, and keep
The throne he should be judged from? Down with him,
That I may trample on the false white head
So long has worn my crown! Where are my soldiers?
Of all my subjects and my vassals here
Not one to do my bidding? Hark! A trumpet!

    The trumpet—
(*He pauses as the trumpet sounds as in Act I., and masked Soldiers
gradually fill in behind the throne.*)

    King (*rising before his throne*)—
Aye, indeed, the trumpet blows

A memorable note, to summon those
Who, if forthwith you fall not at the feet
Of him whose head you threaten with the dust,
Forthwith shall draw the curtain of the Past
About you; and this momentary gleam
Of glory, that you think to hold life-fast,
So coming, so shall vanish, as a dream.

   Segismund—
He prophesies; the old man prophesies;
And, at his trumpet's summons, from the tower
The leash-bound shadows loosened after me
My rising glory reach and overlour—
But, reach not I my height, he shall not hold,
But with me back to his own darkness!

   (*He dashes toward the throne and is inclosed by the soldiers.*)
Traitors!
Hold off! Unhand me! Am not I your king?
And you would strangle him!
But I am breaking with an inward Fire
Shall scorch you off, and wrap me on the wings
Of conflagration from a kindled pyre
Of lying prophecies and prophet kings
Above the extinguished stars—Reach me the sword
He flung me—Fill me such a bowl of wine
As that you woke the day with—

   King—
And shall close,—
But of the vintage that Clotaldo knows.

(He is drugged, returned to the tower, and on waking assured that
the recent taste of freedom and kingship was all a dream, and his
former life in the tower the reality.)

   Segismund—
You know
'Tis nothing but a dream?
   Clotaldo—
Nay, you yourself
Know best how lately you awoke from that
You know you went to sleep on?
Why, have you never dreamt the like before?

191

Segismund—
Never, to such reality.

Clotaldo—
Such dreams
Are oftentimes the sleeping exhalations
Of that ambition that lies smoldering
Under the ashes of the lowest fortune;
By which, when reason slumbers, or has lost
The reins of sensible comparison,
We fly at something higher than we are—
Scarce ever dive to lower—to be kings,
Or conquerors, crowned with laurel or with gold,
Nay, mounting heav'n itself on eagle wings.
Which, by the way, now that I think of it,
May furnish us the key to this high flight—
That royal Eagle we were watching, and
Talking of as you went to sleep last night.

Segismund—
Last night? Last night?

Clotaldo—
Aye, do you not remember
Envying his immunity of flight,
As, rising from his throne of rock, he sailed
Above the mountains far into the West
That burned about him, while with poising wings
He darkled in it as a burning brand
Is seen to smolder in the fire it feeds?

Segismund—
Last night—last night—Oh, what a day was that
Between that last night and this sad To-day!

Clotaldo—
And yet, perhaps,
Only some few dark moments, into which
Imagination, once lit up within
And unconditional of time and space,
Can pour infinities.

Segismund—
And I remember
How the old man they called the King, who wore
The crown of gold about his silver hair,
And a mysterious girdle round his waist,

192

Just when my rage was roaring at its height,
And after which it was all dark again,
Bid me beware lest all should be a dream.

Clotaldo—

Aye, there another specialty of dreams,
That once the dreamer 'gins to dream he dreams.
His foot is on the very verge of waking.

Segismund—

Would it had been upon the verge of death
That knows no waking—
Lifting me up to glory, to fall back,
Stunned, crippled—wretcheder than ev'n before.

Clotaldo—

Yet not so glorious, Segismund, if you
Your visionary honor wore so ill
As to work murder and revenge on those
Who meant you well.

Segismund—

Who meant me!—me! their Prince
Chained like a felon—

Clotaldo—

Stay, stay—Not so fast,
You dreamed the Prince, remember.

Segismund—

Then in dream
Revenged it only.
True. But as they say
Dreams are rough copies of the waking soul
Yet uncorrected of the higher Will,
So that men sometimes in their dreams confess
An unsuspected, or forgotten, self;
One must beware to check—aye, if one may,
Stifle ere born, such passion in ourselves
As makes, we see, such havoc with our sleep,
And ill reacts upon the waking day.
And, by the bye, for one test, Segismund,
Between such swearable realities—
Since Dreaming, Madness, Passion, are akin
In missing each that salutary rein
Of reason, and the guiding will of man:
One test, I think, of waking sanity

193

Shall be that conscious power of self-control,
To curb all passion, but much most of all
That evil and vindictive, that ill squares
With human, and with holy canon less,
Which bids us pardon ev'n our enemies,
And much more those who, out of no ill will,
Mistakenly have taken up the rod
Which heav'n, they think, has put into their hands.

    Segismund—
I think I soon shall have to try again—
Sleep has not yet done with me.

    Clotaldo—
Such a sleep.
Take my advice—'tis early yet—the sun
Scarce up above the mountain; go within,
And if the night deceived you, try anew
With morning; morning dreams they say come true.

    Segismund—
Oh, rather pray for me a sleep so fast
As shall obliterate dream and waking too.

    (*Exit into the tower.*)

    Clotaldo—
So sleep; sleep fast: and sleep away those two
Night potions, and the waking dream between
Which dream thou must believe; and, if to see
Again, poor Segismund! that dream must be.
And yet, and yet, in these our ghostly lives,
Half night, half day, half sleeping, half awake,
How if our working life, like that of sleep,
Be all a dream in that eternal life
To which we wake not till we sleep in death?
How if, I say, the senses we now trust
For date of sensible comparison,—
Aye, ev'n the Reason's self that dates with them,
Should be in essence or intensity
Hereafter so transcended, and awoke
To a perceptive subtlety so keen
As to confess themselves befooled before,
In all that now they will avouch for most?
One man—like this—but only so much longer
As life is longer than a summer's day,

194

Believed himself a king upon his throne,
And played at hazard with his fellows' lives,
Who cheaply dreamed away their lives to him.
The sailor dreamed of tossing on the flood:
The soldier of his laurels grown in blood:
The lover of the beauty that he knew
Must yet dissolve to dusty residue:
The merchant and the miser of his bags
Of fingered gold; the beggar of his rags:
And all this stage of earth on which we seem
Such busy actors, and the parts we played,
Substantial as the shadow of a shade,
And Dreaming but a dream within a dream.

   Fife—
Was it not said, sir,
By some philosopher as yet unborn
That any chimney sweep who for twelve hours
Dreams himself king is happy as the king
Who dreams himself twelve hours a chimney-sweep?

   Clotaldo—
A theme indeed for wiser heads than yours
To moralize upon.

(An insurrection breaking out to reinstate Segismund, a band of soldiers bring him, asleep, from the tower.)

   Captain—
O Royal Segismund, our Prince and King,
Look on us—listen to us—answer us,
Your faithful soldiery and subjects, now
About you kneeling, but on fire to rise
And cleave a passage through your enemies,
Until we seat you on your lawful throne.
For though your father, King Basilio,
Now King of Poland, jealous of the stars
That prophesy his setting with your rise,
Here holds you ignominiously eclipsed,
And would Astolfo, Duke of Muscovy,
Mount to the throne of Poland after him;
So will not we, your loyal soldiery

And subjects; neither those of us now first
Apprised of your existence and your right:
Nor those that hitherto deluded by
Allegiance false, their vizors now fling down,
And craving pardon on their knees with us
For that unconscious disloyalty,
Offer with us the service of their blood;
Not only we and they; but at our heels
The heart, if not the bulk, of Poland follows
To join their voices and their arms with ours,
In vindicating with our lives our own
Prince Segismund to Poland and her throne.

    Soldiers—
Segismund, Segismund, Prince Segismund!
Our own King Segismund, etc.

    (*They all arise.*)

    Segismund—
Again? So soon?—What, not yet done with me?
The sun is little higher up, I think,
Than when I last lay down,
To bury in the depth of your own sea
You that infest its shallows.

    Captain—
Sir!

    Segismund—
And now,
Not in a palace, not in the fine clothes
We all were in; but here, in the old place,
And in your old accounterment—
Only your vizors off, and lips unlockt
To mock me with that idle title—

    Captain—
Nay,
Indeed no idle title, but your own,
Then, now, and now forever. For, behold,
Ev'n as I speak, the mountain passes fill
And bristle with the advancing soldiery
That glitters in your rising glory, sir;
And, at our signal, echo to our cry,
"Segismund, King of Poland!"

    (*Shouts, trumpets, etc.*)

196

Segismund—
Oh, how cheap
The muster of a countless host of shadows,
As impotent to do with as to keep!
All this they said before—to softer music.
    Captain—
Soft music, sir, to what indeed were shadows,
That, following the sunshine of a Court,
Shall back be brought with it—if shadows still,
Yet to substantial reckoning.
    Segismund—
They shall?
The white-haired and white-wandel chamberlain,
So busy with his wand too—the old King
That I was somewhat hard on—he had been
Hard upon me—and the fine feathered Prince
Who crowed so loud—my cousin,—and another,
Another cousin, we will not bear hard on—
And—but Clotaldo?
    Captain—
Fled, my Lord, but close
Pursued; and then—
    Segismund—
Then, as he fled before,
And after he had sworn it on his knees,
Came back to take me—where I am!—No more,
No more of this! Away with you! Begone!
Whether but visions of ambitious night
That morning ought to scatter, or grown out
Of night's proportions you invade the day
To scare me from my little wits yet left,
Begone! I know I must be near awake,
Knowing I dream; or, if not at my voice,
Then vanish at the clapping of my hands,
Or take this foolish fellow for your sport:
Dressing me up in visionary glories,
Which the first air of waking consciousness
Scatters as fast as from the alamander—
That, waking one fine morning in full flower,
One rougher insurrection of the breeze
Of all her sudden honor disadorns

197

To the last blossom, and she stands again
The winter-naked scarecrow that she was!
   (*Shouts, trumpets, etc.*)
   A Soldier—
Challenging King Basilio's now in sight,
And bearing down upon us.
   Captain—
Sir, you hear;
A little hesitation and delay,
And all is lost—your own right, and the lives
Of those who now maintain it at that cost;
With you all saved and won; without, all lost.
That former recognition of your right
Grant but a dream, if you will have it so;
Great things forecast themselves by shadows great:
Or will you have it, this like that dream too,
People, and place, and time itself, all dream—
Yet, being in't, and as the shadows come
Quicker and thicker than you can escape,
Adopt your visionary soldiery,
Who, having struck a solid chain away,
Now put an airy sword into your hand,
And harnessing you piecemeal till you stand
Amidst us all complete in glittering,
If unsubstantial, steel—

(A battle is fought, in which Segismund is victorious; taught by his
former experience, he resolves to be wise and temperate, and closes
with the following moralizing:)

   You stare upon me all, amazed to hear
The word of civil justice from such lips
As never yet seemed tuned to such discourse.
But listen—In that same enchanted tower,
Not long ago, I learned it from a dream
Expounded by this ancient prophet here;
And which he told me, should it come again,
How I should bear myself beneath it; not
As then with angry passion all on fire,
Arguing and making a distempered soul;
But ev'n with justice, mercy, self-control,

As if the dream I walked in were no dream,
And conscience one day to account for it.
A dream it was in which I thought myself,
And you that hailed me now then hailed me King,
In a brave palace that was all my own,
Within, and all without it, mine; until,
Drunk with excess of majesty and pride,
Methought I towered so high and swelled so wide,
That of myself I burst the glittering bubble,
That my ambition had about me blown,
And all again was darkness. Such a dream
As this in which I may be walking now;
Dispensing solemn justice to you shadows,
Who make believe to listen; but anon,
With all your glittering arms and equipage,
Kings, princes, captains, warriors, plume and steel,
Aye, ev'n with all your airy theater,
May flit into air you seem to rend
With acclamation, leaving me to wake
In the dark tower; or dreaming that I wake
From this that waking is; or this and that
Both waking or both dreaming; such a doubt
Confounds and clouds our mortal life about.
And, whether wake or dreaming; this I know,
How dream-wise human glories come and go;
Whose momentary tenure not to break,
Walking as one who knows he soon may wake
So fairly carry the full cup, so well
Disordered insolence and passion quell,
That there be nothing after to upbraid
Dreamer or doer in the part he played,
Whether To-morrow's dawn shall break the spell,
Or the Last Trumpet of the eternal Day,
When Dreaming with the Night shall pass away.

   (*Exeunt.*)

KAREL CAPEK

KAREL CAPEK (Czech, 1890-1938). Most widely known Czech writer, through plays, *R.U.R.* and *The Life of the Insects*. Also author of six novels, short story collections, travel books. Ardent humanitarian, fond of utopian themes. Like his friend Masaryk, strongly under influence of American ideas. Said to have died "of the death of his country."

THE ISLAND

AT one time there lived in Lisbon a certain Dom Luiz de Faria who later sailed away in order to see the world, and having visited the greater part of it, died on an island as remote as one's imagination can picture. During his life in Lisbon he was a man full of wisdom and judgment. He lived as such men usually do, in a way to gratify his own desires without doing harm to others, and he occupied a position in affairs commensurate with his innate pride. But even that life eventually bored him and became a burden to him. Therefore he exchanged his property for money and sailed away on the first ship out into the world.

On this ship he sailed first to Cadiz and then to Palermo, Constantinople and Beiruth, to Palestine, Egypt and around Arabia clear up to Ceylon. Then they sailed around lower India and the islands including Java whence they struck for the open sea again heading towards the east and south. Sometimes they met fellow countrymen who were homeward bound and who wept with joy when they asked questions about their native land.

In all the countries they visited Dom Luiz saw so many things that were extraordinary and well-nigh marvellous, that he felt as if he had forgotten all his former life.

While they sailed thus over the wide sea, the stormy season overtook them and their boat tossed on the waves like a cork which has neither a goal nor anchor. For three days the storm increased in violence. The third night the ship struck a coral reef.

Dom Luiz during the terrific crash felt himself lifted to a great height and then plunged down into the water. But the water hurled him back and pitched him unconscious on a broken timber.

When he recovered consciousness, he realised that it was bright noon and that he was drifting on a pile of shattered beams wholly alone on a calm sea. At that instant he felt for the first time a real joy in being alive.

He floated thus until evening and throughout the night and the entire succeeding day, but not a glimpse of land did he have. Besides, the pile of rafters on which he floated was becoming loosened by the action of the water, and piece after piece detached itself, Dom Luiz vainly trying to tie them together with strips of his own clothing. At last only three weak timbers remained to him and he sank back in weariness. With a feeling of being utterly forsaken, Dom Luiz made his adieu to life and resigned himself to the will of God.

The third day at dawn he saw that the waves were bearing him to a beautiful island of charming groves and green thickets which seemed to be floating on the bosom of the ocean.

Finally, covered with salt and foam he stepped out on the land. At that instant several savages emerged from the forest, but Dom Luiz gave utterance to an unfriendly shout for he was afraid of them. Then he knelt down to pray, sank to the earth and fell asleep on the shore of the ocean.

When the sun was setting, he was awakened by a great hunger. The sand all around him was marked by the prints of bare flat feet. Dom Luiz was much rejoiced for he realised that around him had walked and sat many savages who had discussed and wondered about him but had done him no injury. Forthwith he went to seek food but it had already grown dark. When he had passed to the other side of the cliff, he beheld the savages sitting in a circle eating their supper. He saw men, women and children in that circle, but he took a position at some distance, not being bold enough to go closer, as if he were a beggar from some far-off province.

A young female of the savage group arose from her place and brought him a flat basket full of fruit. Luiz flung himself upon the basket and devoured bananas, figs, both dried and fresh, other fruits and fresh clams, meat dried in the sun and sweet bread of a very different sort from ours. The girl also brought him a pitcher of spring water and, seating herself in a squat position, she watched him eat and drink. When Luiz had had his fill, he felt a great relief in his whole body and began to thank the girl aloud for her gifts and for the water, for her kind-heartedness and for the mercifulness of all the others. As he spoke thus, a deep gratitude like the sweet anguish of an overflowing heart grew in him and poured itself out in beautiful words which he had never before been able to utter so well. The savage girl sat in front of him and listened.

The following day he continued his inspection, encircling the

Dom Luiz felt that he must repeat his gratitude in a way to make her understand and so he thanked her as fervently as if he were praying. In the meantime the savages had all gone away into the forest and Luiz was afraid that he would remain alone in the unfamiliar place with this great joy in his heart. So he began to relate things to the girl to detain her—telling her where he came from, how the ship was wrecked and what sufferings he had endured on the sea. All the while the savage maid lay before him flat on her stomach and listened silently. Then Luiz observed that she had fallen asleep with her face on the earth. Seating himself at some distance, he gazed at the heavenly stars and listened to the murmur of the sea until sleep overcame him.

When he awoke in the morning, he looked for the maid but she had vanished. Only the impression of her entire body—straight and long like a green twig—remained in the sand. And when Luiz stepped into the hollow, it was warm and sun-heated. Then he followed the shoreline to inspect the island. Sometimes he had to go through forests or underbrush; often he had to skirt swamps and climb over boulders. At times he met groups of savages but he was not afraid of them. He noted that the ocean was a more beautiful blue than anywhere else in the world and that there were blossoming trees and unusual loveliness of vegetation. Thus he journeyed all day long enjoying the beauty of the island which was the most pleasing of any he had ever seen. Even the natives, he observed, were far more handsome than other savage tribes.

The following day he continued his inspection, encircling the entire island which was of an undulating surface blessed with streams and flowering verdure, just as one would picture paradise. By evening he reached the spot on the shore where he had landed from the sea and there sat the young savage girl all alone braiding her hair. At her feet lay the timbers on which he had floated hither. The waves of the impassable sea splashed up as far as the rafters so that he could advance no farther. Here Dom Luiz seated himself beside her and gazed at the sweep of the water bearing off his thoughts wave on wave. After many hundreds of waves had thus come and gone, his heart overflowed with an immeasurable sorrow and he began to pour out his grief, telling how he had journeyed for two days making a complete circumference of the island but that nowhere had he found a city or a harbour or a human being resembling himself. He told how all his comrades had perished at sea and that he had been cast up on an island from which there was no return; that he was left alone among low savage beings who spoke another language in which it was impossible to distinguish words or sense. Thus he complained bitterly and the savage maid listened to him lying on the sand until she fell asleep as if rocked to slumber by the grievous lullaby of his tribulations. Then Luiz became silent and breathed softly.

In the morning they sat together on the rock overlooking the sea giving a view of the entire horizon. There Dom Luiz reviewed his whole life, the elegance and splendour of Lisbon, his love affairs, his voyages and all that he had seen in the world and he closed his eyes to vision more clearly the beautiful scenes in his own life. When he again opened his eyes, he saw the savage girl sitting on her heels and looking before her with a somewhat unintelligent gaze. He saw that she was lovely, with a small body and slender limbs, as brown as the earth, and finely erect.

After that he sat often on the rock looking out for a possible passing ship. He saw the sun rise up from the ocean and sink in its depths and he became accustomed to this just as he did to all else. He learned day by day more of the pleasant sweetness of the island and its climate. It was like an isle of love. Sometimes the savages came to him and gazed on him with respect as they squatted in a circle about him like penguins. Among them were tattooed men and venerable ancients and these brought him portions of food that he might live.

When the rainy season came, Dom Luiz took up his abode in the young savage girl's hut. Thus he lived among the wild natives and went naked just as they did but he felt scorn for them and did not learn a single word of their language. He did not know what name they gave to the island on which he lived, to the roof which covered his head or to the woman who in the eyes of God was his only mate. Whenever he returned to the hut, he found there food prepared for him, a couch and the quiet embrace of his brown wife. Although he regarded her as not really or wholly a human being, but rather more nearly like other animals, nevertheless he treated her as if she understood him, telling her everything in his own language and feeling fully satisfied because she listened to him attentively. He narrated to her everything that occupied his mind—events of his former life in Lisbon, things about his home, details of his travels. At first it grieved him that the savage maiden neither understood his words nor the significance of what he was saying but he became accustomed even to that and continued to recount everything in the

203

same phrases and also with variations and always afterward he took her into his arms.

But in the course of time his narrations grew shorter and more interrupted. The adventures he had had slipped the memory of Dom Luiz just as if they hadn't happened or as if nothing had ever happened. For whole days he would lie on his couch lost in thought and silence. He became accustomed to his new life and continued to sit on his rock but he no longer kept a lookout for passing ships. Thus many years passed and Luiz forgot about returning, forgot the past, even his own native speech, and his mind was as mute as his tongue. Always at night he returned to his hut but he never learned to know the natives any more intimately than he had the day he arrived on the island.

Once in the summer he was deep in the forest when such a strange unrest overwhelmed him suddenly that he ran out of the wood to behold out on the ocean a beautiful ship at anchor. With violently beating heart he rushed to the shore to mount his boulder and when he reached it, he saw on the beach a group of sailors and officers. He concealed himself behind the rock like a savage and listened. Their words touched the margin of his memory and he then realised that the newcomers were speaking his native tongue. He rose then and tried to address them but he only gave utterance to a loud shout. The new arrivals were frightened and he gave a second outcry. They raised their carbines but in that instant his tongue became untangled and he cried out, "Seignors,—have mercy!" All of them cried out in joy and hastened forward to him. But Luiz was seized by a savage instinct to flee before them. They, however, had completely surrounded him and one after another embraced him and overwhelmed him with questions. Thus he stood in the midst of the group—naked and full of anguish, looking in every direction for a loophole of escape.

"Don't be afraid," an elderly officer said to him. "Just recall that you are a human being. Bring him meat and wine for he looks thin and miserable. And you—sit down here among us and rest while you get accustomed again to the speech of human beings instead of to screeches which no doubt apes employ as speech."

They brought Dom Luiz sweet wine, prepared meats and biscuits. He sat among them as if in a dream and ate and gradually began to feel his memory returning. The others also ate and drank and conversed merrily rejoicing that they had found a fellow countryman When Luiz had partaken of some of the food, a delicious feeling of gratitude filled him just as that time when the savage maiden had fed him but in addition he now felt a joy in the beautiful speech which he heard and understood and in the companionable people who addressed him as a brother. The words now came to his tongue of themselves and he expressed his thanks to them as best he could.

"Rest a little longer," the old officer said to him, "and then you can tell us who you are and how you got here. Then the precious gift of language will return to you for there is nothing more beautiful than the power of speech which permits a man to talk, to relate his adventures and to pour out his feelings."

While he was speaking a young sailor tuned up and began softly to sing a song about a man who went away beyond the sea while his sweetheart implores the sea and the winds and the sky to restore him to her, the pleading grief of the maiden being expressed in the most touching words one could find anywhere. After him others sang or recited other poems of similar content, each of them a little sadder in strain. All the songs gave voice to the longing for a loved one; they told of ships sailing to far distant lands and of the ever changeful sea. At the last everyone was filled with memories of home and of all whom they had left behind. Dom Luiz wept copious tears, painfully happy in the afflictions he had suffered and in their joyous solution, when after having become unused to civilized speech he now heard the beautiful music of poetry. He wept because it was all like a dream which he feared could not be real.

Finally the old officer arose and said, "Children, now we will inspect the island which we found here in the ocean and before the sun sets we will gather here to row back to the ship. At night we will lift anchor and under God's protection, we will sail back. You, my friend," he turned to Luiz, "if you have anything that is yours and that you want to take with you as a souvenir, bring it here and wait for us till just before sunset."

The sailors scattered over the island shore and Dom Luiz betook himself to the savage woman's hut. The farther he advanced the more he loitered, turning over in his mind just how he should tell the savage that he must go away and forsake her. He sat down on a stone and debated with himself for he could not run away without any show of gratitude when he had lived with her for ten years. He recalled all the things she had done for him, how she had provided his food and shelter and had served him with her body and by her labours. Then he entered her hut, sat down beside her and talked a great deal and very hurriedly as if thus he could the better convince

205

her. He told her that they had come for him and that he must now sail away to attend to very necessary affairs of which he conjured up a great quantity. Then he took her in his arms and thanked her for everything that she had done for him and he promised her that he would soon return, accompanying his promises with solemn vows and protestations. When he had talked a long time, he noticed that she was listening to him without the faintest understanding or comprehension. This angered him and, losing his patience, he repeated all his arguments as emphatically as possible and he stamped his feet in his irritability. It suddenly occurred to him that the sailors were probably pushing off, not waiting for him, and he rushed out from the hut in the middle of his speech and hastened to the shore.

But as yet no one was there so he sat down to wait. But the thought worried him that in all likelihood the savage woman had not thoroughly understood what he had said to her about being compelled to go away. That seemed such a terrible thing to him that he suddenly started back on a run to explain everything to her once more. However, he did not step into her hut but looked through a crack to see what she was doing. He saw that she had gathered fresh grass to make a soft bed for him for the night; he saw her placing fruit for him to eat and he noted for the first time that she herself ate only the poorer specimens—those that were dwarfed or spotted and for him she selected the most beautiful—all the large and perfect samples of fruit. Then she sat down as immovable as a statue and waited for him. Of a sudden Dom Luis comprehended clearly that he must yet eat the fruit set out for him and lie down on the couch prepared so carefully and complete her expectations before he could depart.

Meanwhile the sun was setting and the sailors gathered on the shore to push off to the ship. Only Dom Luiz was missing and so they called out to him, "Seignor! Seignor!" When he did not come, they scattered in various directions on the edge of the forest to seek him, all the time continuing to call out to him. Two of the seamen ran quite close to him, calling him all the while but he hid among the shrubbery, his heart pounding in his breast for fear they would find him. Then all the voices died down, and the darkness came. Splashing the oars, the seamen rowed to the vessel loudly lamenting the lost survivor of the wreck. Then absolute quiet ensued and Dom Luiz emerged from the underbrush and returned to the hut. The savage woman sat there unmoved and patient. Dom Luiz ate the fruit, lay down on the freshly made couch with her beside him.

When dawn was breaking Dom Luiz lay sleepless and gazed out through the door of the hut where beyond the trees of the forest could be seen the sunlit sea—that sea on which the beautiful ship was just sailing away from the island. The savage woman lay beside him asleep but she was no longer attractive as in former years but ugly and terrible to look upon. Tear after tear rolled down on her bosom while Dom Luiz, in a whisper, lest she might hear, repeated beautiful words, wonderful poems describing the sorrow of longing and of vain eternal yearning.

Then the ship disappeared beyond the horizon and Dom Luiz remained on the island but he never uttered a single word from that day during all the years that preceded his death.

GIOSUE CARDUCCI

GIOSUÈ CARDUCCI (Italian, 1835-1907). Protagonist of the Italian classics in post-Risorgimento literature. Favored return to early literary forms, Roman paganism and imperialism. Opposed to Romanticism and Christianity. Poetry preoccupied with history and landscape of Italy: *Iams and Epodes, Barbarian Odes*. Critical works created great stir in their time.

SONNET

Alone my vessel passes, mid the cry
Of halycons, on the stormy waters borne,
Swept on, by thunder of the billows torn,
Beneath the clamours of the lightening sky.
All Memories turn to that far shore gone by
Their faces wet with tears and sorrow-worn,
And all fair Hopes o'erthrown their glances forlorn
Cast on the splintered oars that broken lie.

Yet at the stern still doth my Genius stand,
While to the creaking masts he hearkeneth,
And cries o'er sea and sky his loud command:
'Row on! row on! O guides of desperate breath,
Toward cloudy ports of the forgetful land,
Toward whitening breakers of the reefs of death.'

PANTHEISM

I told it not, O vigilant stars, to you;
To thee, all-seeing sun, I made no moan;
Her name, the flower of all things fair and true,
Was echoed in my silent heart alone.

Yet now my secret star tells unto star,
Through the brown night, to some vague sphery tune;
The great sun smiles at it, when, sinking far,
He whispers love to the white and rising moon.

On shadowy hills, on shores where life is gay,
Each bush repeats it to each flower that blows;
The flitting birds sing, 'Poet grim and grey,
At last Love's honeyed dreams thy spirit knows.'

I told it not, yet heaven and earth repeat
The name beloved in sounds divine that swell,
And mid the acacia-blossom's perfume sweet
Murmurs the Spirit of All—'She loves thee well.'

SNOWFALL

Slowly flutters the snow from ash-coloured heavens in silence;
Sound or tumult of life rises not up from the town;

Not of herbseller the cry, nor rumorous rattle of wagons,
Not love's passionate song joyous in musical youth.

But, from the belfry swaying, hoarsely the hours thro' the evening
Moan like sighs from a world far from the light of our day.

Wandering song-birds beat at my tarnished window panes; friendly
Spirits returning are they, seeking and calling for me.

Soon, O belovèd ones, soon—be calm, heart ever undaunted—
Soon to the silence I come, soon in the shades to repose.

MIGUEL DE CERVANTES Y SAAVEDRA

MIGUEL DE CERVANTES Y SAAVEDRA (Spanish, 1547-1616). Spain's greatest writer and one of foremost in world literature. Wrote poetry and plays, but greatest triumph was novel, *Don Quixote*. Like *Hamlet* and *Faust*, *Quixote* reveals the many contradictions in man's nature. Imbued with deep humanism and gentle humor, Cervantes died same day as his great contemporary, Shakespeare.

SANCHO PANZA IN HIS ISLAND

SANCHO, with all his attendants, came to a town that had about a thousand inhabitants, and was one of the best where the duke had any power. They gave him to understand that the name of the place was the Island of Barataria, either because the town was called Barataria, or because the government cost him so cheap. As soon as he came to the gates (for it was walled) the chief officers and inhabitants, in their formalities, came out to receive him, the bells rung, and all the people gave general demonstrations of their joy. The new governor was then carried in mighty pomp to the great church, to give Heaven thanks: and, after some ridiculous ceremonies, they delivered him the keys of the gates, and received him as perpetual governor of the Island of Barataria. In the meantime, the garb, the port, the huge beard, and the short and thick shape of the new governor, made everyone who knew nothing of the jest wonder: and even those who were privy to the plot, who were many, were not a little surprised.

In short, from the church they carried him to the court of justice; where, when they had placed him in his seat, "My lord governor," said the duke's steward to him, "it is an ancient custom here, that he who takes possession of this famous island must answer to some difficult and intricate question that is propounded to him; and by the return he makes the people feel the pulse of his understanding, and by an estimate of his abilities, judge whether they ought to rejoice or to be sorry for his coming."

All the while the steward was speaking, Sancho was staring on an inscription in large characters on the wall over against his seat; and, as he could not read, he asked what was the meaning of that which he saw painted there upon the wall. "Sir," said they, "it is an account of the day when your lordship took possession of this island; and the inscription runs thus: 'This day, being such a day of this month, in such a year, the Lord Don Sancho Panza took possession of this island, which may he long enjoy.' " "And who is he?" asked Sancho. "Your lordship," answered the steward; "for we know of no other Panza in the island but yourself, who now sit in this chair." "Well, friend," said Sancho, "pray take notice that Don does not belong to me, nor was it borne by any of my family before me. Plain Sancho Panza is my name; my father was called Sancho, my grandfather Sancho, and all of us have been Panzas, without any Don or Donna added to our name. Now do I already guess your Dons are as thick as stones in this island. But it is enough that Heaven knows my meaning; if my government happens to last but four days to an end, it shall go hard but I will clear the island of these swarms of Dons, that must needs be as troublesome as so many flesh-flies. Come, now for your question, good Mr. Steward, and I will answer it as well as I can, whether the town be sorry or pleased."

At the same instant two men came into the court, the one dressed like a country fellow, the other looked like a tailor, with a pair of shears in his hand. "If it please you, my lord," cried the tailor, "I and this farmer here are come before your worship. This honest man came to my shop yesterday, for, saving your presence, I am a tailor, and, Heaven be praised, free of my company; so, my lord, he showed me a piece of cloth. 'Sir,' quoth he, 'is there enough of this to make a cap?' Whereupon I measured the stuff, and answered him, 'Yes,' if it like your worship. Now, as I imagined, do you see, he could not but imagine (and perhaps he imagined right enough) that I had a mind to cabbage some of his cloth, judging hard of us honest tailors. 'Pr'ythee,' quoth he, 'look there be not enough for two caps?' Now I smelt him out, and told him there was. Whereupon the old knave, (if it like your worship,) going on to the tune, bid me look again, and see whether it would not make three. And at last, if it would not make five. I was resolved to humour my customer, and said it might: so we struck a bargain.

"Just now the man is come for his caps, which I gave him; but when I asked him for my money he will have me give him his cloth again, or pay him for it."—"Is this true, honest man?" said Sancho to the farmer. "Yes, if it please you," answered the fellow; "but pray let him show the five caps he has made me." "With all my heart," cried the tailor; and with that, pulling his hand from under his cloak, he held up five little tiny caps, hanging upon his four fingers and thumb, as upon so many pins. "There," quoth he, "you see the five caps this good gaffer asks for; and may I never whip a stitch more if I have wronged him of the least snip of his cloth, and let any workman be judge." The sight of the caps, and the oddness of the cause, set the whole court a laughing. Only Sancho sat gravely considering a while, and then, "Methinks," said he, "this suit here needs not be long depending, but may be decided without any more ado, with a great deal of equity; and, therefore, the judgment of the court is, that the tailor shall lose his making, and the countryman his cloth, and that the caps be given to the poor prisoners, and so let there be an end of the business."

If this sentence provoked the laughter of the whole court, the next no less raised their admiration. For, after the governor's order was executed, two old men appeared before him, one of them with a large cane in his hand, which he used as a staff. "My lord," said the other, who had none, "some time ago I lent this man ten gold crowns to do him a kindness, which money he was to repay me on demand. I did not ask him for it again in a good while, lest it should prove a greater inconvenience to him to repay me than he laboured under when he borrowed it. However, perceiving that he took no care to pay me, I have asked him for my due; nay, I have been forced to dun him hard for it. But still he did not only refuse to pay me again, but denied he owed me anything, and said, that if I lent him so much money he certainly returned it. Now, because I have no witnesses of the loan, nor he of the pretended payment, I beseech your lordship to put him to his oath, and if he will swear he has paid me, I will freely forgive him before God and the world." "What say you to this, old gentleman with the staff?" asked Sancho. "Sir," answered the old man, "I own he lent me the gold; and since he requires my oath, I beg you will be pleased to hold down your rod of justice, that I may swear upon it how I have honestly and truly returned him his money." Thereupon the governor held down his rod, and in the meantime the defendant gave his cane to the plaintiff to hold, as if it hindered him, while he was to make a cross and swear over the judge's rod: this done, he declared that it was true the other had lent him ten crowns, but that he had really returned him the same sum into his own hands; and that, because he sup- posed the plaintiff had forgotten it, he was continually asking him for it. The great governor, hearing this, asked the creditor what he had to reply. He made answer, that since his adversary had sworn it he was satisfied; for he believed him to be a better Christian than to offer to forswear himself, and that perhaps he had forgotten he had been repaid. Then the defendant took his cane again, and, having made a low obeisance to the judge, was immediately leaving the court; which, when Sancho perceived, reflecting on the passage of the cane, and admiring the creditor's patience, after he had studied a while with his head leaning over his stomach, and his forefinger on his nose, on a sudden he ordered the old man with the staff to be called back. When he was returned, "Honest man," said Sancho, "let me see that cane a little, I have a use for it." "With all my heart," answered the other; "sir, here it is," and with that he gave it him. Sancho took it, and giving it to the other old man, "There," said he, "go your ways, and Heaven be with you, for now you are paid." "How so, my lord?" cried the old man; "do you judge this cane to be worth ten gold crowns?" "Certainly," said the governor, "or else I am the greatest dunce in the world. And now you shall see whether I have not a headpiece fit to govern a whole kingdom upon a shift." This said, he ordered the cane to be broken in open court, which was no sooner done, than out dropped the ten crowns. All the spectators were amazed, and began to look on their governor as a second Solomon. They asked him how he could conjecture that the ten crowns were in the cane? He told them that having observed how the defendant gave it to the plaintiff to hold while he took his oath, and then swore that he had truly returned him the money into his own hands, after which he took his cane again from the plaintiff —this considered, it came into his head that the money was lodged within the reed; from whence may be learned, that though sometimes those that govern are destitute of sense, yet it often pleases God to direct them in their judgment. Besides, he had heard the curate of his parish tell of such another business, and he had so special a memory, that were it not that he was so unlucky as to forget all he had a mind to remember, there could not have been a better in the whole island. At last the two old men went away, the one to his satisfaction, the other with eternal shame and disgrace: and the beholders were astonished; insomuch, that the person who was commissioned to register Sancho's words and actions, and observe his behaviour, was not able to determine whether he should not give him the character of a wise man, instead of that of a fool, which he had been thought to deserve.

* * * *

The history informs us that Sancho was conducted from the court of justice to a sumptuous palace, where, in a spacious room, he found the cloth laid, and a most neat and magnificent entertainment prepared. As soon as he entered, the wind-music played, and four pages waited on him, in order to the washing his hands, which he did with a great deal of gravity. And now, the instruments ceasing, Sancho sat down at the upper end of the table, for there was no seat but there, and the cloth was only laid for one. A certain personage, who afterwards appeared to be a physician, came and stood at his elbow, with a whalebone wand in his hand. Then they took off a curious white cloth that lay over the dishes on the table, and discovered great variety of fruit and other eatables. One that looked like a student said grace: a page put a laced bib under Sancho's chin, and another, who did the office of sewer, set a dish of fruit before him. But he had hardly put one bit into his mouth, before the physician touched the dish with his wand, and then it was taken away by a page in an instant. Immediately another, with meat, was clapped in the place; but Sancho no sooner offered to taste it, than the doctor, with the wand, conjured it away as fast as the fruit. Sancho was annoyed at this sudden removal, and, looking about him on the company, asked them whether they used to tantalise people at that rate, feeding their eyes, and starving their bellies? "My lord governor," answered the physician, "you are to eat here no otherwise than according to the use and custom of other islands where there are governors. I am a doctor of physic, my lord, and have a salary allowed me in this island for taking charge of the governor's health, and I am more careful of it than of my own, studying night and day his constitution, that I may know what to prescribe when he falls sick. Now, the chief thing I do is to attend him always at his meals, to let him eat what I think convenient for him, and to prevent his eating what I imagine to be prejudicial to his health and offensive to his stomach. Therefore, I now ordered the fruit to be taken away because it was too cold and moist: and the other dish, because it is as much too hot, and over seasoned with spices, which are apt to increase thirst, and he that drinks much destroys and consumes the radical moisture, which is the fuel of life." "So, then," quoth Sancho, "this dish of roasted partridges here can do me no manner of harm." "Hold," said the physician, "the lord governor shall not eat of them while I live to prevent it." "Why so?" cried Sancho. "Because," answered the doctor, "our great master, Hippocrates, the north star and luminary of physic, says in one of his aphorisms, *Omnis saturatio mala, perdricis autem pessima*; that is, 'All repletion is bad, but that of partridges is worst of all!' " "If it be so," said Sancho, "let Mr. Doctor see which of all these dishes on the table will do me the most good, and least harm, and let me eat my bellyful of that, without having it whisked away with his wand. For, by my hopes, and the pleasures of government, as I live, I am ready to die with hunger; and, not to allow me to eat any victuals, (let Mr. Doctor say what he will,) is the way to shorten my life, and not to lengthen it." "Very true, my lord," replied the physician; "however, I am of opinion you ought not to eat of these rabbits, as being a hairy, furry sort of food; nor would I have you taste that veal. Indeed, if it were neither roasted nor par boiled, something might be said; but, as it is, it must not be." "Well, then," said Sancho, "what think you of that huge dish yonder that smokes so? I take it to be an olla podrida, and, that being a hodge-podge of so many sorts of victuals, sure I cannot but light upon something there that will nick me, and be both wholesome and toothsome." "*Absit*," cried the doctor, "far be such an ill thought from us; no diet in the world yields worse nutriment than those wish-washes do. No, leave that luxurious compound to your rich monks and prebendaries, your masters of colleges, and lusty feeders at country weddings; but let them not encumber the tables of governors, where nothing but delicate unmixed viands, in their prime, ought to make their appearance. The reason is, that simple medicines are generally allowed to be better than compounds; for, in a composition, there may happen a mistake by an unequal proportion of the ingredients; but simples are not subject to that accident. Therefore, what I would advise at present, as a fit diet for the governor, for the preservation and support of his health, is a hundred of small wafers, and a few thin slices of marmalade, to strengthen his stomach and help digestion." Sancho, hearing this, leaned back upon his chair, and, looking earnestly in the doctor's face, very seriously asked him what his name was, and where he had studied. "My lord," answered he, "I am called Doctor Pedro Rezio de Augero. The name of the place where I was born is Tirteafuera, and lies between Caraquel and Almodabar del Campo, on the right hand; and I took my degree of Doctor in the University of Ossuna." "Hark you," said Sancho, in a mighty chafe, "Mr. Doctor Pedro Rezio de Augero, born at Tirteafuera, that lies between Caraquel and Almodabar del Campo, on the right hand, and who took your degree of Doctor at the University of Ossuna, and so forth, take yourself away! Avoid the room this moment, or, by the sun's light, I'll get me a good cudgel, and, beginning with your carcase, will so belabour and rib-roast all the physicmongers in the island, that I will not leave therein one of the tribe, of those, I mean, that are ignorant quacks; for, as for learned and wise physicians, I will make much of them, and honour them like so many angels. Once more, Pedro Rezio, I say, get out of my presence. Avaunt! or I will take the chair I sit upon, and comb your head with it to some purpose, and let me be called to an account about it when I give up my office; I do not care, I will clear myself by saying I did the world good service in ridding it of a bad physician, the plague of the commonwealth. Body of me! let me eat, or let them take their government again; for an office that will not afford a man victuals is not worth two horsebeans."

ADALBERT VON CHAMISSO

ADALBERT VON CHAMISSO (German, 1781-1838). French-born, fled the Revolution with his parents and became page to Queen of Prussia at age of nine. Botanist on round-the-world scientific voyage. Author of romantic poems and the tale of Peter Schlemihl, so widely read it has become an international legend.

PETER SCHLEMIHL, THE SHADOWLESS MAN

I. THE GREY MAN

HAVING safely landed after a fatiguing journey, I took my modest belongings to the nearest cheap inn, engaged a garret room, washed, put on my newly-turned black coat, and proceeded to find Mr. Thomas John's mansion. After a severe cross-examination on the part of the hall-porter, I had the honour of being shown into the park where Mr. John was entertaining a party. He graciously took my letter of introduction, continuing the while to talk to his guests. Then he broke the seal, still joining in the conversation, which turned upon wealth. "Anyone," he remarked, "who has not at least a million is, pardon the word, a rogue." "How true," I exclaimed; which pleased him, for he asked me to stay. Then, offering his arm to a fair lady, he led the party to the rose-clad hill. Everybody was very jolly; and I followed behind, so as not to make myself a nuisance.

The beautiful Fanny, who seemed to be the queen of the day, in trying to pick a rose, had scratched her finger, which caused much commotion. She asked for some plaster, and a quiet, lean, tall, elderly man, dressed in grey, who walked by my side, put his hand in his coat pocket, pulled out a pocket-book, and, with a deep bow, handed the lady what she wanted. She took it without thanks, and we all continued to ascend the hill.

Arrived at the top, Mr. John, espying a light spot on the horizon, called for a telescope. Before the servants had time to move, the grey man, bowing modestly, had put his hand in his pocket and pulled out a beautiful telescope, which passed from hand to hand without being returned to its owner. Nobody seemed surprised at the huge instrument issuing from a tiny pocket, and nobody took any more notice of the grey man than of myself.

The ground was damp, and somebody suggested how fine it would be to spread some Turkey carpets. Scarcely had the wish been expressed, when the grey man again put his hand into his pocket, and, with a modest, humble gesture, pulled out a rich Turkey carpet, some twenty yards by ten, which was spread out by the servants without anybody appearing to be surprised. I asked a young gentleman who the obliging man might be. He did not know.

The sun began to get troublesome, and Fanny casually asked the grey man if he might happen to have a tent by him. He bowed deeply, and began to pull out of his pocket canvas, and bars, and ropes, and everything needed for the tent, which was promptly put up. Again nobody seemed surprised. I felt uncanny; especially when, at the next expressed desire, I saw him pull out of his pocket three fine large horses with saddles and trappings! You would not believe it if I did not tell you that I saw it with my own eyes.

It was gruesome. I sneaked away, and had already reached the foot of the hill, when, to my horror, I noticed the grey man approaching. He took off his hat, bowed humbly, and addressed me.

"Forgive my impertinence, sir, but during the short time I have had the happiness to be near you I have been able to look with indescribable admiration upon that beautiful shadow of yours, which you throw from you contemptuously, as it were. Pardon me, but would you feel inclined to sell it?"

I thought he was mad. "Is your own shadow not enough for you? What a strange bargain!"

"No price is too high for this invaluable shadow. I have many a precious thing in my pocket, which you may choose—a mandrake, the dish-cloth of Roland's page, Fortunati's purse——"

"What! Fortunati's purse?"

"Will you condescend to try it?" he said, handing me a money-bag of moderate size, from which I drew ten gold pieces, and another ten, and yet another ten.

I extended my hand, and exclaimed, "A bargain! For this purse you can have my shadow." He seized my hand, knelt down, cleverly detached my shadow from the lawn, rolled it up, folded it, and put it in his pocket. Then he bowed and retired behind the rose-hedge, chuckling gently.

I hurried back to my inn, after having tied the bag around my neck, under my waistcoat. As I went along the sunny street, I heard an old woman's voice, "Heigh, young man, you have lost your shadow!"

"Thank you," I said, threw her a gold piece, and sought the shade of the trees. But I had to cross a broad street again, just as a group of boys were leaving school. They shouted at me, jeered, and threw mud at me. To keep them away I threw a handful of gold among them, and jumped into a carriage. Now I began to feel what I had sacrificed. What was to become of me?

At the inn I sent for my things, and then made the driver take me to the best hotel, where I engaged the state rooms and locked myself up. And what, my dear Chamisso, do you think I did then? I pulled masses of gold out of the bag, covered the floor of the room with ducats, threw myself upon them, made them tinkle, rolled over them, buried my hands in them, until I was exhausted and fell to sleep. Next morning I had to cart all these coins into a cupboard, leaving only just a few handfuls. Then, with the help of the host, I engaged some servants, a certain Bendel, a good, faithful soul, being specially recommended to me as a valet. I spent the whole day with tailors, bootmakers, jewellers, merchants, and bought a heap of precious things, just to get rid of the heaps of gold.

I never ventured out in daytime; and even at night when I happened to step out into the moonlight, I had to suffer untold anguish from the contemptuous sneers of men, the deep pity of women, the shuddering fear of fair maidens. Then I sent Bendel to search for the grey man, giving him every possible indication. He came back late, and told me that none of Mr. John's servants or guests remembered the stranger, and that he could find no trace of him. "By the way," he concluded, "a gentleman whom I met just as I went out, bid me tell you that he was on the point of leaving the country, and that in a year and a day he would call on you to propose new business. He said you would know who he was."

"How did he look?" Bendel described the man in the grey coat! He was in despair when I told him that this was the very person I wanted. But it was too late; he had gone without leaving a trace.

A famous artist for whom I sent to ask him whether he could paint me a shadow, told me that he might, but I should be bound to lose it again at the slightest movement.

"How did you manage to lose yours?" he asked. I had to lie. "When I was travelling in Russia it froze so firmly to the ground that I could not get it off again."

"The best thing you can do is not to walk in the sun," the artist retorted with a piercing look, and walked out.

I confessed my misfortune to Bendel, and the sympathetic lad, after a terrible struggle with his conscience, decided to remain in my service. From that day he was always with me, ever trying to throw his broad shadow over me to conceal my affliction from the world. Nevertheless, the fair Fanny, whom I often met in the hours of dusk and evening, and who had begun to show me marked favour, discovered my terrible secret one night, as the moon suddenly rose from behind a cloud, and fainted with terror.

There was nothing left for me but to leave the town. I sent for horses, took only Bendel and another servant, a rogue named Gauner, with me, and covered thirty miles during the night. Then we continued our journey across the mountains to a little-frequented watering-place, where I was anxious to seek rest from my troubles.

II. A SOUL FOR A SHADOW

Bendel preceded me to prepare a house for my reception, and spent money so lavishly that the rumour spread the King of Prussia was coming incognito. A grand reception was prepared by the townsfolk, with music and flowers and a chorus of maidens in white, led by a girl of wonderful beauty. And all this in broad sunlight! I did not move in my carriage, and Bendel tried to explain that there must be a mistake, which made the good folk believe that I wanted to remain incognito. Bendel handed a diamond tiara to the beautiful maiden, and we drove on amid cheering and firing of guns.

I became known as Count Peter, and when it was found out that the King of Prussia was elsewhere, they all thought I must be some other king. I gave a grand fête, Bendel taking good care to have such lavish illuminations all round that no one should notice the absence of my shadow. I had masses of gold coins thrown among the people in the street, and gave Mina, the beautiful girl who headed the chorus at my arrival, all the jewels I had brought with me, for distribution among her friends. She was the daughter of the verdurer, and I lost no time in making friends with her parents, and succeeded in gaining Mina's affection.

Continuing to spend money with regal lavishness, I myself led a simple and retired life, never leaving my rooms in daylight. Bendel warned me of Gauner's extensive thefts; but I did not mind. Why should I grudge him the money, of which I had an inexhaustible store? In the evenings I used to meet Mina in her garden, and always found her loving, though awed by my wealth and supposed rank. Yet, conscious of my dreadful secret, I dared not ask for her hand. But the year was nearly up since I had made the fateful bargain, and I look forward to the promised visit of the grey man, whom I hoped to persuade to take back his bag for my shadow. In fact, I told the verdurer that on the first of the next month I should ask him for his daughter's hand.

The anniversary arrived—midday, evening, midnight. I waited through the long hours, heard the clock strike twelve; but the grey man did not come! Towards morning I fell into a fitful slumber. I was awakened by angry voices. Gauner forced his way into my room, which was defended by the faithful Bendel.

"What do you want, you rogue?"

"Only to see your shadow, with your lordship's permission."

"How dare you——"

"I am not going to serve a man without a shadow. Either you show it to me, or I go."

I wanted to offer him money; but he, who had stolen millions, refused to accept money from a man without a shadow. He put on his hat, and left the room whistling.

When at dark I went, with a heavy heart, to Mina's bower, I found her, pale and beautiful, and her father with a letter in his hand. He looked at the letter, then scrutinised me, and said, "Do you happen to know, my lord, a certain Peter Schlemihl, who lost his shadow?"

"Oh, my foreboding!" cried Mina. "I knew it; he has no shadow!"

"And you dared," continued the verdurer, "to deceive us? See how she sobs! Confess now how you lost your shadow."

Again I was forced to lie. "Some time ago a man stepped so clumsily into my shadow that he made a big hole. I sent it to be mended, and was promised to have it back yesterday."

"Very well. Either you present yourself within three days with a well-fitting shadow, or, on the next day, my daughter will be another man's wife."

I rushed away, half conscious, groaning and raving. I do not know how long and how far I ran, but I found myself on a sunny heath, when somebody suddenly pulled my sleeve. I turned round. It was the man in the grey coat!

"I announced my visit for to-day. You made a mistake in your impatience. All is well. You buy your shadow back and you will be welcomed by your bride. As for Gauner, who has betrayed you and has asked for Mina's hand—he is ripe for me."

I groped for the bag but the stranger stopped me.

"No, my lord, you keep this; I only want a little souvenir. Be good enough and sign this scrap." On the parchment was written: "I herewith assign to bearer my soul after its natural separation from my body."

I sternly refused. "I am not inclined to stake my soul for my shadow."

He continued to urge, giving the most plausible reasons why I should sign. But I was firm. He even tried to tempt me by unrolling my shadow on the heath. "A line of your pen, and you save your Mina from that rogue's clutches."

At that moment Bendel arrived on the scene, saw me in tears, my shadow on the ground apparently in the stranger's power, and set upon the man with his stick. The grey man walked away, and Bendel followed him, raining blows upon his shoulders, till they disappeared from sight.

I was left with my despair, and spent the day and night on the heath. I was resolved not to return among men, and wandered about for three days, feeding on wild fruit and spring-water. On the morning of the fourth day I suddenly heard a sound, but could see nobody—only a shadow, not unlike my own, but without body. I determined to seize it, and rushed after it. Gradually I gained on it; with a final rush I made for it—and met unexpectedly bodily resistance. We fell on the ground, and a man became visible under me. I understood at once. The man must have had the invisible bird's nest, which he dropped in the struggle, thus becoming visible himself.

The nest being invisible, I looked for its shadow, found it, seized it quickly, and, of course, disappeared from the man's sight. I left him tearing his hair in despair; and I rejoiced at being able to go again among men. Quickly I proceeded to Mina's garden, which was still empty, although I imagined I heard steps following me. I sat down on a bench, and watched the verdurer leaving the house. Then a fog seemed to pass over my head. I looked around, and— oh, horror!—beheld the grey man sitting by my side. He had pulled his magic cap over my head, at his feet was his shadow and my own, and his hand played with the parchment.

"So we are both under the same cap," he began; "now please give me back my bird's nest. Thanks! You see, sometimes we are forced to do what we refuse when asked kindly. I think you had better buy that shadow back. I'll throw in the magic cap."

Meanwhile, Mina's mother had joined the verdurer, and they began to discuss Mina's approaching marriage and Gauner's wealth, which amounted to ten millions. Then Mina joined them. She was urged to consent, and finally said, sobbingly, "I have no further wish on earth. Do with me as you please." At this moment Gauner approached, and Mina fainted.

"Can you endure this?" asked my companion. "Have you no blood in your veins?" He rapidly scratched a slight wound in my hand, and dipped a pen in the blood. "To be sure, red blood! Then sign." And I took the pen and parchment.

I had scarcely touched food for days, and the excitement of this last hour had completely exhausted my strength. Before I had time to sign I swooned away. When I awoke it was dark. My hateful companion was in a towering rage. The sound of festive music came from the brightly illuminated house; groups of people strolled through the garden, talking of Mina's marriage with the wealthy Mr. Gauner, which had taken place this morning.

Disengaging myself from the magic cap, which act made my companion disappear from my view, I made for the garden gate. But the invisible wretch followed me with his taunts. He only left me at the door of my house, with a mocking "au revoir." The place had been wrecked by the mob and was deserted. Only the faithful Bendel was there to receive me with tears of mingled grief and joy. I pressed him to my heart, and bid him leave me to my misery. I told him to keep a few boxes filled with gold, that were still in the house, made him saddle my horse, and departed, leaving the choice of the road to the animal, for I had neither aim, nor wish, nor hope.

A pedestrian joined me on the sad journey. After tramping along for a while, he asked permission to put his cloak on my horse. I consented; he thanked me, and then, in a kind of soliloquy, began to praise the power of wealth, and to speak cleverly of metaphysics. Meanwhile, day was dawning; the sun was about to rise, the shadows to spread their splendour—and I was not alone! I looked at my companion—it was the man with the grey coat!

He smiled at my surprise, and continued to converse amiably. In fact, he not only offered to replace for the time being my former servant Bendel, but actually lent me my shadow for the journey. The temptation was great. I suddenly gave my horse the spurs and galloped off at full speed; but, alas! my shadow remained behind and I had to turn back shamefacedly.

"You can't escape me," said my compainion, "I hold you by your shadow." And all the time, hour by hour, day by day, he continued his urging. At last we quarrelled seriously, and he decided to leave me. "If ever you want me, you have only to shake your bag. You hold me by my gold. You know I can be useful, especially to the wealthy; and you have seen it."

I thought of the past and asked him quickly, "Did you get Mr. John's signature?" He smiled. "With so good a friend, the formality was not necessary."

"Where is he? I want to know."

He hesitated, then put his hand into his pocket, and pulled out Mr. John's livid body; the blue lips of the corpse moved, and uttered painfully the words: *"Justo judico Dei judicatus sum; justo judicio Dei condemnatus sum."*

Seized with horror, I threw the inexhaustible moneybag into the abyss, and then spoke the final words. "You fiend, I exorcise you in the name of God! Be off, and never show yourself before mine eyes again!"

He glared at me furiously and disappeared instantly.

III. THE WANDERER

Left now without shadow and without money, save for the few gold pieces still in my pocket, I could almost have been happy, had it not been for the loss of my love. My horse was down below at the inn; I decided to leave it there and to wander on on foot. In the forest I encountered a peasant, from whom I obtained information about the district and its inhabitants. He was an intelligent man, and I quite enjoyed the talk. When we approached the wide bed of a mountain stream, I made him walk in front, but he turned round to speak to me. Suddenly he broke off—"But how is that? You have no shadow!"

Unfortunately!" I said, with a sigh. "During an illness I lost my hair, nails, and shadow. The hair and nails have grown again, but the shadow won't."

"That must have been a bad illness," said the peasant, and walked on in silence till we reached the nearest side-road, when he turned off without saying another word. I wept bitter tears, and my good spirits had vanished. And so I wandered on sadly, avoiding all villages till nightfall, and often waiting for hours to pass a sunny patch unobserved. I wanted to find work in a mine to save me from my thoughts.

My boots began to be worn out. My slender means made me decide to buy a strong pair that had already been used; new ones were too dear. I put them on at once, and walked out of the village, scarcely noticing the way, since I was thinking deeply of the mine I hoped to reach the same night, and of the manner in which I was to obtain employment. I had scarcely walked two hundred steps, when I noticed that I had lost the road. I was in a wild virginal forest. Another few steps and I was on an endless ice-field. The cold was unbearable, and I had to hasten my steps. I ran for a few minutes, and found myself in rice-fields where Chinese labourers were working. There could be no doubt; I had seven-league boots on my feet!

I fell on my knees, shedding tears of gratitude. Now my future was clear. Excluded from society, study and science were to be my future strength and hope. I wandered through the whole world from east to west, from north to south, comparing the fauna and flora of the different regions. To reduce the speed of my progress, I found I had only to pull a pair of slippers over my boots. When I wanted money, I just took an ivory tusk to sell in London. And finally I made a home in the ancient caves of the desert near Thebes.

Once in the far north I encountered a polar bear. Throwing off my slippers, I wanted to step upon an island facing me. I firmly placed my foot on it, but on the other side I fell into the sea, as the slipper had not come off my boot. I saved my life and hurried to the Libyan desert to cure my cold in the sun; but the heat made me ill. I lost consciousness, and when I awoke again I was in a comfortable bed among other beds, and on the wall facing me I saw inscribed in golden letters my own name.

To cut things short—the institution which had received me had been founded by Bendel and the widowed Mina with my money, and in my honour had been called the Schlemihlium. As soon as I felt strong enough, I returned to my desert cave, and thus I live to this day.

You, my dear Chamisso, are to be the keeper of my strange history, which may contain useful advice for many. You, if you will live among men, honour first the shadow, then the money. But, if you live only for your better self, you will need no advice.

FRANCOIS-RENE DE CHATEAUBRIAND

FRANÇOIS-RENÉ DE CHATEAUBRIAND (French, 1768-1848). Father of the Romantic Movement in France. Had active, stormy career, both as writer and statesman. Travels in America reflected in *Atala* and *René*, epic romances of "the noble savage." Other major works: *Genius of Christianity* and *The Martyrs*, pleas for Catholicism, and colorful autobiography, *Mémoires d'Outre-Tombe*.

CHACTAS RELATES THE DEATH OF ATALA

The heroine of "Atala" is the daughter of a white man and a Christianized Indian. By her mother's command she took a vow of virginity, but later fell in love with Chactas, a young Indian. When she was tempted by this passion to break her vow she took poison.

As the last rays of light calm the winds and restore serenity to the sky, so the tender words of the hermit appeased the troubles that agitated the breast of my beloved. Her thoughts now rested only upon my grief, which she endeavored to alleviate; and, to fortify my mind to bear the loss, sometimes she told me that she should die happy, if I would dry up my tears; sometimes she talked of my mother, or my native country; seeking to distract my mind from my present sorrow, by awaking other remembrances, she exhorted me to patience and virtue. "Thou wilt not always be unhappy," said she; "if Heaven sends you this severe trial now, it is only to render you more compassionate to the misfortunes of others. The heart, O Chactas, resembles those trees, which yield a balm to heal the wounds of man only when they are wounded by a knife." When she had thus spoken she turned towards the missionary for that comfort which she had administered unto me; and alternately consoling and consoled, she gave and received the word of life upon the couch of death.

The hermit's zeal seemed to increase; his aged limbs were reanimated by the ardor of his charity. He was constantly preparing drugs, re-kindling the fire, attending the couch, and making pious exhortations on God and the happiness of the just. With the torch of religion in his hand, he showed the way to future regions. The humble cell was filled with the splendor of her Christian death; and the celestial spirits, no doubt, attended the edifying scene, where religion struggled with love, youth, and death.

Divine religion triumphed; and the pious melancholy that succeeded in our hearts, to the transports of passion, was the trophy of her victory. Towards the middle of the night, Atala seemed sufficiently revived to repeat the prayers of the holy priest; rising from the side of her couch a short time after, she extended her hand toward me, and in a trembling voice said, "O son of Outalissi, dost thou remember the first night when thou didst take me for the virgin of the last love! Oh! wonderful omen of our future fate." She then stopped, then resumed, "When I think that I am about to leave thee for ever, my heart makes such efforts to revive, that love seems almost to render me immortal; but God, thy will be done." After a short pause, she added, "It now only remains for me to ask your forgiveness for all the uneasiness that I have caused you. I have made you unhappy by my pride and my caprices. Chactas, a little earth will soon separate us, and deliver you from all my misfortunes." "Forgive you," replied I, bathed in tears; "is it not I who have caused your misfortunes?" "Beloved friend," said she, interrupting me, "you have rendered me very happy, and had I to begin life again, I should prefer the happiness of our short love in exile, to a life of tranquillity in my native country."

Here Atala's voice faltered; the films of death covered her glassy eyes and mouth; her wandering hands seemed to seek the shroud, and she whispered to the invisible spirits; then making an effort, she endeavored, but in vain, to untie the golden crucifix that was suspended around her neck; she begged of me to take it off, and in a low voice said, "When I spoke to thee the first time, near the pile, thou observedst this cross by the light of the fire: it is the only property which Atala possesses. Lopez, thy father and mine, sent it to my mother at my birth. Receive it from me as thine inheritance, preserve it as a memorial of our misfortunes: thou wilt doubtless implore the God of the unfortunate, as thou goest through this life of trouble. O Chactas, I have one last request to make to thee: O my dearest friend, our union on this earth could have been but short, but there is a future state which will be more durable; it is everlasting; and how dreadful to be separated forever. I only precede and wait thy arrival in the celestial regions: if thou lovest me, embrace the Christian religion, which will procure for us an eternal reunion. That divine religion performs a great miracle, since it enables me to quit thee without despair. O Chactas! I only wish to exact one single promise from thee. I know too well the consequence of a rash vow. It might deprive thee of some other woman more happy than myself. O my mother! forgive thy distracted child; O Virgin, take pity on me! I fall again into my former weakness, I avert my thoughts from Thee, O God! when they should all be applied in imploring Thy mercy."

Overwhelmed with grief and sobbing, my heart was ready to burst. I promised Atala that one day I would embrace the Christian religion. At these words, the priest rising as if inspired, extended his arms towards the vault of the cell, and exclaimed, "It is time to call here the presence of the Omnipotent."

As he spoke, methought an invisible hand forced me to prostrate myself at the side of Atala's couch. The priest then opened a secret recess, where a golden urn was concealed, covered by a silk veil; he fell on his knees in devout adoration; the whole cell seemed suddenly illuminated by it. Methought I heard the voices of angels, and the sounds of celestial harps. When the hallowed hermit took the sacred urn from the tabernacle, to me it seemed as if I saw the Great Spirit emerging from the rock.

The priest uncovered the chalice, took a wafer as white as snow between his fingers, and approached Atala, pronouncing mysterious words. She raised her eyes towards Heaven, and was in rapture: all her pains subsided: departing life seemed as if collecting on her faded lips; and her mouth, half opened, received the God concealed under the mystic bread: the holy divine then dipped some cotton in consecrated oil, and anointed her forehead, and after looking a few minutes upon Atala, he suddenly uttered these solemn words: "Depart, Christian soul; go and rejoin thy Creator." Then raising my drooping head, and steadfastly looking at the vase which contained the consecrated oil, I exclaimed, "Will that remedy restore life to Atala?" "Yes, my son," said the pious anchoret, falling in my arms, "to life eternal." Atala had just expired.——

Here Chactas was again obliged to interrupt his narration; his tears fell; sobs stifled his utterance. The blind sachem uncovered his bosom, and taking out Atala's crucifix, "Here," said he, "this is the pledge of love and misery; René, my son, thou canst behold it—but I,—no more; tell me after so many years is not the gold changed; have not my tears left some traces on it? Couldst thou perceive a place where a saint pressed it to her lips? Why is not old Chactas a Christian? What frivolous reasons of policy could make me still adhere to the idolatry of my forefathers? No! I will delay it no longer: the earth cries to me aloud, When wilt thou descend to the grave? and what do you wait for to embrace this divine religion? O earth, thou wilt not wait long. As soon as a priest shall have renovated by the baptismal flood a head grown white with age and sorrow, I hope to be united to Atala."—But to continue our narration.

I cannot now, O René, describe the despair that seized my soul when Atala had breathed her last; such a description would require more warmth than remains to my grief-worn spirits. Yes, the moon that spreads her silvery rays around our heads, and over the vast plains of Kentucky shall cease to shine, and the rivers to flow, before my tears for Atala shall be dried up. For two days I was insensible to the advice of the hermit. In endeavoring to calm my distress, this holy man did not use vain and worldly arguments; he only said, "My son, the will of God be done;" and clasped me in his arms. Had I not felt, I never should have thought there could have been so much comfort in those few words of a resigned Christian. The tenderness, compassion, and unalterable affection, of the pious servant of the Most High, conquered my obstinate grief. Ashamed of the tears he had shed on my account, "O father," said I, "let not the passions of a miserable youth disturb thy aged breast; let me take the sad remains of my beloved; I will bury them in some remote corner of the desert, and if I am condemned to live, I shall endeavor to render myself worthy of those eternal nuptials promised by Atala."

The hermit was delighted with my returning fortitude, and enthusiastically exclaimed, "May the blood of Jesus Christ, our divine master, which was shed in compassion to our miseries, have mercy upon this young man; increase his courage, and restore peace to his troubled mind, and only leave in it a useful and humble recollection of his misfortunes."

The holy priest refused to give up the corpse of the daughter of Lopez, but he offered to assemble the inhabitants of the village and to inter her with all Christian pomp, but I refused, saying, "The misfortunes and virtues of Atala are unknown to the rest of mankind; let a solitary grave be dug by our hands to share their obscurity." We agreed to set out the next day by sunrise to inter Atala, at the foot of the natural bridge, and in the entrance to the groves of death.

Towards night we carried the precious remains of this pious saint to the entrance of the cell on the north side. The hermit had enveloped her in a piece of linen cloth of his mother's spinning —the only thing that he had preserved from Europe, and which he intended for his own shroud. Atala lay stretched on a couch of sensitive plants; her feet, head, and shoulders were uncovered, and her hair was adorned with a flower of a magnolia; it was the sensitive flower which I had placed upon the maiden's head. Her lips, that were like a withered rose, seemed endeavoring to smile: dark blue veins appeared upon her marble cheeks, her beauteous eyelids were closed, her feet were joined, and her alabaster hands pressed an ebony crucifix to her heart; the fatal scapulary was suspended on her bosom; she looked as if enchanted by the spirit of melancholy, and resting in the double sleep of innocence and death. Her appearance was quite celestial, and had any one seen her, and been ignorant that she had possessed animation, he would have supposed her the statue of virginity.

The pious anchoret ceased not to pray during the whole night. I sat in silence at the top of Atala's funeral couch: how often had I supported her sleeping head upon my knees, and how often had I bent over her beauteous form listening to her and inhaling her perfumed breath; but now no soft murmur issued from her motionless bosom, and it was in vain that I waited for my beloved to awake. The moon supplied her pale light to the funeral eve: she rose at midnight, as a fair virgin that weeps over the bier of a departed friend: it covered the whole scene with a deep melancholy, displaying the aged oaks and flowing rivers. From time to time the cenobite plunged a bunch of flowers into consecrated water, and bathed the couch of death with the heavenly dew, repeating in a solemn voice some verses from the ancient poet Job.

"Man cometh forth like a flower, and is cut down; he fleeth also as a shadow, and continueth not.

"Wherefore is light given to him that is in misery? and life unto the bitter in soul?"

Thus did the venerable missionary sing; his grave and tremulous voice was re-echoed in the silent woods, and the name of God and the grave was resounded by the neighboring torrents and mountains: the sad warbling of the Virginia dove, the roaring of the waves, and the bell that called travelers, mixed with these funeral chants, and methought I heard in the groves of death the departed spirits join the hermit's voice in mournful chorus. The eastern horizon was now fringed with gold: sparrow-hawks shrieked on the cliffs, and the squirrels hastened into the crevices of old elms: it was the time appointed for Atala's funeral. I carried the corpse upon my shoulders, the hermit preceding me with a spade in his hand. We descended from one mountain to another: old age and death equally retarded our steps. At the sight of the dog which had discovered us in the forest, and who now leaping with joy followed us another road, I could not refrain from tears. Often did the golden tresses of Atala, fanned by the morning gale obscure my eyes, and often was I obliged to deposit my sacred load upon the grass to recover my strength. At last we arrived at the sad spot: we descended under the bridge. O my dear son, what a melancholy sight to see a young savage and an old hermit kneeling opposite each other busily engaged in digging a grave for an innocent virgin, whose corpse lay stretched in a dried ravine.

When we had finished our dismal task we placed the beauteous virgin in her earthly bed: alas! I had hoped to have prepared another couch for her. Then taking a little dust in my hand, and maintaining the most profound silence I scattered it, and for the last time looked at the remains of my beloved; then I spread the earth on a face of eighteen years. I saw the lovely features and graceful form of my sister gradually disappear behind the curtain of eternity. Her snowy bosom appeared rising under the black clay as a lily that lifts its fair head from the dark mold. "Lopez!" I exclaimed, "behold thy son, burying his sister!" and I entirely covered Atala with the earth of sleep. We returned to the cell, when I informed the priest of the project that I had formed of settling near him. The saint, who was thoroughly acquainted with the heart of man, discovered that my thoughts were the effects of sorrow. He said, "O, Chactas, son of Outalissi, whilst Atala lived, I entreated you to remain here, but now that your destiny is altered, you owe yourself to your native land; believe me, my dear son, grief is not eternal; it will sooner or later forsake the heart of man. Return to Meschacébé [Mississippi], and console your mother, who daily weeps and wants your support.

"Be instructed in the religion of your beloved Atala, and never forget the promise you made her to follow the paths of virtue, and to embrace the Christian religion: I will guard the tomb of your sister. Depart my son; God, the soul of Atala, and the heart of your old friend, will follow you."

Such were the words of the hermit of the rock. His authority was so great, and his wisdom so profound, that it was impossible to disobey him. The next day I quitted my venerable host, who, as he clasped me to his arms, gave me his last counsel and benediction, accompanied with tears. I went to the grave of my Atala, I was surprised to see upon it a little cross, that looked like the top-mast of a wrecked ship seen at a distance. I guessed that the priest had come to pray at the tomb, during the night; this mark of friendship and religion filled my eyes with tears, I felt almost tempted to open the grave, that I might once more behold my beloved Atala; I sat on the earth newly turned, my elbows resting upon my knees, my head supported by my hands; I remained buried in deep and sorrowful meditation. Then for the first time I made the most serious reflections upon the vanity of mankind, and the still greater vanity of human projects.

BANKIM CHANDRA CHATTERJEE

BANKIM CHANDRA CHATTERJEE (Indian, 1838-1894). Leading Bengali novelist and literary pioneer. Historical romances, strongly influenced by Walter Scott: *Ānanda Math, Sitārām, Mrinālinī*. His goal was revival of national pride in protest against foreign rule. Also wrote contemporary social novels and *Krishna Charita*, exposition of religious views.

THE BRIDE'S ARRIVAL

No SOONER had Prafulla's boat put in at Bhutnath landing than the news spread through the village that Brajeswar had again brought home a wife; it was whispered she was full-grown, even old. People came running from all directions to see the bride, the young, the old, the blind, the lame, everybody. The cook left her pots and ran; the cutter of fish turned her basket upside down over her fish and ran; the bather came running in wet clothes. The diner went half-hungry. The disputer suddenly agreed with her opponent. The woman spanking her child spared him for once. Off he went in his mother's arms to see the old bride. When the news came a husband was eating. The curry and dhal had been served but not the fish; he had to do without fish that day. An old woman complained to her granddaughter, "How can I go to the pond unless you take me?" At the news of the bride's coming the girl abandoned the old woman and dashed off. The old woman managed somehow to get there too. A young woman, having just been scolded by her mother, was promising not to leave the house again when she heard the news. Her promise was at once forgotten; away she went towards the bride's house. A mother left her baby and ran; the baby toddled after her, crying. A young wife veiled her face and passed shamelessly in front of her seated husband and his elder brother. Running loosened the young women's clothes but they had no time to set them right. Their hair fell down but they did not stop to twist it up again. In their excitement they did not notice what they pulled where. There was an uproar. The goddess of modesty fled in shame.

The bride and bridegroom were standing on a low stool while his mother went through the formalities of reception. People leaned forward to get a look at the bride. She did not relax proprieties and kept her veil three-fourths of a yard long. No one could see her face. During the ceremony her mother-in-law raised the veil once to look at her. She started a little but said nothing, merely murmuring, "The bride is nice." There were tears in her eyes.

The reception over, her mother-in-law took the bride to her room and then addressed the assembled neighbours: "Mothers! My son's wife has come a long way. She is hungry and thirsty. I am going to give them their food immediately. Our daughter-in-law will stay here in our house. You will see her all the time. Go home now and take your own meals."

Disappointed, the village women went away finding fault. The offence was the mother-in-law's but the bride got most of the blame because no one had seen her face. They all expressed their disgust at an old bride. Again they all opined that such were to be found

231

in Kulin families. Then whoever had seen an old bride in a Kulin home began to tell about it. Govinda Mukerjee had married a woman fifty-five years old. Hari Chatterjee had brought a seventy-year-old maiden wife home. Manu Banerjee married an old woman after she had been brought down to the bank of the Ganges to die. All such tales with embellishments grew familiar on the way. Venting itself in this fashion, the village gradually grew quiet.

GEOFFREY CHAUCER

GEOFFREY CHAUCER (English, *ca.* 1340-1400). The Father of English poetry, whose choice of London dialect determined standard speech. Had full, rich life and sound, practical philosophy. *The Canterbury Tales* shows influence of Boccaccio, Petrarch, and others. Remarkable storyteller, creator of character, humorist. Other works: *Troilus and Criseyde, The Legend of Good Women.*

THE PARDONER'S TALE

THERE dwelt one time in Flanders a company of young folk who followed such folly as riotous living and gaming in stews and taverns, where with harps, lutes and citerns they danced and played at dice both day and night, and ate and drank without restraint. Thus they served the Devil in cursed fashion within those Devil's temples by abominable superfluity.

These rioters, three, of whom I speak, long ere any bell had rung for prime had sat down in a tavern to drink. And as they sat, they heard the tinkle of a bell that was carried before a corpse to his grave. One of them called to his boy. 'Be off with you, and ask straightway what corpse is passing by; and mind you report his name aright.'

'Sir,' quoth the boy, 'that needs not be. It was told me two hours before you came here; he was an old fellow of yours, by God, and he was suddenly slain tonight, as he sat very drunk on his bench. There came a privy thief men call death, that slays all people in this countryside, and with his spear he smote his heart in two, and went his way without a word. A thousand he has slain in this pestilence; and master, ere you come into his presence, methinks it were best to be warned of such an adversary. Be ready to meet him ever; thus my mother taught me, I say no more.'

'By St. Mary,' said the taverner, 'the child speaks truth, for over a mile hence, in a large village, he has slain both woman, child, servant and knave. I trow his habitation be there. It were great wisdom to be advised ere he do injure a man.'

'Yea, God's arms!' quoth this rioter, 'is it such peril to meet with him? I will seek him in the highways and byways, I vow by God's bones. Hearken, fellows, we three be like; let each hold up his hand to the other and become the other's brother, and we will slay this false traitor, Death. He that slays so many shall be slain ere night, by God's Dignity!'

Together these three plighted their troth each to live and die for the rest as though he were their sworn brother, and up they then started in this drunken rage, and forth they went toward that village of which the taverner had spoken; and many a grisly oath they swore, and rent Christ's blessed body. —'Death shall be dead if they can but catch him.'

When they had gone not quite a mile just as they were about to go over a stile, an old man and poor met them and greeted them full meekly, and said, 'Lordings, God be with you!'

The proudest of the three rioters answered, 'What, churl, bad luck to you! Why are you all wrapped up save your face? Why live you so long to so great an age?'

This old man began to peer into his visage, and said, 'Because I cannot find a man, though I walked to India, neither in hamlet nor in city, who will change his youth for mine age. And therefore must I keep mine old age as long as it is God's will. Death, alas will not have me! Thus I walk like a restless caitiff, and early and late I knock with my staff upon the ground which is my mother's gate, and say, "Beloved Mother, let me in. Lo, how I wane away, flesh and blood and skin! Alas when shall my bones be at rest? Mother, with you I would exchange my chest, that has been long time in my chamber, yea for an hair-cloth to wrap me in!" But yet she will not do me that favour; wherefore my face is full pale and withered.—But sirs, it is not courteous to speak churlishly to an old man, unless he trespass in word or deed. You may yourselves read in Holy Writ, "Before an old hoary-head man ye shall arise;" wherefore I counsel you, do no harm now to an old man, no more than you would that men did to you in your old age if it be that

233

you abide so long. And God be with you, wherever you go or be; I must go whither I have to go.'

'Nay old churl, you shall not go, by God,' said the second gamester straightway. 'You part not so lightly by St. John! You spoke right now of that traitor Death who slays all our friends in this country side. By my troth, you are his spy! Tell where he is, or by God and the Holy Sacrament you shall die. Truly you are of his consent to slay us young folk, false thief!'

'Now, sirs,' quoth he, 'If you be so lief to find Death, turn up this crooked way; for by my faith I left him in that grove under a tree, and there he will abide, nor for all your boasting will he hide him. See you that oak? Right here you shall find him. May God, Who redeemed mankind, save you and amend you!' Thus said this old man.

And each of these rioters ran till he came to the tree, and there they found florins coined of fine round gold well nigh seven bushels, as they thought. No longer sought they then after Death, but each was so glad at the sight that they sat them down by the precious hoard. The worst of them spoke the first word. 'Brethren,' he said, 'heed what I say; my wit is great, though I jest oft and play. This treasure has been given us by Fortune that we may live our lives in mirth and jollity, and lightly as it comes, so we will spend it. Eh! God's precious dignity! Who would have weened today that we should have so fair a grace! But could this gold be carried to my house or else to yours,—for you know well all this gold is ours,—then were we in high felicity! But truly by day it may not be done. Men would say we were sturdy thieves and hang us for our treasure. This treasure must be carried by night, as wisely and as slyly as may be. Wherefore I advise that we draw cuts amongst us all, and he that draws the shortest shall run with a blithe heart to the town and that full swift and privily bring us bread and wine. And two of us shall cunningly guard this treasure, and at night, if he will not tarry, we will carry it where we all agree is safest.'

One of them brought the cuts in his fist and bade them draw and look where the lot should fall. It fell to the youngest of them and he went forth toward the town at once. So soon as he was gone one said to the other, 'You well know you are my sworn brother, and you will profit by what I tell you. Here is gold and plenty of it, to be divided amongst us three. You know well our fellow is gone. If I can shape it so that it be divided betwixt us two, had I not done you a friendly turn?'

The other answered, 'I wot not how that may be. He knows well the gold is with us two. What shall we do? What shall we say?'

'Shall it be a secret?' said the first wicked fellow. 'I shall tell you in a few words what we shall do to bring it about.'

'I agree,' quoth the other, 'not to betray you, by my troth.'

'Now,' quoth the first, 'you know well we be two and that two should be stronger than one. Look when he is set down; do you arise as though you would play with him, and I will rive him through the two sides while you struggle with him as in sport; and look that you do the same with your dagger. And then shall all this gold be shared, dear friend, betwixt you and me. Then may we both fulfil all our lusts, and play at dice at our will.' And thus, as you heard me say, were these two villains accorded to slay the third.

The youngest, who went to town, revolved full often in his heart the beauty of those bright new florins. 'Oh Lord,' quoth he, 'if so be I could have all this gold to myself, no man living under God's throne should live so merry as I!' And at last the fiend, our enemy, put it into his thought to buy poison with which he might slay his two fellows; for the fiend found him in such a way of life that he had leave to bring him to sorrow, for this was his full intention namely to slay them both and never to repent. And forth he went without tarrying into the town to an apothecary, and prayed him to sell him some poison that he might kill his rats; and there was also a pole-cat in his yard, which he said, had killed his capons and he would fain wreak him upon the vermin that destroyed him by night. The apothecary answered, 'And you shall have such a thing, that, so may God save my soul, no creature in all this world can eat or drink of this composition the amount of a grain of wheat, but he shall at once forfeit his life. Yea, die he shall, and that in less time than you can walk a mile, this poison is so strong and violent.'

This cursed man clutched the box of poison in his hand and then ran into the next street to a man and borrowed of him three large bottles. Into two of them he poured his poison, but the third he kept clean for his drink, for all night long he planned to labour in carrying away his gold. And when this rioter, the Devil take him! had filled his three great bottles with wine, he repaired again to his fellows.

What need to speak about it more? for just as they had planned his death, even so they slew him, and that anon. And when this was done, one spake thus, 'Now let us sit and drink and make merry, and then we will bury his body.' And then by chance, he took one of the bottles where the poison was, and he drank and gave his fellow to drink also. Wherefore anon they both died. And certes, Avicenna wrote never in any canon or any chapter more wondrous sufferings of empoisoning than these two wretches showed ere they died. Thus ended these two murderers as well as the poisoner.

ANTON CHEKHOV

ANTON CHEKHOV (Russian, 1860-1904). Great master of Russian short story, whose style heavily influenced modern writing. Meticulously wrought tales, concerned with introspective, inarticulate emotions rather than with outward events. Grandson of a serf, became the artist of twilight Czarist Russia. His great plays, *The Cherry Orchard, The Sea Gull, Three Sisters, Uncle Vanya*, left indelible mark on modern theater, but never successfully imitated.

THE SLANDERER

SERGEY KAPITONICH AKHINEYEV, the teacher of calligraphy, gave his daughter Natalya in marriage to the teacher of history and geography, Ivan Petrovich Loshadinikh. The wedding feast went on swimmingly. They sang, played, and danced in the parlor. Waiters, hired for the occasion from the club, bustled about hither and thither like madmen, in black frock coats and soiled white neckties. A loud noise of voices smote the air. From the outside people looked in at the windows—their social standing gave them no right to enter.

Just at midnight the host, Akhineyev, made his way to the kitchen to see whether everything was ready for the supper. The kitchen was filled with smoke from the floor to the ceiling; the smoke reeked with the odors of geese, ducks, and many other things. Victuals and beverages were scattered about on two tables in artistic disorder. Marfa, the cook, a stout, red-faced woman, was busying herself near the loaded tables.

"Show me the sturgeon, dear," said Akhineyev, rubbing his hands and licking his lips. "What a fine odor! I could just devour the whole kitchen! Well, let me see the sturgeon!"

Marfa walked up to one of the benches and carefully lifted a greasy newspaper. Beneath that paper, in a huge dish, lay a big fat sturgeon, amid capers, olives, and carrots. Akhineyev glanced at the sturgeon and heaved a sigh of relief. His face became radiant, his eyes rolled. He bent down, and, smacking his lips, gave vent to a sound like a creaking wheel. He stood a while, then snapped his fingers for pleasure, and smacked his lips once more.

"Bah! The sound of a hearty kiss. Whom have you been kissing there, Marfusha?" some one's voice was heard from the adjoining room, and soon the closely cropped head of Vankin, the assistant school instructor, appeared in the doorway. "Whom have you been kissing here? A-a-ah! Very good! Sergey Kapitonich! A fine old man indeed! With the female sex tête-à-tête!"

"I wasn't kissing at all," said Akhineyev, confused; "who told you, you fool? I only—smacked my lips on account of—in consideration of my pleasure—at the sight of the fish."

"Tell that to some one else, not to me!" exclaimed Vankin, whose face expanded into a broad smile as he disappeared behind the door. Akhineyev blushed.

"The devil knows what may be the outcome of this!" he thought. "He'll go about tale-bearing now, the rascal. He'll disgrace me before the whole town, the brute!"

Akhineyev entered the parlor timidly and cast furtive glances to see what Vankin was doing. Vankin stood near the piano and, deftly bending down, whispered something to the inspector's sister-in-law, who was laughing.

"That's about me!" thought Akhineyev. "About me, the devil take him! She believes him, she's laughing. My God! No, that mustn't be left like that. No. I'll have to fix it so that no one shall believe him. I'll speak to all of them, and he'll remain a foolish gossip in the end."

Akhineyev scratched his head, and, still confused, walked up to Padekoi.

"I was in the kitchen a little while ago, arranging things there for the supper," he said to the Frenchman. "You like fish, I know, and I have a sturgeon just so big. About two yards. Ha, ha, ha! Yes, by the way, I have almost forgotten. There was a real anecdote about that sturgeon in the kitchen. I entered the kitchen a little while ago and wanted to examine the food. I glanced at the sturgeon and for pleasure, I smacked my lips—it was so piquant! And just at that moment the fool Vankin entered and says—ha, ha, ha—and says: 'A-a! A-a-ah! You have been kissing here?'—with Marfa;

just think of it—with the cook! What a piece of invention, that blockhead. The woman is ugly, she looks like a monkey, and he says we were kissing. What a queer fellow!"

"Who's a queer fellow?" asked Tarantulov, as he approached them.

"I refer to Vankin. I went out into the kitchen—"

The story of Marfa and the sturgeon was repeated.

"That makes me laugh. What a queer fellow he is. In my opinion it is more pleasant to kiss the dog than to kiss Marfa," added Akhineyev, and, turning around, he noticed Mzda.

"We have been speaking about Vankin," he said to him. "What a queer fellow. He entered the kitchen and noticed me standing beside Marfa, and immediately he began to invent different stories. 'What?' he says, 'you have been kissing each other!' He was drunk, so he must have been dreaming. 'And I,' I said, 'I would rather kiss a duck than kiss Marfa. And I have a wife,' said I, 'you fool.' He made me appear ridiculous."

"Who made you appear ridiculous?" inquired the teacher of religion, addressing Akhineyev.

"Vankin. I was standing in the kitchen, you know, and looking at the sturgeon—" And so forth. In about half an hour all the guests knew the story about Vankin and the sturgeon.

"Now let him tell," thought Akhineyev, rubbing his hands. "Let him do it. He'll start to tell them, and they'll cut him short: 'Don't talk nonsense, you fool! We know all about it.'"

And Akhineyev felt so much appeased that, for joy, he drank four glasses of brandy over and above his fill. Having escorted his daughter to her room, he went to his own and soon slept the sleep of an innocent child, and on the following day he no longer remembered the story of the sturgeon. But, alas! Man proposes and God disposes. The evil tongue does its wicked work, and even Akhineyev's cunning did not do him any good. One week later, on a Wednesday, after the third lesson, when Akhineyev stood in the teachers' room and discussed the vicious inclinations of the pupil Visyekin, the director approached him, and, beckoning to him, called him aside.

"See here, Sergey Kapitonich," said the director. "Pardon me. It isn't my affair, yet I must make it clear to you, nevertheless. It is my duty— You see, rumors are on foot that you are on intimate terms with that woman—with your cook— It isn't my affair, but— You may be on intimate terms with her, you may kiss her— You may do whatever you like, but, please, don't do it so openly! I beg of you. Don't forget that you are a pedagogue."

Akhineyev stood as though frozen and petrified. Like one stung by a swarm of bees and scalded with boiling water, he went home. On his way it seemed to him as though the whole town stared at him as at one besmeared with tar— At home new troubles awaited him.

"Why don't you eat anything?" asked his wife at their dinner. "What are you thinking about? Are you thinking about Cupid, eh? You are longing for Marfushka. I know everything already, you Mahomet. Kind people have opened my eyes, you barbarian!"

And she slapped him on the cheek.

He rose from the table, and staggering, without cap or coat, directed his footsteps toward Vankin. The latter was at home.

"You rascal!" he said to Vankin. "Why have you covered me with mud before the whole world? Why have you slandered me?"

"How; what slander? What are you inventing?"

"And who told everybody that I was kissing Marfa? Not you, perhaps? Not you, you murderer?"

Vankin began to blink his eyes, and all the fibres of his face began to quiver. He lifted his eyes toward the image and ejaculated:

"May God punish me, may I lose my eyesight and die, if I said even a single word about you to any one! May I have neither house nor home!"

Vankin's sincerity admitted of no doubt. It was evident that it was not he who had gossiped.

"But who was it? Who?" Akhineyev asked himself, going over in his mind all his acquaintances, and striking his chest. "Who was it?"

CHIKAMATSU MONZAEMON

CHIKAMATSU MONZAEMON (Japanese, 1653-1725). The Shakespeare of Japan. Wrote for Kabuki theater, also for puppet theater. Author of numerous plays, mostly historical or domestic dramas. Due to conventions of puppet theater, and allusiveness of writing, plays extremely difficult to translate. Most popular: *Battles of Kokusenya, The Double Suicide of Sonezaki.*

ADVENTURES OF THE HAKATA DAMSEL

FOUR days after leaving the capital Soshichi and Kojoro found themselves at Seki, a post-town in the province of Isé. There the foot-worn travellers halted before a stone image of Jizo, a guardian god of children. Fervently were they praying to the deity that he might soften Sozaémon toward them when palanquin bearers accosted them.

"Cannot we serve you, sir?"

"That may be. We are going to the province of Owari. How much will you charge to carry us to the next stage?"

"It is five miles to Ishiyakushi, the next stage, so we ask you for *korori*."

Soshichi was startled.

"I don't know how much *korori* is."

"A hundred *mon*, sir."

"Too much. Come down to seventy."

"Very good, sir."

With the care-worn fugitives within their palanquins the bearers presently began a rapid march, keeping in time in their steps to the cries: *"Sokosei!"*—*"Katasei!"*—*"Makkasei!"* Mile succeeded mile, until Oiwaki was reached, where it was customary to change palanquins and bearers. The carriers therefore stopped. Kojoro stepped out promptly, but Soshichi would not get down, so great was his fear lest the bearers' sign *"korori"* should prove a bad omen. His mind might be said to be fettered with apprehension ere his body was tied to the detective's cord.

"Well, Kojoro," said Soshichi, "you had better change palanquins and go ahead of me."

"I will."

"And wait for me at a place called Yokkaichi."

"I will, my husband."

Kojoro, all unaware of Soshichi's fears, changed palanquins and let herself be carried ahead. A few minutes later a palanquin arrived from the next stage. The newcomers addressed Soshichi's bearers.

"Isn't your passenger the companion of the young woman who's just gone on? Let us exchange passengers."

"That'll suit us nicely. Now, sir, we're going to do an exchange. Please descend."

The bearers lifted the blind of the palanquin for Soshichi. The passenger of the other palanquin had already stepped out. He was lightly dressed in drawers and leggings, carried a packet in his hand and a *hayanawa* in his belt. Soshochi but glimpsed at him